D0500439

Windows and Words: A Look at Canadian Children's Literature in English

25   REAPPRAISALS:
CANADIAN
WRITERS

Windows and Words: A Look at Canadian Children's Literature in English

Edited by
Aïda Hudson and
Susan-Ann Cooper

University of Ottawa Press

REAPPRAISALS
Canadian Writers

Gerald Lynch
General Editor

National Library of Canada Cataloguing in Publication

Canadian Children's Literature Symposium (1999 : University of Ottawa)
Windows and words : a look at Canadian children's literature in English /
   edited by Aïda Hudson and Susan-Ann Cooper.

(Reappraisals, Canadian writers 1189-6787 25)
Seventeen papers from the Canadian Children's Literature Symposium,
   held May 1999 at the University of Ottawa.

Includes bibliographical references.

ISBN 0-7766-0556-9

1. Children's literature, Canadian (English) – Histor and criticism – Congress.
2. Canadian literature (English) – 20th century – History and criticism – Congresses.
I. Hudson, Aïda, 1951–   . II. Cooper, Susan-Ann III. Title. IV. Series.

PS8069 C354 1999   C810.9'9282'0904   C2003-902931-X   PR9193.9.C35 1999

University of Ottawa Press gratefully acknowledges the support extended to its publishing
programme by the Canada Council and the University of Ottawa.

We acknowledge the financial support of the Government of Canada through the Book
Publishing Industry Development Program (BPIDP) for our publishing activities.

UNIVERSITY OF OTTAWA
UNIVERSITÉ D'OTTAWA

Cover illustration: Kim La Fave, *Boy with Book,* digital, 2002

ISBN 0-7766-0556-9
ISSN 1189-6787

© University of Ottawa Press, 2003
   542 King Edward, Ottawa, Ont. Canada K1N 6N5
   press@uottawa.ca   http://www.uopress.uottawa.ca

Printed and bound in Canada

Contents

Introduction

AÏDA HUDSON

O N PARLIAMENT HILL, fireworks shot through the sky New Year's Eve 1999 illuminating a new millennium. The temporal shift from the last thousand years to the next made us Canadians consider who we were, who we are, and what we might become. A few blocks from the Hill at the Canadian Children's Literature Symposium on the campus of the University of Ottawa earlier that same year, a devoted group of Canadian scholars and writers had considered the past, the present, and the future of a small but growing area of our literary landscape. They were concerned with the following questions. What literary legacy do our children have to light up their future? What in the past and in the present in Canadian children's fiction is *literature*?

A nation can be judged by how it enriches its children. What was rediscovered and reaffirmed at the symposium was that Canadians have a national literature for the young that is indeed *literature*, increasingly assured in artistry, increasingly multi-cultural in character, and one that merits and rewards serious scholarly study. From this seed idea grew *Windows and Words: A Look at Canadian Children's Literature in English*, a collection of seventeen studies, formal essays, and commentaries, celebrating the wealth, the multitudinousness of our imaginative literature for the young. Three of the essays presented here are surveys of Canadian children's fiction in English: one a study of all the genres of the last decade, the second a survey of the aboriginal adolescent novel from the 1970s to the 1990s, and the third a consideration of the multi-cultural character of children's books in Saskatchewan. Essays dealing with individual authors and motifs complement the overviews. Of these, six essays confirm the central place of our most internationally acclaimed children's writer, Lucy Maud Montgomery. There are studies about book illustration and visual literacy, and about the dual artistic nature of the picture book and its art design. One of two commentaries that close the volume leads the reader to consider what is "Canadian" about literature for Canadian children, while the final commentary reaffirms the volume's main objective: to treat Canadian children's literature as *literature*.

At the heart of this collection is an essay with a unique perspective on the artistry of writing for children. "The Apprehension of Audience: The Difference Between Writing for Adults and Children," by Tim Wynne-Jones serves as a touchstone for certain issues[1] which have troubled writers of children's literature in the past, and, some critics would say, persist. These too are touched on in other essays in the present volume.

In a number of ways Tim Wynne-Jones's opening essay can be read as a response to two cornerstone studies, one that touches on works for children, and the other centred exclusively on writing for children. Both have long influenced how children's literature is viewed in academia. In his well-known and much-studied essay, J. R. R. Tolkien bemoans the fact that in his time fairy stories were considered suitable only for the young:

> Actually, the association of children and fairy-stories is an accident of our domestic history. Fairy-stories have in the modern lettered world been relegated to the "nursery," as shabby or old-fashioned furniture is relegated to the play-room, primarily because the adults do not want it, and do not mind if it is misused. (2001, 34)

In writing about "*Faërie*: the Perilous Realm itself," Tolkien brought to life the importance of fairy tales and defined Fantasy for scholars, writers, and adult readers, but he did so at the expense of children. Whether he was aware of it or not, his essay confirmed a view of long-standing respectability in the academic world that writing for children is a second-rate endeavour. "[R]elegated to the 'nursery'" and "misused" still resound today, but their derogatory influence was partly mitigated in another well-known essay, "On Three Ways of Writing for Children," by C. S. Lewis, Tolkien's longtime friend and fellow member of The Inklings (a group of friends at Oxford who met informally to read aloud their compositions). There, the creator of the Narnian tales explains why he felt compelled to write a fairy tale for children "or burst" (1980, 213): "The third way, which is the only one I could ever use myself, consists in writing a children's story because a children's story is the best art-form for something you have to say" (208).

What is the connection between these two essays and Tim Wynne-Jones's address? How does Wynne-Jones flesh out this delving into the motives of literary creation? Tolkien may have shown how fairy-stories can be Art, but he indeed can be seen to do so at the expense of children, and C. S. Lewis states that a children's story can be the "best art-form" for what an author has to say. Wynne-Jones's address confirms Lewis's statement, but then goes one step further by showing that *the way in* which he constructs for children is a deeply artistic endeavour as well. In other words, he shows that when he writes for children he apprehends the needs of a young audience as intently and as artistically as when he apprehends the needs of an adult audience. There is nothing second-rate about the attention a children's author "relegates" to the young. It is equally a part of his or her creative imagination.

Tim Wynne-Jones is against compartmentalizing literature for children according to age. Every child progresses differently. His attitude underscores another dilemma that is not always generally understood: that the boundary between children's literature and adult literature changes. He is not the only contributor to *Windows and Words* whose argument concerns this boundary. In her contribution to the present study, "Brian O'Connal and Emily Byrd Starr: The Inheritors of Wordsworth's 'Gentle Breeze,'" Margaret Steffler reveals how she had "to struggle once again with the artificial boundaries we seem to impose between literature concerned with the child and children's literature" (87–88). She is uncomfortable with a boundary that categorizes one work as an adult novel about a child, and the other a children's novel. She insists *Who Has Seen the Wind* and *Emily of New Moon* inhabit a "shadowy border area" (88). Today there are many works that blur this boundary. Dennis Lee's poems for the young are enjoyed as much by children as by adults. *Anne of Green Gables* continues to delight the young and old. How ironic that Tolkien, who wrote "On

Fairy-Stories" because fairy tales were mistakenly relegated to the young, wrote *The Lord of the Rings* for adults, that, together with Richard Adams's *Watership Down* became the "rage" in the 1970s with adults and children alike (Egoff and Sutton 1996, 387). The Harry Potter books and the Pullman trilogy *His Dark Materials*, both written for children, have been read as avidly by adults as by children. As is well known, special "adult" book jackets have been made for the Potter books, so that adults won't be embarrassed being seen reading "kids' books." Here are books "relegated" to adults! Perhaps this phenomenon confirms what Lewis wrote so many years ago, namely, that a good children's story would attract the attention of readers of any age (Lewis 1980, 209).

Perhaps too, it is time to consider the advantages of an entire family enjoying the same book and time to recognize that such familial/familiar comforts unashamedly be counted among one of the pleasures of reading. But the phenomenon of a children's book delighting adults may also confirm one of the abiding pleasures—one of the treasures—of children's stories that Tim Wynne-Jones addresses, that of story itself. It may be as well that story has been banished for too long from modern adult fiction, shouldered aside by more complex considerations of narrative, narratology, and the like lit-crit constructs. Story contributes a large part to the pleasure of reading, and perhaps adults, tired of fiction that is dominated by style, crave the story in children's books. Tolkien himself argued in "On Fairy-Stories" that "the fairy tale element," is thrown in with figures from Myth and History into the "Cauldron of Story" and that it "has has always been boiling" (2001, 29). For Tolkien the literature of man is the "Tree of Tales" (56); story is literature and the domain of all readers. Increasingly, university teachers who lecture on children's literature find that their students are taking courses in this field not only because many of them will be working with children in some capacity, but also because they enjoy children's literature themselves. University students reading such books for young adults as Tim Wynne-Jones's *The Boy in the Burning House* and Janet Lunn's *The Root Cellar* find that they cannot put the books down. This, of course, does not mean that children's books are avidly read entirely because of story, whether the readers are adults or children. Kenneth Oppel's bat trilogy is an epic that explores life and death, the afterlife and the underworld as Dantean and Miltonic as any adult would expect in an adult work of fiction. Writers for the young are well aware that their works must grow along with the children who read them if those works are to hold meaning for readers even when they are older, even when they grow into adults.

Several other issues keep recurring in *Windows and Words*. These include social and moral strictures on writing for children, the highlighting of the artistic character and merit of picture books, and national, racial, and ethnic issues.

One issue that continues to be of profound interest is the protection of childhood. Childhood is itself a concept that changes with changing social customs, rites of passage, wealth, and work, but childhood can still usefully be defined as that period from infancy to adolescence when there is little awareness of sexuality. The English Romantics idealized childhood, especially its innocence, and vestiges of this idealization are still with us today. The violation of a child's innocence remains a serious concern in the Canadian public consciousness and undoubtedly influences how authors write (and don't write) for children. Wynne-Jones's handling of sexual intimacy has its beginnings in "the seeds of [a work's] final form" which dictate the audience that he apprehends (19). In her essay, "The Eros of Childhood and Early Adolescence in Girl Series: L. M. Montgomery's *Emily* Trilogy," Irene Gammel shows how L. M. Montgomery herself was frustrated with publishers' constraints about the realistic depiction of a girl's bodily changes and sexual awareness as she crosses the threshold between childhood and adolescence. Gammel examines the *Emily* trilogy using modern feminist body theory, as well as the root meaning of erotic. Her argument makes clear that, despite publishers' constraints, Montgomery created a realistic but unusual adolescent girl. Forced to be reticent or formal at times when dealing with the pubescent Emily, Montgomery, nevertheless, had the artistic power to suggest, to allude, and to imply without offending the innocence of her young audience.

In their essay, "Secrecy and Space: Glenn Gould and Tim Wynne-Jones's *The Maestro*," Alan West and Lee Harris touch on the violation done to the childhood of Burl Crow, the hero of *The Maestro*. They examine the inspiration of the musical genius Nathaniel Orlando Gow (who is based on Glenn Gould) and how his artistic "secrecy" and "space" protect and nurture Burl. This influence revives Burl's self-respect, and in a curious way "fathers" his childhood after years of neglect and abuse by his own father. Gow may be self-absorbed and his interest in Burl may be painfully brief, but he helps to heal and mentor Burl Crow, long after his death. As a side note, West and Harris examine how essential fairy tales are, not only in initially shaping Burl's own secrecy and space, but also as the basis for his quest. Another essay that touches on childhood innocence is Sandra Beckett's wide-ranging and entertaining "Retelling 'Little Red Riding Hood' Abroad and at Home." Although this article is concerned with the often humorous character of modern retellings throughout the Western world, Little Red Riding Hood herself remains a tantalizingly persistent innocent. Perhaps it is the ambiguous character of her innocence that is at the heart of the retellers' fascination with her.

We turn now to a consideration of the artistic merit and artistry of picture books and illustrated novels. Janet Lunn discusses her work with illustrators, not only maintaining that the picture book is an art form, but that a large measure of its artistry rests on the *equal* marriage of picture and word. In "Publishing Children's Picture Books: The Role of Design and Art Direction," Michael Solomon deals with the picture book as artefact, as an object of design and of typographical art. He provides us with a rare look into how picture books are made, and into the impact computer technology and the global market have made in shaping picture books. In "The Changing Faces of Canadian Children: Pictures, Power, and Pedagogy," Andrea McKenzie insists on the importance of "reading" illustrations in order to get the full meaning of an illustrated novel or a picture book. Pictures give words new meaning, in particular telling child readers of their changing place in their literature and even in their own country. Judith Saltman's overview of Canadian picture books in her survey shows that today Canadian picture books also enjoy an international reputation.[2]

What are the national, racial, and ethnic concerns that are reflected in *Windows and Words?* In "The Rise of the Aboriginal Voice in Canadian Adolescent Fiction 1970-1990," Beverley Haun shows that literature of or about First Nations peoples deserves a presence on the national stage as literature, and also as a social and political commentary. She writes with sensitivity about Natives' relationships to outside cultures and how they dealt with the repercussions of European domination in colonial times, as well as their emergence from and reaction to a way of life imposed by other cultures. Cecily Devereux, in "'not one of those dreadful new women': Anne Shirley and the culture of imperial motherhood," examines how the vestiges of British imperialism in a young Canada shaped the very concept of motherhood for L. M. Montgomery. She argues that Anne "realizes" the "idea of woman as imperial 'mother of the race'" (125) and that this concept cannot be ignored in trying to understand "first-wave" feminism. Examining methodologies from the point of view of a cultural anthropologist and using Montgomery's work as her central case study, Virginia Careless demonstrates that literary critics must be aware of the social and cultural background of any work of fiction, particularly when making literary comparisons. In "A Parliament of Stories: Multiculturalism and the Contemporary Children's Literature of Saskatchewan," Gregory Maillet insists it is misguided to consider as minor the children's literature of the multi-cultural community in Saskatchewan. He provides a very different approach to what ought to be the corpus of children's literature in our country, arguing that scholars interested in Canadian children's fiction should be aware that there are works out of the Métis and ethnic cultures of Saskatchewan that should not be ignored. His title, "A Parliament of Stories," underscores the scholarly need to do justice to the "parliament" of cultures that *is* Canadian culture. John Sorfleet's commentary "The Nature of Canadian Children's Literature" is a homely confirmation of our identity as a nation. He provides a meeting place for all the cultural perspectives in the present volume. The most basic distinction about the Canadianness in the last century's literature for the young is that the imaginative landscape changed to "home ground"—to the landscape of our own country. In the closing commentary of *Windows and Words*, Elizabeth Waterston brings us back to a consideration of what children are and how they grow and change, and insists that scholars, teachers, and writers should focus on their *literary* needs.

Some papers have been left in their original, somewhat unorthodox, format for what may be called reasons of authenticity. One of these is Tim Wynne-Jones's address, which opened the symposium. So enthusiastically was it received that it seemed fitting that readers of the present volume have the opportunity to read his words as they were spoken. Given space limitations and the editors' objectives, some submissions on Montgomery had to be left out. If the aim had been a book on Montgomery, there were enough excellent essays to create one. The six essays selected represent the wide range of scholarly approaches Montgomery's novels inspire, from Irene Gammel's feminist approach to John Sorfleet's classic study of the Christian progress of the entertainingly wayward Anne Shirley, as well as Helen Siourbas's timely discussion of the canonical status of Montgomery's novels. The prominence of Montgomery's work in *Windows and Words* should be viewed as a tribute to her central place in Canadian children's literature; the editors hope that such extensive interest will serve as a model for the kind of attention subsequent writers of children's literature deserve, many of whom are presented in Judith Saltman's overview, as well as in Beverley Haun's and Gregory Maillet's more specialized surveys. And finally, for variety, the editors left three informal commentaries in their original format in this collection made up predominantly of formal essays.

In closing, the editors would like to thank the Canadianists' Committee of the Department of English at the University of Ottawa for their advice and kind support: Gerald Lynch, Frank Tierney, Glenn Clever, Camille La Bossièrre, Peter Stich, Cynthia Sugars, John Moss, Seymour Mayne, David Staines, Gwendolyn Guth, and Linda Morra. We would like to thank (then) Chair Keith Wilson for opening the symposium on Canadian Children's Literature, and thank Linda Morra a second time for the energy with which she assisted us in organizing the conference and in helping with the initial stages of this book. We are grateful to the Department of English and the National Library of Canada for hosting and helping to sponsor the Canadian Children's Literature Symposium. Mary Jane Starr, Randall Ware, and Mary Collis (retired children's librarian of the National Library) were generous with their time and efforts in making the readings and workshop associated with the conference such a success; Daniel St-Hilaire assisted in the technical reproduction of the illustrations in *Windows and Words*. The conference and the publication of *Windows and Words* would not have been possible without the financial assistance of the Social Sciences and Humanities Research Council, and the Faculty of Arts Research and Publication Committee as well as the University Research Fund of the University of Ottawa.

NOTES

1. I focus on "issues" that are common to the essays within the collection, some of which reflect abiding issues in children's literature in America and in Britain as well. For Canadian historical overviews, the following works are invalu-

able: Sheila Egoff and Judith Saltman, *The Republic of Childhood: A Critical Guide to Canadian Children's Literature in English* (Toronto: Oxford University Press, 1990), Judith Saltman, *Modern Canadian Children's Books* (Oxford University Press, 1987), and Elizabeth Waterston, *Children's Literature in Canada* (New York: Twayne, 1992). For critical background on Canadian children's literature, see the academic journal *Canadian Children's Literature (CCL)*, and on children's literature in America, Britain, and Canada, see Sheila Egoff et al. *Only Connect: Readings on Children's Literature* 2nd ed. (Toronto: Oxford University Press, 1980), and Sheila Egoff et al. *Only Connect: Readings on Children's Literature*. 3rd ed. (Toronto: Oxford University Press, 1996), which includes an entirely different collection of essays from the second edition. For a critical guide see Raymond E. Jones and Jon C. Stott, *Canadian Children's Books: A Critical Guide to Authors and Illustrators* (Don Mills: Oxford University Press, 2000), and for an award-winning historical survey and critical guide to French-Canadian children's literature, see Françoise Lepage, *Histoire de la littérature pour la jeunesse: Québec et francophonies du Canada* (Orléans: Les Éditions David, 2000). Useful websites and other electronic reference aids are included in Appendix B to Jones's and Stott's *Canadian Children's Books* listed above.

2.   Judith Saltman also has a website, *Canadian Children's Illustrated Books in English* http://www.slais.ubc.ca/saltman/ccib/background.html

WORKS CITED

Egoff, Sheila and Wendy Sutton. "Epilogue: Some Thoughts on Connecting." In *Only Connect: Readings on Children's Literature*. 3rd ed. Ed. Sheila Egoff, Gordon Stubbs, Ralph Ashley, and Wendy Sutton. Oxford: Oxford University Press, 1996.

Lewis, C. S. "On Three Ways of Writing for Children." In *Only Connect: Readings on Children's Literature*. 2nd ed. Ed. Sheila Egoff, G. T. Stubbs, and L. F. Ashley. Toronto: Oxford University Press, 1980.

Tolkien, J. R. R. "On Fairy-Stories." In *Tree and Leaf Including the Poem Mythopeia and the Homecoming of Beorhtnoth Beorhthelm's Son*. Preface by Christopher Tolkien. London: Harper Collins, 2001.

The Apprehension of Audience: The Difference Between Writing for Adults and Children

TIM WYNNE-JONES

IT'S AN HONOUR TO BE HERE FOR THIS SYMPOSIUM. A little spooky, perhaps, considering that the banner under which this annual spring event takes place is "Reappraisals: Canadian Writers." I don't feel quite dead enough yet to be reappraised, personally. But certainly there is a healthy body of Canadian children's literature out there very worthy of scholarly attention. Other speakers, this weekend, will be looking at subjects ranging all the way from L. M. Montgomery to . . . well, L. M. Montgomery. A third of the presentations will deal in one way or another with the redoubtable Maud. I think Virginia Careless perfectly captures our enduring fascination with our greatest literary export in the title of her paper, "L. M. Montgomery and Everybody Else."

My talk tonight, however, is entitled "The Apprehension of Audience: The Difference Between Writing for Adults and Children." When Aïda Hudson invited me to this symposium, she asked specifically if I would address this topic. I am pleased to do so because it is a subject about which I am prone to prevaricate. Tonight I will attempt to tell all.

"There is no difference; it's all just writing." I've been known to say that, with a defensive *whinge* in my voice, as if the question veils dreary implications. Of course there are differences. But I suppose I would rather people concentrate on the similarities: interesting and original characters, effective dialogue, a persuasive narrative voice, colourful figures of speech, and a well-turned story line. If, indeed, these are the ingredients of good fiction. We shall see . . . .

In a less querulous frame of mind, I might say, "When I write for children, I leave out things they are not likely to find interesting, things like a morbid preoccupation with degenerative cartilage, for instance, or mutual funds." I do not say, mind you, things children will not understand. I can claim no expertise in what children may or may not understand and, for that matter, I'm only ever guessing when I make a decision about what children may or may not find interesting. Any adult who sets himself up as an expert in this regard is, I think, probably a charlatan, or writing curriculum for the Ontario Government.

I recall sitting next to the noted children's illustrator, Ted Harrison, as we listened to a stirring speech by Monica Hughes. She was recalling the classics she had enjoyed as a child and there was a certain amount of sighing in the audience as nostalgic favourites were mentioned. Ted leaned over to me and said, behind his hand, something to the effect of, "When I was eleven, the only thing I wanted to read was *Mein Kampf*."

Anything might interest one child or another. What's more, I'm quite certain anything can be made clear to a child by a diligent writer, if it suits his or her dramatic purposes.

When I was at university, I lived with a gaggle of artsy-types in a house called The Toadstool. We had a good friend, Don Plewes, who was doing graduate work in physics and who visited The Toadstool when he needed distraction. We were genuinely interested in Don's work and he took great pains to explain it to us. No, I should say he took great *joy* explaining it to us. Indeed, he felt strongly that if he could not explain himself in a manner we could grasp, there was probably something fundamentally wrong with his approach to the work. This is an important point. Don did not assume, as specialists are wont to do, that his work was beyond our humble scope. It was his job as a storyteller to give us the goods in an accessible fashion. That is the job of a children's writer.

As an addendum to this anecdote, I have to say that I visited Don recently, not having seen him in ten years. He is now internationally renowned in the field of cancer research. With great exuberance, he recalled his delivery of a paper at a conference held in Chicago. Although his audience was comprised entirely of scientists involved in similar research, there was a point he was not sure they would be able to understand if described in words alone, since it involved some tricky molecular activity. So he enlisted his son to make a computer generated cartoon to illustrate his point. His son was fifteen.

I think of Don and his son Britten whenever someone tells me that something is beyond a child's understanding. Not all children are wizards. But I would rather appeal to the tiny bit of wizard that may reside in the soul of a dullard than target my work at the statistical dullness ascribed to the so-called average kid. Average—ordinary—is something children of a certain difficult age aspire to if they are not blessed with extraordinary good looks or athletic prowess. I do not see it as part of my mandate to encourage these aspirations to shallowness. But rather to encourage a child to challenge the tyranny of opinion and the group imperative to conform; to encourage a child to look beyond the Procrustean bed of school and the school-yard. To my mind, Wonder is the antidote to ordinariness and the pre-eminent content of good children's fiction. While there are many superlatives one might apply to fine adult literature, wonderful, in the strictest sense of the word, is seldom one of them, with notable exceptions. *One Hundred Years of Solitude*, for instance, is indeed full of wonder.

I have entitled my presentation the "apprehension" of audience rather than the "targeting" of audience. There is an important difference, if only semantic. For one thing, targeting suggests that one's audience is also one's victim . . . .

To target an audience is a term more appropriate to marketing books rather than to writing them, a point I stress when speaking to new authors. Our job, as writers, is to write—not to package. Targeting takes for granted the non-existent "average kid." It presumes a set of consumer desires. It suggests a shopping list of themes and plots and character-types. It hints at formula. Every genre has a recognizable form and the writer who does not instinctively understand that is usually doomed.

But form is not formula.

The Name of the Rose by Umberto Eco and *I the Jury* by Mickey Spillane are both mysteries and follow the form of that genre, though they could not be more different in length or breadth or in any other way. (For one thing, Mike Hammer's Latin is decidedly vulgate.)

In my use of the phrase apprehension of audience, I mean to suggest arresting one's audience as opposed to killing them. But the word also suggests a kind of anxiety about that reader's response, which—as long as the anxiety is not debilitating—is not such a bad idea. One should never take one's audience for granted or underestimate it. Among children's writers this is especially important, since one must be careful from one's lofty height neither to patronize nor to pontificate.

The novelist sits at a keyboard and, like a pianist, is able to produce on that one instrument a work of many voices, tones, and colours, many melodies and counter melodies. The result, of course, may be grand or merely upright. The writer, however, who addresses more than one audience in his or her work—adults and children, for instance—or who writes across a range of genres—from romance to mystery, let's say—might better be compared to an organist, who further modifies the creative process with an array of stops and pedals, brought into play not so much to better target the work, but to better suit it to varying reader expectations.

Genre writing, which includes writing for children, depends upon a recognizable form, however far the envelope is pushed. Writing for adults, on the other hand, by which I mean the books reviewed under the banner of Literature, is, I believe, in this last chapter of the twentieth century, primarily about form. In children's fiction, style is the handmaiden of story, whereas, in adult Literature, story is often the handmaiden of style.

I say Literature to distinguish a category of writing that would rather not be genre-fied, which is to say, it is not historical fiction, crime fiction, romance, what have you. Those genres tend, like children's fiction, to put story foremost.

Carol Shield's *Swann, A Mystery* nicely exhibits the point I am trying to make here. It is a novel that cleverly uses the form of the mystery genre to its literary ends, while at the same time, being enough of an actual mystery to win the Crime Writers of Canada's Arthur Ellis Award. It is a very clever, very stylish piece, the last third of which, subtitled *The Swann Symposium*, is written as a film script. This is the kind of playing around with reader expectations that distinguishes the best of contemporary adult fiction. But the artful disintegration of the text into a film script is revealing.

I sometimes think that the Literature-set have handed over the job of storyteller to the filmmaker, in the same way painters, earlier in the century, handed over the job of realistic representation to the photographer.

Perhaps you experienced the same curiosity in seeing the movie, *The English Patient*, as did I, having already read the book. I barely recognized it at all. I had enjoyed the book and I very much enjoyed the film. What the screenwriter and director, Anthony Minghella, had done, with surpassing craft, was to pull from the complex fabric of Michael Ondaatje's text a golden thread of story.

The thread of story from a weighty postmodern novel like, let's say, Martin Amis's *The Information* would be a mere scrap of a thing, certainly not something you could tie in a bow. But that is not to scoff at Amis's achievement. It is, in its way, a monumental work; story was never the point of *The Information*.

Recently I heard Jane Hamilton referring to her award-winning novel, *The Book of Ruth*. She said, "There really is no plot in the book; it's driven by [Ruth's] voice."

Voice, theme, pattern, style, assaults on formal structure—these are the forces at work in contemporary adult fiction. If there is Story, the author often winks to the reader as if it's kind of a shared joke—but not to worry, he's not going to resolve it, or, if he does, it will be in an ironic key.

According to French philosopher Jean-François Lyotard "our postmodernity consists of our inability to believe any longer in the grand narratives—such as the Jewish, Christian, Marxist eschatologies—that hitherto have bestowed meaning on history."

So everything is meta this and meta that—Literature is metastasizing all over the place. The results can be truly fascinating. The adult in me loves the intellectual foreplay, the lengths to which words can be used to unlock meaning, the semiotic challenge of hypertext. The adult in me grasps the notion that the interpretations of a narrative are inexhaustible, that as Derrida insists, the text is merely a "trace." And so the adult in me reads *The Unbearable Lightness of Being*. But the child in me reads *The Golden Compass*. Something with direction. The child in me still wants something that begins and ends with a muddle in the middle and a satisfying resolution. Unlike Maud Montgomery, I do not insist on a happy ending, only that the resolution amply discharges the debt, the conflict, out of which the story grew. The child in me craves coherence.

Story is what makes a children's novel tick. Apparently there is a boom in biography in North America. It seems the adult reading public still yearns for stories. If they have to, they'll even settle for real ones.

Writing is a performance art. Unless one is writing in a diary one is always writing with an audience of others in mind. But it is important to me not to think of that audience as an amorphous, faceless, targetable entity. Nor do I wish to write for an exclusive group. I try to write for one and all, inclusively: one and all, excluding no one simply by dint of age or sex.

I might further dissemble and say that I only write for me. I have, after all, been many ages. In me somewhere lurks a six-year-old listening to *The House at Pooh Corner*, an eleven-year-old giggling helplessly over the adventures of *Freddy the Pig*. There skulks a teen reading *Tom Swift Junior* in his bedroom and his older sister's copy of *Peyton Place* in the bathroom. I am a twenty-five-year-old reading *Trout Fishing in America*, a thirty-year-old washed up on *Brighton Rock*. In me is a fifty-year-old reading Nick Homby and Barbara Kingsolver and Tim Findley. And in me is the raw material, at least, of a seventy-five-year-old. (I should be so lucky.) At that point I hope to return to *The House at Pooh Corner*, if Eeyore doesn't mind the company.

There is a difference in writing for children, perhaps, but it is important to me never to relegate the child to the ghetto of childhood, but rather to see childhood as part of a continuum. I have said, elsewhere, that I write for adults who were once kids and for kids who will one day be adults. This is coy, I know; the kind of thing you say on the radio to divert an interviewer from a thorny topic.

So let me try now to make clear the most important aspects of difference, beyond the importance of Story, between a book for adults and a book for children.

In a children's book there must be a child's window onto the story. By this, I mean something more than simply a child's point of view—how low the sill is, so to speak. I mean also the transparency of the glass, itself. In a book, the medium through which we see the story unfold is language.

I love language. Words tend to carry me away, if I'm not careful. In adult fiction, this lexical abduction is permissible. But in a children's book, the words mustn't get in the way. In adult fiction, one is allowed the luxury of stained glass, if you will, of deliberately drawing the attention of one's audience to the decorative surface tension, the shimmer and glow of the language itself. There is, I think, in this an existential belief that the view—the world at large—is not really seeable, anyway. It is enough that the medium be translucent, shed a little light on the utterly unknowable. To put it another way, the story may not—*cannot*—resolve, but one is resolved to that insolubility.

A child's window must be made of clearer stuff. Resolution, however difficult, is expected and the medium, the language of the book, must have within it, as Frank Kermode calls it, a "sense of an ending." One attempts to write plainly, which is not to say that one must always write in words of one syllable or stifling short sentences, meant to telegraph meaning. I cannot resist word play and, from what I hear from young readers, they like it too. But I must be sparing with it.

On a side note, I seldom swear in children's books. I don't think of myself as prudish in this regard and I don't think it is inappropriate for other children's writers to use obscenities. My day-to-day speech is far from immaculate. My decision to buy the Collins Concise Dictionary was based upon the fact that it had all of the four-letter words adequately explained and thumb-indexed for easy access. I do not think of myself as hypocrite for censoring myself in this way, nor is it done to avoid tempest-in-a-tea-pot scandals from outraged teachers, although that is undoubtedly a factor in children's fiction writing. Mostly, I leave out obscenities because they are tired and depleted of real force. They're too easy.

So when Cal Crow calls Burl a "dumb stump-for-brains," or shouts, "When you gonna act your age, boy, and not your shoe size," there's a chance my reader has not heard those expressions before; whereas the reader has probably heard "shit-for-brains" and "When you gonna fuckin' grow up."

As a writer for children I do not pull out all the stops. But I hope I am never proscriptive, at least in my use of language. Age-appropriate vocabulary lists, an idea fostered by publishers eager to capitalize on the literacy-boom, are anathema to me and a death certificate to culture. As Umberto Eco says, the Truth is an ongoing negotiation between empirical evidence and culture, and the negotiating team is, he suggests, the linguistic community, by which he means those whose command of language is not fettered, who can find the words to give shape to the truth. Children need words, the more the merrier.

Another side note: I refer often to works which might be considered part of the Canon of children's literature. I regularly cite *Alice's Adventures in Wonderland* or *Winnie-the-Pooh*. In my collection of short stories, *Lord of the Fries*, the title story is a deconstruction of "Rumpel-stiltskin." "The Anne Rehearsals" is about a trio of girls who call them-selves the Rillas, who celebrate everything Anneish, and what happens to them during a disastrous school production of *Anne of Green Gables*. And the two main characters of my story "The Bermuda Triangle" are none other than Jim Hawkins and Billy Bones. Relatively few kids today will read *Treasure Island*, but it strikes me as worthwhile, where fitting, to keep these reading adventures of another era alive if only by allusion. (Actually, my hope is that one day a kid who has read my stuff will pick up *Treasure Island* and say, "Hey, Stevenson stole Wynne-Jones's characters.") These allusions are not meant as a sly literary conceit. It is not meant to exclude the kid who does not get the reference, but rather to encourage the kid who does. "Hey, you've read a thing or two, by gum!" It is also, obviously, a debt to pleasure recognition of heritage. A statement: books are where I come from.

My son's seventh-grade teacher recently mentioned, in passing, a line from a nursery rhyme, "Jack Spratt could eat no fat," only to discover that only five students had ever heard the line before.

So I make a point of getting the old words into the mouths of chil-dren. Not in a didactic way or in the sense of spoon-feeding them doses of vocab. so that they will be able to successfully negotiate a letter from Rev-enue Canada. Nothing really prepares you for that! I am more interested in supplying the valuable resource of delight. I tell kids that the Dictio-nary is a Lost and Found. And that found words are the property of the finder. Words like "mazuma" and "epistaxis" give new meaning—not to mention pizzazz—to plain old money or the common nosebleed. Then there is "snitchy" and "oragious"—perfectly useful expressions to describe, respectively, an irritable teacher, let's say, or a tempestuous hockey game. Then there is "floccinaucinihilipilification." "Floccinaucinihilipilifica-tion" means the "habit of estimating as worthless." Kids understand that well enough. I have passed a school yard and heard a kid using that mar-velously excessive word a year after my school visit.

Words inform my writing—take me places I had not expected to go. But in writing for kids, I try never to let this happen at the expense of story. So one soft-pedals language, avoiding both obfuscation and verbal effusion, while mindful of the opportunity to play with words that might arise in a character like the Maestro. Nathaniel Orlando Gow is a character who shows little restraint in *his* fooling around with words, and thus allows me the liberty of doing the same.

My novel *The Maestro* came about because I was asked to write a radio drama based in one way or another on Glenn Gould. The drama, had I written it, would have been most definitely for adults, since CBC radio has no children's programming. The invitation came in May of 1993 from a CBC producer, Bill Lane, for whom I had written a dozen plays. There was to be a big celebration of Gould that fall and CBC wanted proposals. However, by the time I was approached, the proposals were due the following week. I gave it a shot and came up with the idea of Gould having a secret hideaway in his beloved Northland. He would need a piano, of course, so I airlifted one to him by helicopter. That image was about all I really had by the deadline, and, as Bill Lane noted, as striking as the image was, it wasn't going to go over so well on radio.

The image, mercifully, did not fly away. It went underground where my unconscious worked on it. And in August, three months later, I woke up early in the morning and wrote down the first chapters of the novel.

I woke up with a boy, Burl Crow, and a pressing motivation, his cruel father, Cal. I woke up with a conflict already in progress. I woke up with someone to *see* that airborne grand piano.

That it was witnessed from the point of view of a thirteen-year-old needn't necessarily have prohibited the story evolving into an adult work. I toyed seriously with it. After all, at the time, I had written three adult novels and no children's novels.

Had I done so, I could have explored Cal's infidelity more explicitly, his abuse more graphically. Cal's dialogue would have, inevitably, been riper. In an adult novel I might even have decided that young Burl should have some kind of an affair, however fleeting, with the lonely genius he found in the pyramid on the shore of Ghost Lake.

None of these ideas, finally, captivated me enough to propel me in that direction. My guess is, in retrospect, that the initial expression that early August morning had within it the seeds of its final form and not simply because the protagonist was an adolescent.

In that first outburst of story-structured words, as Aidan Chambers would call them, there was something stronger at work than what a child might find interesting, or what issues I might wish to explore. There was the voice of the narrator.

Philip Pullman recently mentioned at a conference that the most important character in any novel is the narrator. I think I knew this but couldn't be sure if I had ever heard it articulated before.

The voice of the narrator is not the voice of the author. I knew that well enough. The voice I used to narrate *Odd's End*, my first adult novel, could not possibly have narrated any of the stories in *Some of the Kinder Planets*, let alone *Zoom at Sea*. The narrator's voice is not neutral. It is engaged in the goings on to a greater or lesser degree. It is omniscient to a greater or lesser degree.

Though my writing process varies from book to book, it inevitably begins with a scene that is vivid to me, though I have no fixed idea of where it may be leading. In that first committal to the page, the narrator's voice, however, is more or less fixed, I think.

In children's fiction, a writer tends to show rather than to tell. This is the last important difference I wish to make between children's fiction and adult fiction. When I am trying to explain this concept, I use the following example.

"After Lydia's phone call, Lyle was hurt and angry." That's a telling sentence. Whereas, "After Lydia's phone call, Lyle photocopied her portrait forty-three times, stapled them to his flesh and threw himself in the fish pond in the lobby of the school." That is a showing sentence. And it is obviously more potent. It transmits an image—one begins to see Lyle. It is, of course, equally effective in writing for adults to show rather than to tell, but there are things one wants simply to tell one's reader: a bit of the character's history, an event which is outside the story but impacts upon it. Whatever. The narrator takes on this parenthetic task. However, when the narrative voice in one of my young people's stories takes over, my editor is bound to affix a post-it note that says, "This is very told, don't you think."

The idea is, for an age of children more attuned to images than words, paint a picture. And I like to do that. What's more, it is important for young readers, especially those who write themselves, to be shown by example that abstractions like "hurt" and "angry" let alone "love" are so generic as to be almost useless forms of expression.

But at some point, it is also wonderful to simply tell a story within the context of the larger story. This is generally frowned upon in contemporary children's fiction. There is this fear, I suppose, that the young reader's interest is tenuous at best and one should not stray too far from the main character, or from the path of the narrative, not gather too many flowers along the way, but get straight to Granny's lest the reader be consumed by the big bad wolf of Boredom.

So let me summarize: I think that the five elements which most importantly differentiate children's fiction from adult fiction are:

1. The relative importance of Story in the Aristotelian sense;
2. The window onto the events;
3. The relative transparency of the language;
4. The narrator's voice; and
5. The degree to which the story is told.

There is nothing in this list about the relative literary quality or seriousness of one form over the other. Every book I write is the best book I can possibly write. I do not feel that the stops and pedals which modify a children's text lessen it, anymore than I believe a sonnet is a lesser poem than one written in blank verse. A short story by Alice Munro or a poem by William Stafford are not lesser items than a novel because of their relative brevity. They are the forms best suited to the job at hand, the forms best suited to the voice of the narrator.

Graham Greene, the seminal influence of my early adulthood, referred to his lighter fair, books like *The Third Man* as "entertainments," whereas books like *The Power and the Glory* he considered to be more substantial works, examining grander themes. Nowhere in his two autobiographies, however, does he suggest that the two kinds of books were aimed at different readers. The categorization merely expressed his intention, not his audience. He also said, "It is only in childhood that books have any influence on our lives." If that is true, then my childhood seems to live on and on. I have never lost the taste for Story. It is, inevitably, what's on my mind when I sit down at the keyboard to play.

Thank you.

Canadian Children's Literature at the Millennium

JUDITH SALTMAN

IN ATTEMPTING TO DECIPHER trends and patterns in Canadian children's literature at the millennium, it is important to remember that Canada is a young country and our children's literature, in comparison to the more than 300-year-old British children's literature, is also still young. Many publishers, writers, and critics have observed that our children's literature may go back over 100 years, but that it has only shown significant growth in the last twenty-five to thirty years.

A survey of our literary history, from the first Canadian children's books of the Victorian period, written by visitors to Canada or immigrants, reveals a body of children's stories rooted in the challenging Canadian landscape, in the genres of the outdoor adventure survival story, the retelling of First Nations and Inuit legends, and the wild-animal biography. These genres dominated the early Canadian children's books of the late nineteenth and first half of the twentieth century. Although L. M. Montgomery, Ernest Thompson Seton, and Sir Charles G. D. Roberts received international acclaim in the early twentieth century, very few Canadian children's books were written and published until the 1970s. Canada was known for the paucity of its literature: approximately fifty to sixty books for children were published annually in the 1960s. Realistic fiction and fantasy emerged slowly. Fantasy had no storehouse of Arthurian magic and myth to draw upon in this land of Native legend, and realistic fiction was still blithely skipping across the tundra well into the 1970s at a time when American children's books battled tumultuously with the new, harsher social realism. Historical fiction continued as a lacklustre, didactic genre.

In the late 1960s and early 1970s, new, small, nationalistic children's publishing houses, such as Groundwood Books, Kids Can Press, Annick Press, Women's Press, Tundra Books, and James Lorimer, exploded into the world of Canadian publishing and joined the larger publishing houses with a commitment to Canadian children's literature, such as Oxford University Press, to begin the process of building an indigenous children's literature. By the 1980s, Canadian children's publishers had diversified and began to market themselves internationally. Our writers expanded their range into new genres and themes. The results were stories of a multicultural society, the beginnings of a young adult literature, novels of social history, time travel fantasy, and first-class picture books. Over the last thirty years our children's literature has achieved an international presence. At the end of the 1990s, we can say that Canadian children's literature has emerged as a force.

In retrospect, the decade of the 1990s is most notable for the remarkable increase in the volume of Canadian children's book publishing. Today, up to 400 books are published annually. However, consider for context that the United States and England each bring out approximately 6,000 children's titles a year. Picture books and non-fiction books represent almost two-thirds (one third each) of new children's book production in Canada through the 1990s. Children's fiction follows, ranging from one-fifth to one-quarter. Young adult fiction lags behind at generally one-tenth of new books.

The picture book and fiction genres, in particular, have benefited from the contributions of new illustrators and writers who have emerged to practise their art with talented proficiency through the 1990s.

The years since 1990 have also seen artistic growth and the exploration of new terrain by many authors who ushered in the new Canadian children's literature of the 1970s and 1980s, among them, Michael Bedard, Martha Brooks, Brian Doyle, Sarah Ellis, Monica Hughes, Welwyn Wilton Katz, Jean Little, Janet Lunn, Kevin Major, Kit Pearson, Diana Wieler, Budge Wilson, and Tim Wynne-Jones. In addition, recognized writers for adults have turned to children's books. Margaret Atwood,

George Bowering, Roch Carrier, Thomas King, P. K. Page, and W. D. Valgardson shifted audiences from adults to children with greater success than earlier writers.

Meanwhile, francophone works translated into English are slowly increasing in picture books, but not noticeably in fiction. Although picture book authors and illustrators, such as Roch Carrier, Stéphane Poulin, Marie-Louise Gay, and other notable talents, are published in English-language editions, and often illustrate English-language texts, generally translation into English from French-Canadian children's literature is inadequate. Multilingual and bilingual books have plummeted from a high in the late 1980s.

Canada's cultural diversity has been increasingly reflected in Canadian children's literature, especially in picture books. This reflection has moved from the superficial treatment of multiculturalism as a confined issue in the early books of the 1960s and 1970s to a richer examination of life within a variety of cultures. Writers and illustrators of the 1990s tend to address cultural diversity in a broader and more considered exploration. The texts and illustrations of such creators as Harvey Chan, Luis Garay, Richardo Keens-Douglas, Tololwa Mollel, Paul Yee, and Song Nan Zhang have deepened the representation of diversity in Canadian children's literature.

The picture book genre has undergone a dramatic increase in new writing and illustration talent since 1990 as a wave of immigration brought new writers and illustrators to Canada in the 1980s and 1990s. In another trend in picture books, several children's authors of award-winning older fiction, including Michael Bedard, Monica Hughes, Jean Little, Janet Lunn, Barbara Smucker, and Paul Yee, have turned their hands to the younger picture book genre in the 1990s.

In the 1970s, Tundra Books, and its author-illustrators Ann Blades and William Kurelek, pioneered picture books with strong Canadian content and setting. After a trend toward the predominance of fantasies and domestic tales throughout the 1980s, picture books set definitively in a contemporary or historical Canadian context have reappeared with a new vitality in the 1990s, transporting the reader to the west coast, in Paul Yee's *Ghost Train* and Sheryl McFarlane's *Waiting for the Whales*; the Prairie regions, in W. D. Valgardson's *Sarah and the People of Sand River* and Jo Bannatyne-Cugnet's *A Prairie Alphabet*; the Arctic, in Michael Kusugak's

Northern Lights; and Newfoundland, in Geoff Butler's *The Killick*. Diverse Canadian histories, geographies, and cultural backgrounds are presented to children through these books, as they are in the recent burgeoning of multi-ethnic picture books considering the immigrant experience, such as Jim McGugan's *Josepha: A Prairie Boy's Story.*

While rich with a sense of place and true to cultural, geographical, psychological, and emotional experiences, these evocative books are not the ones to which young children are most endeared—perhaps because of their often weighty subject matter and serious tone. Despite the integrity and art of these recognizably Canadian picture books, it appears to be the simple delight, hilarity, appealing characters, and frequently serial nature of humorous stories, fantasies, and domestic family picture books that particularly regale young children. While the now canonical generation of 1970s and 1980s picture book characters—Bonnie McSmithers, Mortimer, and Brenda and Edward—endure as unforgettable and beloved characters, Mrs. Ming, Farmer Joe, Jillian Jiggs, Zoom the cat, and Franklin the turtle engage a new audience of young readers.

Among the many voices of different cultures in 1990s picture books are those of aboriginal picture book creators, including Thomas King, Michael Kusugak, George Littlechild, William Kent Monkman, Shirley Sterling, C. J. Taylor, Jan Bourdeau Waboose, and Leo Yerxa. These writers and illustrators, published by mainstream publishing houses, have added to the substantial body of aboriginal stories from a growing number of First Nations presses and Native cultural groups, such as Fifth House, Theytus, Pemmican, and others.

In addition to creating single-tale picture books, a significant number of First Nations writers and editors have focused on anthologizing and retelling Native legends for children. This movement began in the 1960s, parallel with the publications of Christie Harris and other non-Native retellers, and in the strong work of George Clutesi, who cleared a path for other aboriginal writers in the 1970s and 1980s such as Basil Johnston and Inuit artist Agnes Nanogak. These retellers worked to preserve their cultural heritage and sustain the oral tradition, reshaping tales in an authentic aboriginal voice, often from elders' memories. Through the 1990s, anthologies have diminished in number and have been overwhelmed by the plethora of single-tale Native legends from such reteller-illustrators as C. J. Taylor. These picture books, while forceful and articulate in themselves, lack the scope and depth of the mythological power of story and culture found in the weave of tales in collections of legend. The questions that Native and non-Native storytellers continue to face, such as the problem of how much of a culture is translatable and how to sustain an authentic voice, have gained a more serious dimension in the 1980s and 1990s, encompassing the divisive issue of cultural appropriation.

Since 1990, Canadian authors have retold folk tales for children that originate in many different worldwide cultures, reflecting Canada's diversity. This is most notable in the illustrated picture book tales, which are successfully marketed internationally. Titles such as the Jewish *Something from Nothing* by Phoebe Gilman, the Chinese *The Cricket's Cage* by Stefan Czernecki, the African *Orphan Boy* by Tololwa Mollel, the Caribbean *La Diablesse and the Baby* by Richardo Keens-Douglas, and others, exemplify the breadth and vitality of this trend. Unfortunately, the majority of these 1990s oral tradition picture books have not drawn on Canadian folklore. Perhaps the move to market picture books internationally has resulted in fewer reflections, in both anthologies and picture books, of Canadian folk identity, including that of French-Canadian folklore, pioneer folktales, and Inuit mythology.

The historically tentative development of poetry for Canadian children has been nourished in the 1990s by David Booth's *Til All the Stars Have Fallen: Canadian Poems for Children*. This anthology draws from Canadian poetry written originally for both adult and children's audiences, and furthers the momentum provided in the 1960s by Mary Alice Downie and Barbara Robertson's first collection of adult poetry selected for children, *The Wind Has Wings: Poems from Canada*.

In the 1970s and 1980s, Dennis Lee performed an infectiously humorous alchemy in *Alligator Pie* and other titles, playing with place, history, and the power of naming to create a new Canadian nursery and nonsense lore. Robert Heidbreder and Lois Simmie both followed Lee in the 1980s and 1990s with different signature styles remarkable for their wit and lyricism, qualities that also characterize Sheree Fitch's poetry, noted for its active, performance-oriented voice. The challenge of producing a rich body of poetry for children is evident throughout children's literature worldwide. While the development of a Canadian body of children's poetry still rests with a small group of writers, the emerging talent of the following nature and lyric poets is taking poetry in new directions: Barbara Nichol in *Biscuits in the Cupboard*, Sue Ann Alderson in *Pond Seasons*, and Robert Priest in *Day Songs, Night Songs*. These writers present exciting possibilities beyond the nonsense and light verse that have characterized Canadian poetry to date.

The foundation genre of Canadian children's literature, realistic fiction, has also benefited from the emergence of new writers in the 1990s, particularly in young adult fiction and the children's and young adult short story. A new magic realism at times accompanies the enduring regionalism of Canadian writing in these genres. The outdoor adventure narrative and consideration of the immigrant experience continue while subgenres such as the realistic wild-animal biography are rarely found. As works of family and child life stories are characterized by a deeper social and psychological authenticity, so too are contemporary and historical stories strengthened by culturally diverse perspectives.

From the late nineteenth century, the survival story distinguished early Canadian children's realistic fiction and it continues to do so to the present day. Farley Mowat and James Houston produced exemplary outdoor survival stories in the mid- to late twentieth century. Through the 1970s and 1980s, the writing of both Monica Hughes and Jan Truss plumbed the psychological and emotional resonance of these stories, and in the 1990s both contemporary and historical settings provided the context for continued examination of Canadian youths' relationship to the wilderness. Many of the survival sagas combine more than one style or content of narrative. While an atmosphere of harsh realism dominates the survival narrative in Tim Wynne-Jones's *The Maestro*, it is subtly juxtaposed with that of magic realism. In *The Hollow Tree*, the history of the Loyalists comes alive through the powerful wilderness survival saga crafted by Janet Lunn.

Lunn's central protagonist is a teenage girl—a strong female adolescent in a genre that has been decidedly male. For many decades, the fictional setting for a young Canadian woman's connection with place has been L. M. Montgomery's pastoral landscape in her *Anne* stories. It was not until Jan Truss's *Jasmin* in the early 1980s that the Canadian wilderness presented a place of self-discovery for a solitary young female character. In the 1990s, we are introduced to a new group of adolescent protagonists whose survival stories and identification with the land focus on psychological and emotional, rather than physical, concerns. The

Canadian wilderness is a powerful metaphor for both the pain and healing in the female protagonists' lives in the coming-of-age novels *Sharla* by Budge Wilson, *Keri* by Jan Andrews, *Juliana and the Medicine Fish* by Jake Macdonald, and *Bone Dance* by Martha Brooks.

Beyond the survival and outdoor adventure stories, most realistic fiction since 1990 is urban in setting. Controversial subjects have gained a greater presence in contemporary child and teenage life stories, and have contributed to the continuing expansion and emotional breadth of young adult fiction in particular. There is a greater seriousness felt in Canadian domestic realism for the intermediate-age reader. Many younger books are now imbued with the harsh naturalism of adolescent fiction, but they are not issue-dominated. It is not plot or issue but character that is central to these episodic stories. In the realistic fiction of Julie Johnston, Sarah Ellis, and W. D. Valgardson, adult and child characters alike are real and memorable. Realistic stories also incorporate older protagonists than those published in previous decades. The publication of both young adult and culturally diverse stories has also grown, and in both, the measure of familial dysfunction, personal tragedy, and social conflict increases with the age of the central protagonist.

In recent years, historical and contemporary narratives of cultural diversity have become more numerous. Most of these works describe experiences of diaspora, the struggle of life in a new culture, and the experience of intolerance, as in the works of Paul Yee. In this body of writing, Canadian society is rarely accepting of cultural difference, as evidenced in Michèle Marineau's tragic *The Road to Chlifa*. With the exception of novels and short stories by such authors as Tim Wynne-Jones, Sarah Ellis, and Brian Doyle, and a few others, it is rare for the narrative to engage a multicultural group of adults and children in harmonious social interaction without the tension of intolerance. By contrast, Canadian picture books describe a more inclusive environment.

Lightness of spirit is also rare in young adult and culturally diverse fiction. The emotional tonality of works in this area is heavier, even painfully sombre. The delightful wit in works by Sarah Ellis, Teresa Toten, and Brian Doyle is the exception. Humour is more commonly found in works for younger readers, as in the mystery series by Linda Bayley, and the clever slapstick of Gordon Korman and Martin Godfrey.

While Canadian writers of young adult fiction approach dilemma and conflict with a painful naturalism, as found in the writings of Beth Goobie, Diana Wieler, William Bell, and Martha Brooks, their work is rarely marked by gratuitous despair. Their young adult characters exhibit, for the most part, dignity and moral sensibility in their decision-making. Many of the writers for young adults are practitioners of the short story. Gillian Chan, Bernice Friesen, Martha Brooks, Linda Holeman, Tim Wynne-Jones, R. P. MacIntyre, and Budge Wilson write stories of character and epiphany, a tradition in Canadian short stories for adults.

Similar to realistic fiction, in Canadian historical fiction since 1990, which often incorporates the theme of coming-of-age, we find older protagonists. Single, specific events in Canadian history are the subject of a minority of recent novels. John Ibbitson writes of the War of 1812; Marian Brandis of the 1837 Upper Canada MacKenzie Rebellion. The engaging dynamics of Canadian history come alive in these novels through the fictional experiences of ordinary adolescents swept up in large historical events. Actual political and historical figures are no longer the rough caricatures found in earlier historical fiction, but are rather depicted as fully-formed, complex individuals.

Most Canadian historical fiction explores Canadian life of the last few centuries. As with survival stories, there has been an increase in the number of female protagonists. Continuing in the path of 1980s publishing, social histories that describe life as lived in other periods through the portrayal of social behaviours, values, and daily incident are published in greater number than fictional works of specific, historical events. Primarily set in the late nineteenth or early twentieth century, these stories are given the weight of reality through their generous level of detail and their subtle exploration of the coming-of-age of young men and women, the immigrant experience, and labour history.

Of particular note are the strong narratives of nineteenth-century immigration and the Depression era. The cruel challenges of arrival and survival in a harsh land and the rewards of a new life are captured in works such as Jean Little's *The Belonging Place*, Linda Holeman's *Promise Song*, and Janet McNaughton's *To Dance at the Palais Royale*. The intense hardships of prairie life at the end of the Great War are made real in such stories as Celia Lottridge's *Wings to Fly*.

It is to stories of the Second World War, however, that a powerful group of historical fiction writers have lent their talents. Perhaps the stories of relatives or childhood memories have in recent times influenced authors to consider this period which was largely ignored prior to 1990. While many of these works are near-memoirs, others show evidence of the influence of historical research. These narratives are predominantly set in Europe, as in Carol Matas's holocaust fiction, or the British war stories of James Heneghan, Gerald Holt, and Monica Hughes. Kit Pearson's *The Sky Is Falling* and sequels is a trilogy with clear Canadian connections in its depiction of the war guest children's experiences in Toronto.

On the whole, historical fiction, echoing realistic young adult literature, is often harsh in tone and atmosphere, showing the physical hardships, relentless labour, prejudices towards cultural groups, and restrictions facing girls and women in past eras. However, the writing also demonstrates the resilience and integrity of the child and adolescent protagonists and offers faith in their psychological and emotional growth in this new land.

Canadian fantasists of the 1990s have explored an expanding number of subgenres, including time-slip fantasy, comic fantasy, psychological fantasy, and ghost stories. Much Canadian comic or light fantasy is written for a young audience. It is humorous and playful, and, on occasion, reflective. Such authors as Sandra Birdsell, Hazel Hutchins, Mordecai Richler, and Richard Scrimger enliven Canadian fantasy through creative innovations of character, plot, and theme.

Canadian time-slip fantasy of the 1970s and 1980s tended to focus on travel into the recent past and family history. Time-slip fantasy of the 1990s ventures into the more dramatically historical, even mythical past. Concern with the injustice of past social and political events has a more frequent presence in the 1990s than the unobtrusive, more private observance of ancestors found in earlier time travel fantasy. Julie Lawson's *White Jade Tiger* combines both trends.

The 1990s have also seen the emergence of a new form of fantasy in Canadian writing—the psychological fantasy, which often subsumes psychic phenomena as well as elements from other fantasy subgenres, such as time-travel or ghosts. Rather than relying on the traditional use of magic as a motivator of plot, authors use the acceptance of extrasensory perceptions and other supernatural powers to alter the shape of plot resolution and character development common from earlier fantasies. Michael Bedard and Welwyn Wilton Katz write in this mode. In many of these works, the psychological transformation of the protagonist takes precedence over the fantasy elements. This character maturation often echoes patterns familiar from the young adult realistic novel such as coming to terms with complex ethical dilemmas and, therefore, requires older characters with emotional and intellectual maturity and sense of identity. Canadian history and landscape have only just begun to figure in psychological fantasies, such as *Out of the Dark* by Katz.

In comparison to psychological fantasy, Canadian epic or high fantasies, such as Karleen Bradford's *Dragonfire*, are less developed as a genre. They incorporate the high adventure of the ongoing struggle of good and evil set in a Secondary Reality, but do not handle the imagery of the heroic quest as subtly as Canada's first high fantasist, Ruth Nichols.

Revisionist fantasies that imaginatively subvert folklore and fantasy elements are a new trend of the 1990s. The experimentation with irony and the use of intertextuality and allusion yields complex, dark revisionings of traditional fantasy and folklore tropes. Such works as Sarah Ellis's *Back of Beyond* and Priscilla Galloway's *Truly Grim Tales* are provocative and appeal to crossover adult audiences.

Canadian ghost fantasies, such as Kit Pearson's *Awake and Dreaming* and works by the prolific Margaret Buffie, explore and expand a new subgenre in children's fantasy. They diverge from the folklore idiom of the ghost story, as they attest to the endurance of the human spirit and the continuum that links past and present. They often slide between time-travel and psychological fantasies.

There has been little development of animal fantasy in Canada in the 1990s, with the notable exception of Kenneth Oppel's secondary created world of bat life, history, and mythology in the compellingly written *Silverwing* and sequels. Monica Hughes reigns as Canada's internationally celebrated science fiction writer for youth. Her stories are set in a future earth (often the Canadian north or the prairies) or on another planet, and subtly reflect Canadian social philosophies, cultural diversity, and values. While inventive, creative, and often distinctive, recent Canadian fantasies are not consistently successful in the difficult creation of an entirely plausible Secondary Reality that is convincing in its structure and code of logic and laws.

In conclusion, Canadian children's literature is very much alive and flourishing, a commanding body of writing and illustration. The scope of our literature has broadened greatly to include many more literary forms and styles than in the past. Many of the strongest of our writers and illustrators continue to reflect the sweep and range of the Canadian landscape and experience. As Canadian adults we can take pride in this new wave of

Canadian authors and illustrators and enthusiastically pass on to our children their country's literary inheritance.

WORKS CITED

1.   Picture books

Bannatyne-Cugnet, Jo. *A Prairie Alphabet*. Illus. by Yvette Moore. Montreal: Tundra Books, 1992.

Butler, Geoff. *The Killick: A Newfoundland Story*. Montreal: Tundra Books, 1995.

Kusugak, Michael Arvaarluk. *Northern Lights: The Soccer Trails*. Illus. by Vladyana Krykorka. Toronto: Annick Press, 1993.

McFarlane, Sheryl. *Waiting for the Whales*. Illus. by Ron Lightburn. Victoria, B.C.: Orca Book Publishers, 1991.

McGugan, Jim. *Josepha: A Prairie Boy's Story*. Illus. by Murray Kimber. Northern Lights Books for Children. Red Deer, Alta.: Red Deer College Press, 1994.

Valgardson, W. D. *Sarah and the People of Sand River*. Illus. by Ian Wallace. A Groundwood Book. Vancouver/Toronto: Douglas & McIntyre, 1996.

Yee, Paul. *Ghost Train*. Illus. by Harvey Chan. A Groundwood Book. Vancouver/ Toronto: Douglas & McIntyre, 1996.

2.   The Oral Tradition

Czernecki, Stefan. *The Cricket's Cage*. Winnipeg: Hyperion Press, 1996.

Gilman, Phoebe. *Something from Nothing*. Richmond Hill, Ontario: North Winds Press/Scholastic Canada, 1992.

Keens-Douglas, Richardo. *La Diablesse and the Baby: A Caribbean Folktale*. Illus. by Marie LaFrance. Toronto: Annick Press, 1994.

Mollel, Tololwa M. *The Orphan Boy*. Illus. by Paul Morin. Toronto: Oxford University Press, 1990; Toronto: Stoddart Publishing, 1995.

3.   Poetry

Alderson, Sue Ann. *Pond Seasons*. Illus. by Ann Blades. A Groundwood Book. Vancouver/Toronto: Douglas & McIntyre, 1997.

Booth, David, ed. *Til All the Stars Have Fallen: Canadian Poems for Children*. Toronto: Kids Can Press, 1989.

Downie, Mary Alice, and Barbara Robertson, eds. *The Wind Has Wings: Poems from Canada*. Illus. by Elizabeth Cleaver. Toronto: Oxford University Press, 1968.

Lee, Dennis. *Alligator Pie*. Illus. by Frank Newfeld. Toronto: Macmillan of Canada, 1974.

Nichol, Barbara. *Biscuits in the Cupboard*. Illus. by Philippe Béha. Toronto: Stoddart Kids, 1997.

Priest, Robert. *Day Songs, Night Songs*. Illus. by Keith Lee. A Groundwood Book. Vancouver/Toronto: Douglas & McIntyre, 1993.

4.   Fiction

Andrews, Jan. *Keri*. A Groundwood Book. Vancouver/Toronto: Douglas & McIntyre, 1996.

Bradford, Karleen. *Dragonfire*. Toronto: HarperCollins, 1997.

Brooks, Martha. *Bone Dance*. A Groundwood Book. Vancouver/Toronto: Douglas & McIntyre, 1997.

Ellis, Sarah. *Back of Beyond*. A Groundwood Book: Vancouver/Toronto: Douglas & McIntyre, 1996.

Galloway, Priscilla. *Truly Grim Tales*. Toronto: Lester Publishing, 1995; Toronto: Stoddart Publishing, 1996.

Holeman, Linda. *Promise Song*. Toronto: Tundra Books, 1997.

Katz, Welwyn Wilton. *Out of the Dark*. A Groundwood Book. Vancouver/Toronto: Douglas & McIntyre, 1995.

Lawson, Julie. *White Jade Tiger*. Victoria, B.C.: Beach Holme Publishing, 1993.

Little, Jean. *The Belonging Place*. Toronto: Viking/Penguin Books Canada, 1997.

Lottridge, Celia Barker. *Wings to Fly*. Illus. by Mary Jane Gerber. A Groundwood Book. Vancouver/Toronto: Douglas & McIntyre, 1997.

Lunn, Janet. *The Hollow Tree*. Toronto: Alfred Knopf Canada, 1997.

MacDonald, Jake. *Juliana and the Medicine Fish*. Great Plains Fiction Series. Winnipeg: Great Plains Publications, 1997.

McNaughton, Janet. *To Dance at the Palais Royale*. St. John's, Nfld.: Tuckamore Books/Creative Publishers, 1996.

Marineau, Michèle. *The Road to Chlifa*. Trans. by Susan Ouriou. Northern Lights Young Novels. Red Deer, Alta.: Red Deer College Press, 1995.

Oppel, Kenneth. *Silverwing*. Toronto: HarperCollins Publishers, 1997.

Pearson, Kit. *Awake and Dreaming*. Toronto: Viking/Penguin Books Canada, 1996.

———. *War Guests Trilogy: The Sky Is Falling; Looking at the Moon; The Lights Go on Again*. Toronto: Viking/Penguin Books Canada, 1989-1993.

Truss, Jan. *Jasmin*. A Groundwood Book. Vancouver/Toronto: Douglas & McIntyre, 1982.

Wilson, Budge. *Sharla*. Toronto: Stoddart Kids, 1997.

Wynne-Jones, Tim. *The Maestro*. A Groundwood Book. Vancouver/Toronto: Douglas & McIntyre, 1995.

The Rise of the Aboriginal Voice in Canadian Adolescent Fiction 1970-1990

BEVERLEY HAUN

OVER THE PAST FEW YEARS I compiled a database of Canadian fiction for adolescents published between 1970 and 1990 and still in print today. The study begins in 1970 in order to take account of conditions immediately before and after the 1973 Royal Commission on Publishing, and ends in 1990 to allow for the time it takes a novel to show staying power. Novels with an Aboriginal focus stood out from all the rest as preoccupying many of the authors of Canadian adolescent fiction. These are novels written by and or about Canadian Aboriginal and Métis people for an adolescent audience, but also include novels with significant Aboriginal elements even if the characters themselves are not primarily Aboriginal, such as novels with a central focus on specific Aboriginal cultural artefacts or ceremonies or attitudes toward the land. No other interest over the two decades of the study captured the imagination of writers to such an extent. Because Aboriginal literature is the most observable trend evident in the database, I chose to examine it in detail, first to determine its shape and values, and then to explore the forces and events that have contributed to Aboriginal literature's growing to represent more than a quarter of Canadian adolescent novels in print.

At the beginning of the period under discussion, an emerging sensitivity to Native issues developed in large part as a response to the federal government's 1969 white paper on Indian policy. The white paper "sought to end the collective rights of Aboriginal people in favour of individual rights." It included "plans to eliminate the protection for reserved lands, to terminate the legal status of Indian peoples, and to have services delivered to them by provincial governments." Although Native Canadians denounced its main terms and assumptions, the resulting bitterness and sense of betrayal helped strengthen the resolve of Aboriginal organizations to work together to bring about a change. This marked the beginning of a new phase in Aboriginal/non-Aboriginal relations, identified by the recent Royal Commission on Aboriginal Peoples as the "period of negotiation and renewal" that is "characterized by non-Aboriginal society's admission of the manifest failure of its interventionist and assimilationist approach" (Royal Commission on Aboriginal Peoples, 1996).

At the same time as political events were helping alter perceptions about the reality of coexisting in Canada, Native issues were being presented to all North Americans through popular culture media. In fact *Little Big Man* (1970) and *Dances With Wolves* (1990), both American films, bracket the two decades covered by this study, and are demonstrations of a shift, in one branch of popular culture, from a settler/invader view of Amerindians towards one more postcolonial in its outlook. This new outlook was instrumental in affecting the perceptions of thoughtful non-indigenous Canadians and helping them to reconsider and realign their attitudes towards the First Nations of the country and towards what it means to be Canadian.

Many non-Native Canadians find themselves feeling like outsiders when they try to discover a way of identifying directly with, or articulating specifically, what it means to be a Canadian. In "The Representation of the Indigene," Terry Goldie argues that non-Native Canadians look at a Native Canadian and see someone who is Other and therefore alien to themselves. But the Native is indigenous and cannot be alien (1995, 234). So the non-Native Canadian must be alien. But how can the Canadian be alien within Canada? Goldie suggests there are two possible solutions to this dilemma. One is that the non-Native culture attempts to incorporate the Other, superficially through appropriation of Aboriginal dress, jewellery, or names like Oneida Camp or Pontiac car. The alternative, more thoughtful, approach is through fiction. An attempt is made to understand aspects of Aboriginal culture by entering into it imaginatively as in novels by Rudy Wiebe, M. T. Kelly, and Peter Such. Conversely, suggests

Goldie, the non-Native culture may reject or erase the indigenous culture with the attitude that "[t]his country really began with the arrival of the whites" (234).

Goldie does not think the importance of the alien within can be overstated. In their need to become Aboriginal, to belong here, many non-Natives in Canada have adopted a process of co-opting indigenous values and experience. For many writers the only chance for "Indigenization" has seemed to be through writing about the people who are truly indigenous, the First Nations and the Inuit. However, the Aboriginal Canadian character constructed by these non-Native writers has become in literary circles a part of the Canadian imagination, rather than a representation of a contemporary or even a plausible historical Aboriginal. Instead, the literary Aboriginal is the sort of wise person who might persuade a non-Aboriginal Canadian to look to the First Nations for personal role models (Goldie 1995, 234).

Increasingly, as new immigrants to Canada continue the cultural practices of their native countries, and as the descendants of the older settler element of Canadian society reject the values associated with imperialism and the popular culture of the United States, the cultural values of Canadian indigenous peoples have become an attractive alternative. The strength of this need to identify with Native Canada is demonstrated by the contents of the database in this study. Since 1970 there has been an increase in the number of Aboriginal adolescent novels written, with a dramatic number of them staying in print. Of the 464 novels in the Bibliography of Canadian fiction for adolescents published from 1970 to 1990, forty-five or 9.7% fall into the category covered by the definition of Aboriginal Literature. But of the 134 novels that are still in print, thirty-four are Aboriginal Literature, a 25% share. These thirty-four Aboriginal titles can be divided into three subsets, each speaking to a different element of postcolonial discourse: thirteen novels reflect the values of the middle-class that postcolonial values have formed in reaction to; fourteen novels reflect the postcolonial desire to embrace Aboriginal philosophies or atone for invader atrocities; and seven novels by Aboriginals address a resistance to their displacement by the settler society and embrace a desire to live within or reconstruct their own culture. Because it is content driven, adolescent fiction provides an excellent context for the interrogation or promulgation of these values. I will examine each subset in turn.

The first group of novels focuses largely on Aboriginals yet reflects the values of the middle class. Although most authors chose an Aboriginal character either as the centre of the story, or as one of a pair of protagonists, and although the action of many of the novels centres on Aboriginal practices or artefacts, the final emphasis is on a "non-Native" resolution to the conflicts dealt with throughout the text.

False Face (1987) by Welwyn Wilton Katz is perhaps the best known of the novels that fall into this first group. It won the International Fiction Contest, the only Canadian adolescent novel published before 1990 to do so. It has a complex plot that weaves together three themes: concern for the fate of Aboriginal artefacts; concern for the environment; and concern about the corruption behind our social masks. It is the story of Laney, a teenage girl, who fights with her antique-dealer mother for the possession of False Face Society masks found in a bog near their home in London, Ontario. Laney wants to see the bog preserved as a wildlife habitat and to prevent its development into a subdivision by letting the public know it is an ancient Aboriginal site. Her mother wants to sell the masks quietly to a collector, without revealing their source. The "power" of the masks is used to reveal the mother's true feelings of animosity towards a daughter who resembles too closely, in both physical and emotional make-up, the husband she has divorced. The father was able to leave and build a new life, but the same opportunity is not given to Laney. Why the daughter cannot live with her father is never explained. This is one of the very few adolescent novels that does not have a happy ending.

A Métis classmate of Laney's is introduced in order to offer an Aboriginal point of view on this situation. Thoughtful questions are raised about Canada's dominant culture's right to disturb Aboriginal artefacts. Should they be allowed to decay in nature, or should they be preserved through appropriation or by artificial means? When non-Aboriginal Canadians find them, to whom do they belong? Who has a right to display them? Should they be "studied," or revert to the First Nation from whence they came? Ultimately the masks in the novel are not sold, studied, or displayed. They are returned to the bog by the Aboriginal character to protect the land from development through their powerful magic. Although an Aboriginal solution to the discovery of the masks is put forward by the author, the part played by the Aboriginal character is peripheral to the main story of unhealthy middle-class family dynamics that revolve around the mask.

What we do know of the Métis character, Tom, is that he lived his first fourteen years on a Mohawk reserve, and wants desperately to return. Before the death of his Mohawk father, he had been looking forward to coming of age and being initiated into the Society of Faces—to learn the Society's lore and participate in its ceremonies. Having used the masks to reveal decay and corruption in the dominant middle-class world, and having presented the politically expedient solution to the fate of the masks that were disturbed in the bog, and to the bog itself, however, Katz is done with her subplot. Tom is not allowed the option of initiation. He was introduced to present a Native point of view on the artefacts themselves and is not offered resolution to his own feelings of displacement. Katz sidesteps the issues she created for Tom and consigns him to an unfulfilled future in London with his white mother. At his father's grave he reflects that his father, though a "pure-bred Mohawk," had loved and married a white woman. "He had seen people as people, regardless of the colour of their skin. He belonged to a world that didn't yet exist" (105). With this model of behaviour in mind, Tom's last thought in the novel is, "white, Indian, Half-breed, what did it matter? Nobody was free, and nobody was safe. Everybody had to choose what to let himself be" (153). Here we have a politically expedient solution to the question of identity that models for the reader a position that would have all Canadians separate themselves from issues of race or identification with a specific ethnic group and select a path that Katz sees as leading to the greater good. But the greater good for whom? A comfortable middle-class status quo? This attitude may resolve racial conflicts between disparate groups, but leaves unaddressed questions about heritage and a right to practise and live one's culture. It echoes past official Canadian policies of assimilation of the Aboriginals of this country into the fabric of the dominant culture—not just with the intent of sharing the dominant culture, but with the sinister agenda of eliminating the Aboriginal ones, reducing them to historical records and artefacts to be studied or examined, displayed or sold. *False Face*, as I indicated, won a major literary award offered by the dominant sector in society.

All of the novels in this first subset maintain the values of the dominant segment of Canadian society while at the same time acknowledging the presence of the Aboriginal element of that society and beginning, however tentatively, to engage it in an imaginative dialogue.

Postcolonial Desires

The second subset express postcolonial desires. It is only when authors writing about Aboriginal Canadians leave behind what postcolonial theorists regard as the Imperialist or Western European values of Canada's dominant middle class that literary movement can be made toward any meaningful discourse between the indigenous and the non-indigenous cultures.

Some of this counter-textuality takes the form of novels that have been and are being written by authors, both non-Aboriginal and Aboriginal, of Aboriginal adolescent fiction who speak out of the postcolonial discourse, advocating that Aboriginals in Canada recapture their Native heritage. Non-Native writers who feel responsible for the degradation that Aboriginal cultures have undergone since the arrival of settlers in Canada advocate recognizing their responsibility for that degradation and joining the Aboriginal peoples of today in reclaiming their heritage. As well, they look to Aboriginal spirituality and environmental philosophies for ways to heal the social ills of the postcolonial society we now live in. Diana Brydon points out in "The White Inuit Speaks: Contamination as Literary Strategy" (1990, 196) that there is a current flood of books by non-Native Canadians embracing Aboriginal spirituality. For some, these books serve the need to feel at home in this country; for others they substitute a spiritual system of belief connected to the land to replace conventional Western forms of worship. In these books the writers place perceived inadequacies of the dominant culture in contrast to indigenous belief systems and ways of living harmoniously with the land and its creatures. They view the present moral and social corruption of our age against the pre-acculturated values of the First Nations that they see romantically as untainted by any of the evils of contemporary society.

One of the best of the fourteen novels in this category, *Blood Red Ochre* (1989) by Kevin Major, creates a complex but clear moral paradigm. Major's novel tells the story of the last of the Beothuk Nation and a teenage contemporary of the fishermen who destroyed the Beothuk meeting across time. There is no doubt as to the assignment of responsibility or the direction of condemnation and sympathy. It is worth noting that while colonial/Aboriginal history is rife with incidents of atrocious invader and settler behaviour, these incidents are often addressed in a minor way in adolescent novels because the didactic nature of adolescent fiction means that models of right action take precedence over depictions of grievous wrongs. Resistance as a postcolonial trait largely gives way in these narratives to models of idealized social reconstruction with indigenous and non-indigenous characters cooperating and coexisting.

Of these fourteen novels, half are historical fiction, two are science fiction, and the rest are works of contemporary realism. The novels divide into two distinct groups: those that acknowledge settler guilt in displacing and destroying Aboriginal cultures, and those that celebrate Aboriginal ways of living in the world.

The writers of Canadian adolescent Aboriginal fiction come full circle in these first two groups, from trying to assimilate the Aboriginals to non-Aboriginal ways to abandoning those ways and joining the Aboriginals in theirs. Neither seems a satisfactory answer to the Canadian cultural dilemma for each would deny or absorb one of the cultures and leave all Canadians the poorer for its absence.

Aboriginal Voices

The final subset is Aboriginal Voices. Aboriginals displaced by the settler occupation are also seeking to reposition themselves in this country. A large part of postcolonial discourse in Canada concerns itself with questions about contemporary models of coexistence between the group that exercises dominance in the society and the groups indigenous to the country that have been socially and culturally marginalized. Two main choices seem to present themselves in this discourse: a return to Aboriginal "authenticity" or the creation of a form of "hybridization."

The notion of authenticity is not an Aboriginal one, but one created from within the discipline of anthropology. Anthropologists, in their imperial "project of naming and thus knowing indigenous groups," imported to Canada "a notion of aboriginality, of cultural authenticity, which is now proving difficult to displace" (Ashcroft et al. 1995, 214). Yet the very notion of authenticity is questionable because it is not possible to return to, or rediscover, an absolute precolonial cultural purity or authenticity, nor possible "to create national or regional formations entirely independent of their historical implications in the European colonial enterprise" (195–196). Although authenticity is not a model that would end the marginalization of the First Nations in Canada, it does have validity as a metaphor "that permits collective self-fashioning" (Loomba 1998, 182). One may not, in fact, be able to return to the world of one's ancestors, but one can claim to be doing so, with political effect (183). By holding up ancestral cultural ideals, Canadian Aboriginals can offer a positive and healthy image to their children to counter the less positive image they often absorb from the attitudes that still prevail in the dominant culture of the land. The Aboriginal adolescent fiction analyzed in this study that holds up ancestral cultural ideals has tended to be written so far by non-Native writers with postcolonial sensibilities. The novels being written by the Aboriginals themselves are still focused on working through stages of anger at the lack of self-worth they have internalized through years of mistreatment and marginalization, anger, resistance, and restructuring. As anger and resistance are worked through in First Nations' life and literature, a movement towards literary celebration should follow.

The second choice that presents itself in the Canadian postcolonial discourse is hybridity. The Aboriginal resisting colonization and working to restructure a new sense of self cannot return to authenticity but is herself a new hybrid entity, engendered by the encounter between the two conflicting systems of belief (Gandhi 1998, 130). While hybridity seems inevitable, it is also a complex set of conditions that need to be distinguished one from the other.

As well as the negative hybridity of forced assimilation and internalized self-rejection so strongly developed through the residential school system, "political co-optation" and "social conformism" were other kinds of hybridity encouraged by the colonizers in Canada. Most forms of hybridity have negative connotations, and cannot lead to coexistence on equal terms. However, at least one can be seen as a model for healthy pluralism and coexistence within Canada: this is what Ella Shohat calls "creative transcendence" (Loomba 1998, 178).

Just as authenticity is best regarded as a tool that can serve liberation, so creative transcendence serves as a tool and does not define a particular political program (Loomba 1998, 182). It uses language appropriation for destabilizing sites of colonial power. Using the language of the dominating culture the indigenous writer is able to challenge that culture by "twisting old authoritarian words into new oppositional meanings" (Gandhi 1998, 147). Aboriginal writers are thus able to protest out of and not just against the cultural vocabulary of colonialism, both recognizing and subverting "the authority of imperial textuality" (148). In doing so, according to Elleke Boehmer quoted in Ghandhi, Aboriginal writers engage in "a double process of cleaving": cleaving from colonial definitions and cleaving to "the ideological, linguistic, and textual forms of the colonial power" (148). The subsequent hybridized colonial and indigenous ideas can then be used to assert a positive and empowered form of cultural alterity (Loomba 1998,176), an apartness, according to Mikhail Bakhtin as cited in Ashcroft, that stands as a precondition of dialogue, across and between differences of culture, gender, class, and other social categories (Ashcroft et al. 1998, 12). In this space of hybridized colonial and indigenous ideas exists what Diana Brydon describes as the "concept of contamination as literary device"; the bringing of differences together into creative contact, which she suggests is a central activity of postcolonial and postmodern literature (Brydon 1990, 191).

The cross-cultural imagination that Brydon calls contamination is not, however, just a literary device for creative transcendence, but also a cultural and even a political project. Canadian adolescent literature, created out of the postcolonial discourse surrounding transcendental hybridity, is a powerful tool for modelling how to actively, consciously choose to coexist in harmony and diversity, creating from that diversity a national vision of cultural plurality. A third space can be created, neither colonized nor unacculturated, but rather, as Homi Bhabba suggests, a space of communication, negotiation, and translation—a space of hybridity (Homi Bhabba in Gandhi 1998, 131).

Three Canadian Aboriginal leaders, Jeanette Armstrong, Duke Redbird, and Mary Lou Fox Radulovich, each emphasize different aspects of the changes necessary to reach a hybridized coexistence among all Canadians: to heal Aboriginal peoples through cultural affirmation, to alter the dominant culture's historical perceptions and current view of Aboriginals, and to offer all Canadians the best aspects of Aboriginal philosophies in order for all to create a more culturally integrated and balanced country.

Jeanette Armstrong, author of the novel *Slash*, expressed her views in an address to the Saskatchewan Writer's Guild 1990 Annual Conference subsequently published as "The Disempowerment of First North American Native Peoples and Empowerment Through Their Writing." She first refers to the "total subjective control" over her peoples "through various coercive measures" and the direct removal of "political, social, and religious freedoms" (208). Out of this bleak history she describes a new Canadian order governed by multicultural policies of equality in which "domination is not possible because all cultures are valued" (210). She then specifically addresses Native writers telling them they can empower their people through writing. She sees them as having the task of examining "the past and culturally [affirming] a new vision for all our people in the future, arising out of the powerful and positive support structures that are inherent in the principles of co-operation" (210).

Armstrong's vision is not just to repair the damage done to her own people and to share their "principles of co-operation" with the rest of Canada. She sees the responsibility of the Native writer as world-wide in "light of these times in which world over, solutions are being sought to address the failed assimilationist measures originating out of conquest, oppression, and exploitation, whether under the socialist or capitalist banner" (210). With a paradigm shift in cultural paternalism she maintains that Native writers must express their message clearly "to the people who have no way to know that there are good alternatives and that instead of losing control we can all grow powerful together" (210). Such a sentiment, although well intended, bears an uncomfortable similarity to the mandate of early colonial missionaries to various colonized indigenes.

Duke Redbird, like Armstrong, focuses on the contribution Native Canadians can make to the shaping of a new "North American." *We Are Métis* (1992) was written by Redbird as an interdisciplinary Masters thesis for York University (515). His is a cultural theorist's approach, abandoning political confrontation for cultural infiltration into mainstream media, presenting Aboriginal culture before the Canadian masses as something irresistible, seductive, desirable (122–126). "The media generated by natives" will penetrate "into the majority culture, even into the academic world of the universities" (123). He argues that the revival of Native awareness will also raise the self-image of Native children. More contentiously, he asserts that "all the races and ethnic groups in Canada are being integrated into the psychological and geophysical reality that is North America and that the Métis are the only ethnic group indigenous to the continent" (125). He maintains that "all other races, including Indian and Inuit, came from elsewhere at some other time" (125). He recognizes that hybridization requires movement from both the centre and the margin, although he does not appear to recognize that that centre can form around wealth and power as well as privileged ethnicity. "Integration is a two-way street and the white majority society is reflecting the native reality more and more specifically as the years go by" (125). Without making allowances for gender, he concludes by saying that what the Métis "have to do is go out into the world and become the manifestation of what the real North American is going to become—the ideal, whole man" (126).

Redbird's version of hybridity is a cultural merger: indigenous and non-indigenous Canadians assuming one identity. Armstrong, with a more political than cultural agenda, would replace capitalist and socialist "systems" with Aboriginal ones. Mary Lou Fox Radulovich's emphasis, like Redbird's, is on culture, but as the foundation to all other imported cultures in the society—a vision of hybridity that leaves room for pluralism. When she addressed the Loughborough International Seminar on Canadian Writers held in Toronto in August 1975, Radulovich declared that Aboriginal culture is common to all Canadians. (Her address was subsequently published as "Native People's Cultural Resurgence.") She states that "the heritage of the North American Indian is the basic cultural strain of the Americas" (66), even though the heritage of many other countries is vitally important to a multicultural society. It is this heritage—that of the First Americans—which makes all of us on this continent unique. "Unfortunately," she continues, "this basic truth has never been reflected in the curricula of our elementary schools, high schools, colleges, or universities" (66).

Radulovich offers a model of decolonization that positively acknowledges the cultures of the non-Aboriginal, returns the culture of the Aboriginals to a central place of importance, and, in a generous translation of hybridity, offers to share that Aboriginal culture with the displaced non-Natives who are seeking a way to identify with the foundation culture in order to feel more fully they belong to Canada. Of the three models—Armstrong's healing, Redbird's merger, and Radulovich's foundation—the last seems the best for constructing an inclusive and pluralistic future cultural identity for Canada and Canadians.

The notion of hybridity is central to the creation of Canadian Aboriginal novels. Just as Aboriginal voices were appropriated by non-

Aboriginal writers to create several of the novels examined in the first section of this essay, so the Aboriginal writers have had to appropriate the English language and English literary forms (Ashcroft et al. 1989, 38). They have also had to assimilate the educational values and methods of the dominant middle class in order to write to it and to themselves. The results can be found in the seven novels by Aboriginal writers, and one by a teacher living and working with Aboriginals, that have stayed in print from 1970 to 1990.

A viewpoint that dominates five of these novels and grows out of colonization is a kind of "double vision" that does not readily occur to indigenous writers of cultures that have not been invaded (Ashcroft et al. 1989, 26). To a large degree the personal identity of contemporary Aboriginals in Canada is constituted by difference. As they seek to define their ideal selves, part of their definition is in relation to what they are not and do not want to be—reflections of the settler/invaders, dominators consuming and altering the land. Because of the failed non-Native attempts to assimilate Canadian Aboriginals, the other part of their double vision stems from a sense of alienation within their own land. This sense of displacement creates the tension that gives urgency to their need to define themselves and to participate in a larger discourse that insists that the rest of Canada redefine itself and move to meet in a commonly shared middle ground.

None of these novels has villains from the dominating culture, while ten of the twenty-eight Aboriginal novels authored by non-Natives have specifically white and often prejudiced villains in conflict with the Aboriginal protagonists. These Aboriginally-authored novels diffuse instead a general anger or frustration with the dominant political, economic, or social systems throughout the narratives. Since the novels are written with a didactic purpose to empower Natives and to alter the perceptions of the larger non-Native audience, it seems politic not to antagonize targeted readers. *Spirit of the White Bison* (1985), by Beatrice Culleton, for example, is the story of the destruction of the bison as an expansionist economic policy to rid the Plains Indians of their food source and force them onto reserves, thereby opening the prairies for farming and grazing. In a very angry and powerful novel for young readers, Culleton discreetly has a non-Native loner save the bison narrator and later be saved during a stampede by the same bison, giving a non-Native reader a role model with whom to identify.

Honour the Sun (1987), by Ruby Slipperjack, stands apart in this group of Aboriginal novels as being especially gentle, almost pastoral. It is a celebration of life close to the land, and of progression through childhood, the seasons, and the years in a small matriarchal community along railroad tracks in northern Ontario. It moves through the days, recounting the seasonal routines of berry picking, fish netting, and living as a large family whose main conflict seems to be coping with violent local drunks. Questions of identity or place do not arise and a merging of Aboriginal and non-Aboriginal cultures is taken for granted as a way of life. Time and the evolution of cultural history will eventually reveal to what extent this kind of novel is an aberration or a new direction for Aboriginal novels.

I have looked in this paper at Aboriginal fiction as one of the largest subsets of recent Canadian adolescent novels. The fact that it is being created by more than one of the cultural strands of the Canadian literary community, each bringing a different point of view to the enterprise, lends complexity and strength to Canada's evolving vision of itself. The emphasis of non-Aboriginal writers has been divided between maintaining the dominant cultural position, or atoning for it and embracing an Aboriginal world view, and the emphasis of Aboriginal writers has been to recapture and celebrate their cultures while finding a way for all to coexist. As these writers for adolescents, with their strong sense of didactic purpose, create a new inclusive and equally valued version of their different selves and their relations to one another, they help shift the perceptions of their adolescent readers away from the current centrist position of the middle class and into a new cultural narrative of coexistence.

WORKS CITED

Armstrong, Jeannette. "The Disempowerment of First North American Native Peoples and Empowerment Through Their Writing." In *An Anthology of Canadian Native Literature in English*. Ed. Daniel D. Moses and Terry Goldie. Toronto: Oxford University Press, 1992.

Ashcroft, Bill, Gareth Griffiths and Helen Tiffin, eds. *The Empire Writes Back: Theory and Practice in Post-Colonial Literatures*. London: Routledge, 1989.

———, eds. *Key Concepts in Post-Colonial Studies*. London: Routledge, 1998.

———, eds. *The Post-Colonial Studies Reader*. London: Routledge, 1995.

Brydon, Diana. "The White Inuit Speaks: Contamination as Literary Strategy."

48

In *Past The Last Post: Theorizing Post-Colonialism and Post-Modernism*. Ed. Bill Ashcroft and Helen Tiffin. Calgary: University of Calgary Press, 1990.

Canada. Royal Commission on Aboriginal Peoples. *Report*. Ottawa, 1996. As published by Libraxus.com.

Culleton, Beatrice. *The Spirit of the White Bison*. Winnipeg: Pemmican Publications, 1985.

Gandhi, Leela. *Postcolonial Theory: A Critical Introduction*. New York: Columbia University Press, 1998.

Goldie, Terry. "The Representation of the Indigene." In *The Post-Colonial Studies Reader*. Ed. Bill Ashcroft, Gareth Griffiths, and Helen Tiffin. London: Routledge, 1995.

Katz, Welwyn Wilton. *False Face*. Toronto: Douglas & McIntyre, 1987.

Loomba, Ania. *Colonialism/Postcolonialism*. London: Routledge, 1998.

Major, Kevin. *Blood Red Ochre*. New York: Laurel Leaf Contemporary/Dell, 1989.

Radulovich, Mary Lou Fox. "Native People's Cultural Resurgence." *Canadian Children's Literature* 4 (1976): 66–70.

Redbird, Duke. "We Are Métis." In *An Anthology of Canadian Native Literature in English*. Ed. Daniel D. Moses and Terry Goldie. Toronto: Oxford University Press, 1992.

Slipperjack, Ruby. *Honour the Sun*. Winnipeg: Pemmican Publications, 1987.

A Parliament of Stories: Multiculturalism and the Contemporary Children's Literature of Saskatchewan

GREGORY MAILLET

ONE OF THE CENTRAL QUESTIONS facing Canadian literary culture, and indeed Canadian society in general, is how to respond to our nation's ever increasing multiculturalism. Children's literature is probably not the first kind of text that intellectuals expect to explore this difficult issue, and Saskatchewan may be the last place, perhaps, that most Canadians expect to produce an answer. However, anyone familiar with this province's large First Nations and diverse immigrant population—which includes English, French, Métis, German, Ukrainian, Scottish, Irish, Scandinavian, Russian, Hungarian, Polish, and other Eastern Europeans, including some Jews, and many other more recent immigrants—should not be surprised that multiculturalism still flourishes (Archer 1980, 139–141). In fact, the Multicultural Council of Saskatchewan estimates that the province now includes "more than 200 cultures," and that its people "speak more than 80 languages" (Multicultural Council of Saskatchewan 1999, 1). Even if these figures are exaggerated, festivals such as Regina's popular "Mosaic" provide annual, tangible evidence of multicultural variety. Equally vital, and again in sharp contrast to its rustic pioneer image, is Saskatchewan's literary culture, a significant part of which is children's literature. Again, statistics cannot define this vitality, but in the Saskatchewan Writer's Guild guide, no fewer than forty-seven of the 145 guild writers list children's literature as their primary vocation (Saskatchewan Writer's Guild

1994, 182–186). These authors have abundantly harvested Saskatchewan's rich multicultural legacy for the past several decades, but few, outside the province's children, have feasted thereon. For Canadian literary critics to do likewise, they first require a conception of "multicultural children's literature" that does not exclude the exceptional achievement of this unique province.

Such exclusion generally results from two opposed but equally flawed approaches to multiculturalism. The first is better termed "minority-culturalism" in that it proposes study of only minority groups. Since for many areas of North America this means people of colour who often are economically disadvantaged, this approach tends to see skin colour and economic class as the primary variants of culture, and results in a definition of "multicultural literature" like that given by American Donna Norton in her textbook for children's literature, *Through the Eyes of a Child*. For Norton, "multicultural literature is literature about racial or ethnic minority groups that are culturally and socially different from the white Anglo-Saxon majority in the United States, whose largely middle class values and customs are most represented in American literature" (1991, 531). Whatever the validity of this definition in the U.S., it clearly cannot apply to Saskatchewan, which does not have an Anglo-Saxon majority, and whose whites retain diverse ethnic traditions that often are not defined by economic factors; certainly, as well, non-white ethnic writers have written much of Saskatchewan's children's literature.

Opposite to Norton's approach is an exceptionally broad definition of culture, such as "the way of life of a people, including their attitudes, values, beliefs, arts, sciences, modes of perception, and habits of thought and activity" (Blackburn 1994, 90). This approach helps us to see the complexity of culture, but by being so inclusive it can also subsume individuals within broad categories that ignore the unique tone and emphases stressed by real human beings living their culture. On a political level, this approach results in a republican, U.S.-style federalism that melts culture down in the service of nationalism. A parallel approach, and even diction, can be found in Egoff and Saltman's *The New Republic of Childhood*, which tells us that the prolific children's literature produced by the immigrant writers of our "multicultural society" will surely "increase to the point where the presentation of various cultures will no longer be considered ethnic but simply Canadian" (1990, 18). Expanding on this point later in their influential book, they note the growth of "multi-ethnic" children's literature, but then argue, "It is to be expected, and welcomed, that differences in culture will be subsumed into childhood experiences that take precedence over a specific culture. There is, after all, a 'republic of childhood'" (Egoff and Saltman 1990, 181). Although a degree of common childhood—indeed human—experience is in my view indisputable, to welcome the effacement of the unique cultural life within which such experience develops—for better or worse—is at best naive and at worst destructive.

Within literary culture, such an approach leads to an overvaluing of works such as Manitoban William Kurelek's award winning *A Prairie Boy's Winter and Summer*, which Egoff and Saltman believe has exported well, despite its "local background and ambience," because its "pictures speak a universal language" (Egoff and Saltman 1990, 311). Kurelek's work does show us aspects of prairie life—such as hauling hay, skating in frozen ditches, spring runoff, and gopher hunting—which to some degree are shared by most, if not all, of the prairie's children. Indeed, its portrayal of commonplace prairie life has been successfully updated for the 1990s by Saskatchewan's Jo Bannatyne-Cugnet in her *A Prairie Year* and *A Prairie Alphabet*. Such texts are not in themselves harmful or false, but simply incomplete; what is damaging is when readers interpret them as truly representative of the historical or imaginative reality of life on the Canadian prairies. No text alone could ever be fully representative, of course, but as critics we can acquire an empirical openness to the intertextual, and intratextual multiculturalism that children's literature often includes, and learn to ask cross-cultural questions of specific, individual texts, perhaps in the manner suggested by Ron Jobe in his *Cultural Connections* and *Canadian Connections*. In doing so, however, critics must acknowledge separateness as much as connectedness, as well as the inadequacy of stereotypes within a complex multicultural world, a point that Jobe himself often stresses. The limitations of each critic's cultural horizons will make every multicultural inquiry incomplete, but at least critics may acknowledge this and listen attentively for those elements that people proclaim, or writers see, as central to a culture's existence, and can try to avoid reducing the complexity, and beauty, of our unique variety of cultural expression. More radically, for readers unfamiliar with a culture—which in Canada must be a very common literary experience—multicultural literature can act as an iconoclastic force that replaces stereotypes with an understanding of the actual people who have inspired a literature and a way of life.

Numerous writers with strong Saskatchewan roots have produced a children's literature that is "multicultural" in this sense, but one whose career is especially instructive is David Bouchard. One of his most popular works for children seems like another generic prairie guide, and does in fact focus on climactic features familiar to all prairie residents, but it also draws attention to their unique cultural experience: "If you're not from the prairie," Bouchard stresses, "you can't know my soul" (1994, 28). A Regina teacher and principal for almost two decades, Bouchard particularly explores the Native prairie soul (and soil, the two being so intertwined) in books such as *White Tails Don't Live in the City* and *The Meaning of Respect*. Both are told in the first person voice of an urban native youth who gradually learns to regain an appreciation of the native ways of preserving nature; yet this does not come naturally, as the youth explains:

> My Uncle Louis also uses the word respect a lot. Me, I've got trouble relating the word respect to fish and I find it even more difficult relating respect to plants. My Moshum says you've gotta respect all life on the reserve, even **the bush!** Can you believe that, respect the BUSH??? (Bouchard 1994 [21]).[1]

Since moving to Vancouver in the mid-1990s, Bouchard has further extended his multicultural horizons in *The Great Race*, a presentation of the Chinese Zodiac for children.

Many other authors originally from or now living in Saskatchewan continue to portray the province's unique blend of cultures. William Roy Brownridge's *The Moccasin Goalie* is a heartwarming, largely autobiographical story of a crippled boy who succeeds as a hockey goalie, despite injuries that force him to wear moccasins instead of skates. The story is shaped by the nearly universal role that hockey plays in small town Saskatchewan life, but its authenticity is also enhanced by the ethnic diversity that the story's illustrations emphasize: blond, dark, or native children play happily together, until at story's end a Frenchman, Mr. Matteau, takes them to "Chong's Café," an example of the Chinese restaurants that are spread all over the Canadian prairies. French culture is also celebrated in Sue Bland's *Madame de Toucainville's Magnificent Hat*, the comical story of a woman who revels in bicycle rides through prairie fields, and who regularly attends events such as the "Pheasant Creek Horticultural Society," but whose taste in hats would make her fashionable in Montreal (she shops using the Montreal *Gazette)*—or even Paris. Augmenting the atmosphere of the entire book are Bland's comical, colourful imitations of French impressionist paintings. Another ethnically homogenous but culturally diverse work is Alison Lohans's *Nathaniel's Violin*, the story of a "wizened old woman's" (1996, [4]) gift of classical music to a rustic farm home. Scorned at first, the violin music eventually inspires prosperous work for the farmer, his wife, their son Nathaniel, and even the farm's cows and chickens, whom the "old man could've sworn were singing along"(1996, [19]). The classical art of pottery inspires another Reginan, Jacolyn Caton, whose work *The Potter* is a "creation of art" myth that shows a wizened old potter in some ancient, seaside culture, diligently working until he builds art of such beauty that people come to rob him. The potter then spins himself into a lump of clay and scatters bits of his work everywhere. When found, even in the dry land of Saskatchewan, they inspire one to "dream of sitting in a small room at a wheel that spins and spins," or, perhaps, writes and writes, for Caton concludes: "I am the potter's daughter. I pick up the pot and carry it home to my small room. The earth spins and spins" (1992, [29]).

Our spinning globe has brought artists as well as art to Saskatchewan, and one other example of the unique multiculturalism thereby created is the work of Peter Eyvindson. Of Icelandic heritage, Eyvindson, to say the least, avoids earnest seriousness about his own ethnicity; rather, *The Backward Brothers See the Light: A Tale from Iceland* presents the three Bakkabraedur brothers, who "seemed to have only one brain between them for they often acted in a strange and backward manner" (1991, [3]). For instance, they light their tiny, ill-made house by carrying in sunlight by the cupful from outside, a technique that for some reason works better by day than by night. Eyvindson brings this same kind of humour and, ah, northern solar awareness to *The Missing Sun*, a work that juxtaposes the explanations for the seasons' changes offered by western science and Inuit mythology, while showing affection and respect for both. A respect for practical Native wisdom also imbues Eyvindson's *Jen and the Great One*, though this work was inspired by his father who, like many immigrants to the bare prairies, "planted, nurtured, and always loved trees." The "Great

One" is the lone surviving tree of a large forest, and as the young Native girl Jen sits under it, listening to the wind, the old tree tells her how "Big Businessman," then "Mighty Politician," and finally "Road Builder" had together destroyed the forest and its environment. Jen is horrified and runs off, but soon returns with her friends, whom the book's illustrations make clear are from multicultural backgrounds. From one of the Great One's cones, they plant many seedlings, renewing the tree's spirit, and sense of humour: "'Ah, children,' chuckled the Great One. 'Children of the World. It is you who give me hope'"(1990, [41]).

The most hopeful area of Saskatchewan's multicultural children's literature, certainly, is found in First Nations authors. No longer can it be said, as Egoff and Saltman did in 1990, that in our children's literature "only the illustrations show that the families are Indian or Inuit" (181). Supported in part by the Saskatchewan Indian Federated College (SIFC), which as part of the University of Regina teaches a broad range of First Nations languages, there now exist dual language editions of Native children's literature. *Two Little Girls Lost in the Bush* is a Cree tale told by Nehiyaw, or Glecia Bear, a seventy-eight-year old great-grandmother who recalls being lost in the forest with her little sister when the two were eleven and eight years old. The story becomes explicitly multicultural when "all segments of the community," (Ahenakew 1991, 1) such as Catholic priests and Hudson's Bay workers, take part in the search, and intracultural boundaries are also challenged when owls become signs of hope rather than danger, as is often the case for the Cree (1). The culture that produced *Byron Through the Seasons*, a Dene-English storybook, is even more complex. Created by Ducharme Elementary School in La Loche, Saskatchewan, it includes the ideas, writing, and art of over 400 students, a dozen elders, and a teacher committee of six—all to create a story told by "Grandfather Jonas" for his grandson, Byron, in which the yearly cycle of Dene life is recreated and preserved for future generations.

Other First Nations authors show native children within contemporary Canadian society. The short works of Darrell Pelletier, an SIFC graduate, use humane simplicity to portray Native children, such as "Alfred" and "Lisa," who live ordinary but joyful contemporary lives. Bernelda Wheeler grew up on a Saskatchewan Native Reserve, where she "listened to the birds and loved their songs," but was also "beaten and brutalized" at the local school, she recalls, "because I was aboriginal" (Canadian Children's Book Centre 1994, 319–320). Today, Wheeler combats such attitudes in works like *Where did you get your moccasins?*, which portrays a young native girl explaining to her very multicultural classmates how her "Kookum," or grandmother, has made leather from a deer killed by her father. But as for the moccasins' beautiful beads, she comically concludes by admitting that they were bought "from the store"(1986, [26]).

Perhaps the most creative of Saskatchewan's authors, though, represent one of Western Canada's first multicultural groups, the Métis (Giraud 1986, 319–356), who also have a supportive college in Regina, the Gabriel Dumont Institute. Sherry Farrell Racette, who is of First Nations and Irish descent and who worked at the Dumont Institute for a number of years, created *The Flower Beadwork People*, which summarizes Métis history, pictured in vivid colours, and shows how this unique people "borrowed some of their ideas from their mothers' way of life and some from their fathers'" and then "put them together in their own special way" to create "a new kind of people" (1991, 6). Racette here stresses the beauty of Métis traditions, but much more politically conscious is the extraordinary *Stories of the Road Allowance People*, which Racette illustrated and acclaimed Métis author Maria Campbell "translated" from "michif," the unique French and First Nations dialect spoken by Métis elders (Crawford 1985, 231–240). Then, Campbell presented the elders' eight stories as narrative poems that phonetically reproduce contemporary Métis' "village English" (Marken 1995, 5). In this way, Campbell lets us "hear the voices—breathing, laughing, sighing human voices" (Marken 1995, 5) of the elders, while allowing today's English speaking children to learn the authentic values of the historic Métis culture.

The first story in *Stories of the Road Allowance People*, a farce about a familiar young boy caught under another man's bed, shows the boy escaping with his life after pretending to be "Good Dog Bob," but it is more than an entertaining book: it concludes with the boy resolving to "never / bodder no one else hees bed after dat" (1995, 13). The second story also deals with a domestic issue: the storyteller, "Crow," rescues a battered woman, who in turn defends the two of them when her husband attacks. More specifically Native issues are explored in stories such as "Big John," about a Métis "Farm-Instructor" (70) who betrays a "Treaty" native by working with Indian Affairs against him, while "Joseph's Justice" tells the unfamiliar, yet inspirational story of a Métis who successfully wins compensation after being falsely arrested during the Riel Rebellion. A less happy episode in Métis history is movingly told in "Jacob": in this tragic tale, a Métis refuses to let his own children attend the Catholic residential schools, because for him they had cut off all connection to his own language and history. The "prees" informs Jacob of his dead Native father's name (97), but unbeknownst to either of them, this is also the father of Jacob's wife; upon hearing the name, she runs off and kills herself. For the rest of his life, Jacob writes a book of Native genealogy, and "fight[s] dah government to build schools on the / reservation" (103).

Yet Campbell's *Stories* are by no means anti-white, or anti-Catholic, which would grossly simplify Métis culture. It is an Irish lawyer who helps Joseph win justice against the British (119), while the story "La Beau Sha Shoo" refers to the title of a "kinda wile"(65) song that Jesus taught to "Ole Arcand," a stylish Métis singer and fiddler, when he had spent a night in heaven after almost dying, and had done "some serious drinking" (63) with the Lord. An even more complex consideration of the role of Catholicism in Métis culture comes in "Rou Garous," the title referring to humans who, in Métis belief, can at night turn into dogs or even wolves. George L'Hirondelle doesn't believe in such creatures, because "he don believe on nutting. / Not even dah Jesus" (37); yet once George actually sees a "rou garou," who by day is the wife of his friend, for "dah firs time he knowed he was part of / someting dat was evil," and then "for dah firs time in many years / he call dah Jesus an dah Virgin Mary" (47). The narrator's mother is upset, saying "dah Prees he win again an he give anudder / woman a bad name / jus to make good Catlics out of dah peoples" (49), but the narrator concludes ambiguously: "But me / I don know. I jus never know who hees right / my Mudder or dah mans an dah Prees" (49). Certainly, Campbell's ultimate purpose is not to blame others for Métis problems, but rather to give her own people the strength of self-knowledge. Her final story, "Dah Teef," opens, "You know me / I talk about dah whitemans like dere dah only / ones dat steal. But dats not true you know / cause some of our own peoples dey steal too" (126).

The tale goes on to recount comically how a thief's actions force an elderly, old-fashioned, but ardently courting couple to spend a night together in the woman's home, where they are embarrassed to be found the next morning by her young grandson. Laughter aside, the story continues one of the central themes linking all of Campbell's stories, the need for young people to respect "dem peoples dat belong in dah old days" (14), but also concludes by reminding young people that individual crimes are not their ultimate problem:

> Dah real bad ting is your kids and all your grandchildren. / Dey don got no good stories about you if your a teef. / An dah stories you know / Dats dah bes treasure of all to leave your family. / Everyting else on dis eart he gets los or wore out. / But dah stories / dey las forever. (143–144)

This, certainly, is the hope, and promise, of all of Saskatchewan's multicultural children's authors—that the stories they tell will, in ages to come, continue to nourish their descendents and sustain their unique cultures. Literary critics can aid this goal not by valuing only children's literature that fits into a "universal republic" of common childhood experience (Egoff and Saltman 1990, xii) or that satisfies political criteria such as whether or not "nonwhite characters" have "stereotypically exaggerated facial features or physiques" (Norton 1991, 535). Nor, though, should we limit our study to works which, according to Egoff and Saltman, further "the true beginnings of children's literature . . . delight rather than didacticism" (1990, 3). Multicultural children's literature does have many important things to teach us as it delights us, but in its particular case the premier criterion of value must simply be whether or not the culture's distinctive traits—however undelightful we might find them—are in fact represented.

Rather than Egoff and Saltman's "republic," a preferable political model might be a parliament, but hopefully one that represents a far greater diversity of people than actual legislatures typically do. In writing books that elect a "parliament of stories," Saskatchewan's children's authors have been fortunate to live in a province that is ethnically diverse, economically co-operative, and politically supportive of the arts, but these blessings do not invalidate their model of multiculturalism. More important than any of these factors, and equally possible among all Canadians, is the presence in Saskatchewan of people, especially children, who resist stereotypical categories, and generic, inhuman labels, and are instead willing to reveal who they are. Because children's authors from Saskatchewan have accepted the people of Saskatchewan as such, and have listened to both their realistic stories and their imaginative fables, so now can we.

58

NOTE

1.   Most of the picturebooks cited in this article are not paginated; the author has added page numbers in square brackets for unpaginated works [ ] as guides for easy reference. Editors' note.

WORKS CITED

Ahenakew, Freda. Introduction. *Two Little Girls Lost in the Bush: A Cree Story for Children*. Told by Nehiyaw (Glecia Bear). Ed. and trans. by Freda Ahenakew and H. C. Wolfart. Illus. by Jerry Whitehead. Saskatoon: Fifth House, 1991.

Archer, John Hall. *Saskatchewan, a history.* Saskatoon: Western Producer Prairie Books, 1980.

Bannatyne-Cugnet, Jo. *A Prairie Alphabet.* Art by Yvette Moore. Montreal: Tundra Books, 1992.

———. *A Prairie Year.* Art by Yvette Moore. Montreal: Tundra Books, 1994.

Blackburn, Simon. *The Oxford Dictionary of Philosophy.* Oxford: Oxford University Press, 1994.

Bland, Sue. *Madame de Toucainville's Magnificent Hat.* Red Deer: Red Deer College Press, 1994.

Bouchard, David. *The Great Race.* Paintings by Zhong-Yang Huang. Vancouver: Raincoast Books, 1997.

———. *If you're not from the prairie.* Images by Henry Ripplinger. Vancouver: Raincoast Books and Summer Wild Productions, 1993.

———. *The Meaning of Respect.* Illus. by Les Culleton. Winnipeg: Pemmican Publications, 1994.

———. *White Tails Don't Live in the City.* Paintings by Ken Lonechild. Winnipeg: Whole Language Consultants, 1989.

Brownridge, William Roy. *The Moccasin Goalie.* Victoria: Orca Book Publishers, 1995.

Campbell, Maria, trans. *Stories of the Road Allowance People.* Paintings by Sherry Farrell Racette. Penticton: Theytus Books, 1995.

Canadian Children's Book Centre. *Writing Stories, Making Pictures: Biographies of 150 Canadian Children's Authors and Illustrators.* Toronto: Canadian Children's Book Centre, 1994.

Caton, Jacolyn. *The Potter.* Pictures by Stephen McCallum. Regina: Coteau Books, 1992.

Children of La Loche and Friends. *Byron Through the Seasons: A Dene-English Story Book.* Saskatoon: Fifth House, 1990.

Crawford, John C. "What is Michif?: Language in the Métis tradition." In *The New Peoples: Being and Becoming Métis in North America.* Ed. Jacqueline Peterson and Jennifer S. Brown. Winnipeg: University of Manitoba Press, 1985.

Egoff, Sheila and Judith Saltman. *The New Republic of Childhood: A Critical Guide to Canadian Children's Literature in English.* Toronto: Oxford University Press, 1990.

Eyvindson, Peter. *The Backward Brothers See the Light: A Tale from Iceland.* Illus. by Craig Terlson. Red Deer: Northern Lights, 1991.

————. *Jen and the Great One.* Illus. by Rhian Brynjolson. Winnipeg: Pemmican Publications, 1990.

————. *The Missing Sun.* Illus. by Rhian Brynjolson. Winnipeg: Pemmican Publications, 1993.

Giraud, Marcel. *The Métis in the Canadian West.* Trans. by George Woodcock. Edmonton: University of Alberta Press, 1986.

Jobe, Ron. *Cultural Connections: Using literature to explore world cultures with children.* Markham: Pembroke, 1991.

Jobe, Ron and Paula Hart. *Canadian Connections: Experiencing Literature with Children.* Markham: Pembroke, 1991.

Kurelek, William. *A Prairie Boy's Winter and Summer.* Montreal: Tundra Books, 1973, 1975.

Lohans, Alison. *Nathaniel's Violin.* Illus. by Marlene Watson. Victoria: Orca Book Publishers, 1996.

Marken, Ron. Foreword. *Stories of the Road Allowance People.* Trans. by Maria Campbell. Paintings by Sherry Farrell Racette. Penticton: Theytus Books, 1995.

Multiculturual Council of Saskatchewan. *Why Multiculturalism?* Regina: Multicultural Council of Saskatchewan, 1999.

Nehiyaw (Glecia Bear). *Two Little Girls Lost in the Bush: A Cree Story for Children.* Ed. and trans. by Freda Ahenakew and H. C. Wolfart. Illus. by Jerry Whitehead. Saskatoon: Fifth House, 1991.

Norton, Donna E. *Through the Eyes of a Child: An Introduction to Children's Literature.* 3rd ed. New York: Macmillan, 1991.

Racette, Sherry Farrell. *The Flower Beadwork People.* Regina: Gabriel Dumont Institute, 1991.

Saskatchewan Writer's Guild. *Saskatchewan Writes!: A Learning Resource Guide about Saskatchewan Writers and their Works.* Regina: Saskatchewan Writers Guild, 1994.

Wheeler, Bernelda. *Where did you get your moccasins?* Illus. by Herman Bekkering. Winnipeg: Pemmican Publications, 1986.

ADDITIONAL REFERENCES

Pelletier, Darrell W. *Alfred's First Day at School.* Regina: Gabriel Dumont Institute, 1992.

———. *Alfred's Summer.* Regina: Gabriel Dumont Institute, 1992.

———. *The Big Storm.* Regina: Gabriel Dumont Institute, 1992.

———. *Lisa and Sam.* Regina: Gabriel Dumont Institute, 1992.

———. *The Pow-Wow.* Regina: Gabriel Dumont Institute, 1992.

Retelling "Little Red Riding Hood" Abroad and at Home

SANDRA L. BECKETT

IN RECENT YEARS the retelling of traditional fairy tales has become a very widespread international trend in children's literature, and it will come as no surprise to anyone that the most retold tale of all is *Little Red Riding Hood*. More than three hundred years after her literary debut in France, Little Red Riding Hood is alive and well and thriving in contemporary children's literature around the world. The tricentenary of the publication of Charles Perrault's *Histoires ou Contes du temps passé* in 1997 inspired a rash of new reversions, particularly in France. However, retellings of the familiar tale abound in many countries, as I illustrated at the tricentenary conference held at the Institut International Charles Perrault, in a paper titled "Le Petit Chaperon rouge globe-trotter" which considered hypertexts from England, Norway, Sweden, the Netherlands, Switzerland, Italy, Spain, Australia, United States, Brazil, and Colombia.[1] The tale's popularity as an intertext in so many countries is a reflection of its privileged status in the literary heritage of Western children.

Canada is no exception if we are to believe Perry Nodelman's article "'Little Red Riding Hood' as a Canadian Fairy Tale," published in *Canadian Children's Literature* in 1980. However, almost twenty years later, when I began investigating the persistence of the tale as an intertext in children's fiction, I was surprised to discover how relatively few original retellings are to be found in the works of contemporary Canadian children's authors. In fact, the few Canadian retellings in my corpus were all from Quebec. This symposium seemed an ideal opportunity to attempt to fill that gap.

One can only marvel at the seemingly endless variety of ways in which *Little Red Riding Hood* has been recycled in contemporary children's fiction. Reference to the tale range from a single brief allusion (either textual or pictorial) to extensive rewritings in novel form. Red Riding Hood and company have been appropriated for books of almost every genre from the picturebook to the comic book, from science fiction to detective stories. In his foreword to *¡Te pillé, Caperucita!*, Carles Cano warns his young readers that the title really tells them almost nothing, "because it could be a spy story, a horror story, a detective story, an adventure story, or even a fairy tale, couldn't it?" (1995, 17). The familiarity of the tale makes even a subtle allusion easily recognizable by young readers and likely to evoke a network of associations. The Italian children's author Gianni Rodari suggests that the series of words—girl, woods, flowers, wolf, grandmother—immediately brings to mind *Little Red Riding Hood*, even for very young children (1996 [1973], 34). In fact, words are not even necessary. One has only to think of the tiny image of Little Red Riding Hood and the wolf in *Anno's Journey*, where the literary figures take their place among the countless icons of European culture. Often the intertextual reference occurs only in the illustrations of a picture book. Anthony Browne's numerous allusions to *Little Red Riding Hood* in *The Tunnel* are confined to the illustrations (e.g., Rose's red cape, her brother disguised as a wolf, the framed illustration in her bedroom). It is not surprising to find *Little Red Riding Hood* on the bookshelves of the baby wolf who can't sleep because he is terrified there is a nasty little boy under his bed in Elsa Devernois' *Grosse peur pour bébé loup*, but how do we explain its presence in Mireille Levert's illustration for *Jeremiah and Mrs. Ming*? Like the baby wolf, Jeremiah is unable to fall asleep because, as he puts it, "All of my books are reading their stories" (Levert 1995, [3]).[2] The first of the three books suspended in the air above his bed is *Little Red Riding Hood*, with the wolf in grandmother's clothing escaping from the confines of the cover. It would seem that *Little Red Riding Hood* is *the* archetypal bedtime story.

Perhaps Levert was already thinking about the *Little Red Riding Hood* she would publish five years later in her uniquely funny style, a version that nonetheless remains quite faithful to that of the Grimms'. No doubt the delectable Little Red Riding Hood was irresistible to an illustrator who admits that she "eats books" (Jennings 1990, dustcover), and who dedicates her *Little Red Riding Hood* to "all the big bad wolves"! The representation of Little Red Riding Hood on the cover of the book in *Jeremiah and Mrs. Ming* is strikingly similar to that on the cover of Levert's version of the tale, thus strangely foreshadowing the later book and adding an interesting intratextual dimension to the intertextual play with *Little Red Riding Hood*.[3]

As studies like Jack Zipes's *Fairy Tales and the Art of Subversion* show, modern retellings transfigure and generally subvert traditional fairy tale motifs to convey new messages and present modern social problems. However, one cannot help but be struck by the number of authors who recycle fairy tales apparently for the sole purpose of provoking a good laugh. At a conference on women's writing and children's literature in France a few years ago, Sophie Quentin claimed that the retellings most easily obtained today are written by men, and that these versions generally rely on humour and parody for their effect (1995, 207, 209).[4] This does seem to be the case in a number of European countries, notably Perrault's France and the Grimms' Germany, but also in Italy, Spain, the Netherlands, and England. To give you an indication of the number of male reversions that emphasize humour and ludic play, I'd like to take you on a whirlwind world tour highlighting some of the best known. France offers an almost endless list: Marcel Aymé's "Le Loup," Philippe Dumas' "Le Petit Chaperon Bleu Marine," Grégoire Solotareff's *Le Petit Chaperon vert*, Cami's *Le Petit Chaperon vert*, Jean Claverie's *Le Petit Chaperon rouge*, Yvan Pommaux's *John Chatterton détective*, Philippe Corentin's *Mademoiselle Sauve-qui-peut*, Jean-Loup Craipeau's *Le Petit Chaperon bouge*, Marcel Gotlib's "La triste histoire du loup végétarien marqué par son hérédité," and "Little Red Riding Hood" "reruminated" by Tomi Ungerer, to name only a few. Moving beyond French borders, we find Janosch's "Das elektrische Rodkäppchen" in Germany; Ivo de Wijs's *Roodkapje en de zeven geitjes* in the Netherlands; Bruno Munari's *Cappuccetto Rosso Verde Giallo Blu e Bianco* and Gianni Rodari's "A sbagliare le storie" ("Little Green Riding Hood") in Italy; Roald Dahl's "Little Red Riding Hood and the Wolf," James Marshall's *Red Riding Hood*, and Allan Ahlberg's "Wilfred," in *Ten in a Bed*, in England; José Luis García Sánchez's *El Último Lobo y Caperucita*, Àlvaro Del Arno's *Caperucita cuenta*

"*Caperucita,* "and Carlos Cano's *¡Te pillé, Caperucita!* and *Caperucita de colores* in Spain; Luis María Pescetti's *Caperucita Roja (tal como se lo contaron a Jorge)* in Argentina; Tony Ross's *Little Red Riding Hood* in Australia; and Jon Scieszka's "Little Red Running Shorts" in *The Stinky Cheese Man and Other Fairly Stupid Tales* in the United States. In this lengthy list that is far from exhaustive, you will have noticed the conspicuous absence of Canada. I have yet to find a single contemporary Canadian retelling of Little Red Riding Hood for children by a male author, let alone one that falls into the humorous category.

Sophie Quentin's hypotheses certainly cannot be applied universally. There are obviously many retellings of Little Red Riding Hood by women authors. Quentin herself mentions a few, notably Patricia Joiret's *Mina je t'aime* and Pierrette Fleutiaux's "Petit Pantalon Rouge, Barbe-Bleue et Notules" (the latter was not published in a children's edition, but is popular with adolescents). Nor can one divide the retellings into clear-cut categories along gender lines. Some women authors use the techniques of humour and parody that Quentin considers typical of the male versions, for example Catherine Storr's "Little Polly Riding Hood," Mary Rayner's *The Small Good Wolf,* Marion Zor's *La Terrible Bande à Charly P.,* Anne Rocard's *L'étrange monsieur Garou,* and Mercè Company's *Las Tres Mellizas y Caperucita Roja.* Once again, I failed to find an example among English-speaking Canadian authors, but Quebec provided Jasmine Dubé's *Le Petit Capuchon rouge.*

The allusions to *Little Red Riding Hood* are quite transparent in Jasmine Dubé's picturebook, but they are used to tell a very different story. *Le Petit Capuchon rouge* begins with the traditional incipit "Once upon a time," but Clotilde lives in a large city and her grandmother's house is far away on the seashore. The title immediately evokes the well-known fairytale, but the substitution of "*capuchon*" (hood or cowl) for "*chaperon*" alerts the reader that this is perhaps not just another version of the familiar story of the little girl and the wolf. The cover illustration of the bottom of the sea further disorientates the reader. Although the first page does present a little girl and her grandmother, the reader soon learns that *Le Petit Capuchon rouge* is not Clotilde, but the little red fish her grandmother gives her for her birthday. Dubé integrates motifs and dialogue from the hypotext into the new story with almost too much cleverness, but the result is nonetheless amusing. The familiar cakes are provided by grandmother herself, but there is no need for the little pot of butter, as they are butter cakes. Dubé's grandmother is typical of the many gourmand grandmothers in contemporary retellings of *Little Red Riding Hood*. After leaping out of his fish bowl into the sea while Clotilde is fishing with her grandmother, Capuchon is warned by another fish not to dawdle on the way to the caves or he might be eaten by the "*loup*." Dubé engages in the wordplay that is characteristic of most humorous retellings. The "*loup*," Capuchon learns, is "*le loup de mer*," which means a sea dog or experienced sailor. However, "*loup*" is also a type of fish, and the strange fish with the warped sense of humour and a penchant for puns introduces himself as "*Loulou, le loup de mer*," assuring Capuchon that he is not "*méchant*." The familiar litany is taken up word for word by Capuchon and Loulou, but the last line "The better to eat you with, my child!" is followed by an explanation that contains yet another play on words, as the wolf, who loves "little round, red fish" has a "*faim de loup*" (in French, the saying is to be as hungry as a "wolf"). The *loup*'s greediness is his downfall, as he swallows the worm on Clotilde's and her grandmother's fishing line. Roles are humorously reversed in the ending that is a parody of the Grimms', as grandmother cuts open the "wolf's" stomach and out pops Capuchon, much to their surprise. The little girl and her grandmother get their revenge that night by feasting on the *loup*.

Contemporary retellings in the humorous mode are generally situated in time and place, quite often in an urban or suburban setting. The humour frequently derives from the resulting anachronisms: details about setting (scrapyards, highways, zoos, police stations); characters' appearance (duffle coats, anoraks, jogging gear, false teeth); or everyday life (pizza, knitting, newspapers, television, videos, telephone, bikes). The integration of the values and preoccupations of modern society (technology, ecology, physical fitness and well-being, gender issues, the elderly, the physically challenged, "political correctness") is also a common source of humour in these retellings. Many of the authors of subversive tales, those Jack Zipes calls "counter-cultural fairy tale writers," often seem to be far less concerned with "transforming the civilizing process" (Zipes 1991, 179) than they are with simply telling a funny story. Their attack on social conventions, established values, and taboos is merely a pretext for laughter, that ingredient of children's literature that has become so profitable in recent years (see Lypp 1995, 189). However, the witty, ironical, sometimes even derisive tone that characterizes these versions may seem to address adults more than children. When humour is used to deconstruct the traditional tale, oftentimes no effort is made to elaborate a serious, positive alternative from the debris.

The strategy used to subvert the traditional tale is generally a very simple one, such as the reversal of roles proposed by Rodari: "Little Red Riding Hood is bad, and the wolf is good . . ." (1973, 35). Sometimes the strategy focuses on the plot, which may be revised, modernized, inverted, fractured, continued, embedded, or completely abandoned. The subversion may take place on the level of the narration, involving a change of focalization or a transgression of the reading pact. Quentin claims that male authors make a game of transgressing the reading pact of the traditional tale, establishing the norms only to indicate immediately their intention of subverting them (1995, 208). Solotareff embeds in *Le Petit Chaperon vert* a version of *Little Red Riding Hood* that remains quite faithful to the Grimms', but it is presented as the fabrication of an incorrigible little liar who wears a red hood, Little Green Riding Hood's worst enemy. Various techniques of exaggeration or surprise are common in these retellings, but as Quentin pointedly states, the surprise is not disconcerting or disturbing (1995, 208). This is in stark contrast to the shocking ending that Patricia Joiret reserves for readers of *Mina je t'aime*, in which Carmina's three would-be suitors or seducers become dessert for her grandmother she-wolf, or that Elise Fagerli serves up her readers in *Ulvehunger*, where the little girl eats her tough, old grandmother.

The retellings of *Little Red Riding Hood* by male authors tend to be playful and witty, intent upon subverting, inverting, even perverting the traditional tale. Quentin wonders if the techniques used in these particularly humorous versions don't hide "the sadistic pleasure" that they feel "in establishing, once and for all, that the girl was eaten by the wolf" (1995, 209), but this seems unlikely because the wolf is generally presented as the victim. However, the sheer number of these versions would seem to suggest that they constitute an attempt to use laughter to dissipate the uneasiness that the traditional story creates in male authors. On a deeper level, many of these retellings may reveal what Jean Perrot describes as "the anguish of modern man in the face of the mysterious, unexpected, and unfathomable desires of the modern girl and woman" (1993, 298).

Although women authors also write playful reversions and may adopt a similar tone to that of their male counterparts, more often their retellings of *Little Red Riding Hood* are written in a much more serious, sometimes even a minor mode. Oftentimes, they are longer stories, either rather lengthy short fiction or novels. A few examples which come to mind, are *Wolf* by Gillian Cross, *Caperucita en Manhattan* by Carmen Martín Gaite, and *Bye Bye Chaperon rouge*, which Quebec author Viviane Julien adapted from a film. The only novel-length retelling for children by a male author that has come to my attention is *Caperucito Azul* by the Ecuadoran author Hernán Rodríguez Castello, one of the very few versions to have a male protagonist. Perhaps the most innovative version by a male author is Paul Biegel's rather lengthy tale, *Wie je droomt ben je zelf* (What you dream, you are yourself), which shares a number of characteristics with the longer retellings by women.

These more serious and complex retellings use traditional fairy tale imagery and motifs to address important psychological and metaphysical problems such as fear, independence, compassion, dreams, and death. Rather than demythologizing or demystifying the traditional tale, these authors make the mythic content meaningful for contemporary readers. This doesn't mean that they don't challenge and subvert the traditional tale. On the contrary, they do so in a much more subtle, complex, and significant manner. By presenting open texts that can be read on different levels and interpreted in multiple ways, they oblige readers to engage in their own dialogue with both the retelling and the traditional tale. In her article "Real 'wolves in those bushes:' readers take dangerous journeys with *Little Red Riding Hood*," Cornelia Hoogland insists on the importance of enhancing "children's ability to carry on an imaginative dialogue with the tale" (1994, 20). The kind of emotional and imaginative involvement that she claims Olga Broumas's poem encourages (1971, 8), characterizes the retellings of *Little Red Riding Hood* by many women authors—abroad (Patricia Joiret, Carmen Martín Gaite, Gillian Cross) as well as in both French-speaking and English-speaking Canada (Viviane Julien's *Bye Bye Chaperon rouge* and Patricia Galloway's "The Good Mother," in *Truly Grim Tales* to which the rest of this paper will be devoted).

In most contemporary retellings, character types are abandoned in favour of an individualization of the characters. Little Red Riding Hood generally has a name: Sonia, Lorette, Fanny, Cassy, Sara. However, several women authors take care to choose a modern name that retains the original colour symbolism. The variety of "red" names ranges from Patricia

Joiret's Carmina (Mina to her friends), with its seductive connotations, to Priscilla Galloway's Ruby, that evokes the idea of something to be cherished and treasured like a precious gem. Whereas many of the playful versions either appropriate the familiar title (Ungerer, Claverie, Ross), establishing an immediate link with the hypotext, or offer a blatant deviation from the original title that cannot fail to awaken very familiar echoes, by merely changing the colour, the item of clothing, or by substituting another qualifier (Solotareff, Cami, Dumas, Munari, Szieska, Janosch), the title of Patricia Galloway's retelling, "The Good Mother," does not evoke reminiscences of the intertext. However, the transparent play on the word "grim" in the title of the collection, *Truly Grim Tales*, naturally leads readers to seek the source of these modern tales in those of the Brothers Grimm and they will not be long establishing a link between "The Good Mother" and "Little Red Cap." Recognition is ensured by familiar motifs such as the heroine's distinctive piece of clothing, not a red cap, but a crimson velvet cape. At the same time, there is a modernization of the motif, because Ruby's close encounter with a giant clam obliges her to substitute tight leggings and a short jacket for her "precious cape" when they go to her grandmother's island (Galloway 1995, 76).

The title Galloway gives to her collection is somewhat ambiguous and could be interpreted as meaning that these are really Grimm tales or that they are really grim tales, that is to say grimmer than the Grimms'. However, not all of the tales she retells are inspired by the Grimms' *Kinder-und Hausmärchen*. "The Voice of Love" is a retelling of Hans Christian Andersen's "The Little Mermaid" and "Blood and Bone" reworks "Tom Thumb." Many authors of contemporary retellings of fairy tales acknowledge their debt—often in a decidedly irreverent manner—to an illustrious predecessor, in a peritextual element of their work (title, dedication, introduction, postface). Galloway's "acknowledgements" pay homage to all those who have ever been involved in telling tales: "Whoever plays with the grand old stories owes a huge debt to centuries of storytellers who have gone before, those who have told and retold, and those who have written down and collected" (ix).

Some contemporary authors pretend, tongue in cheek, to tell the true version of the tale, to fill in gaps, or to offer the sequel. Galloway adopts a very serious tone when she claims to complete the story, to tell the untold story that lurks behind the well-known tales. "I've always known they left out a lot and were unaware of even more. It has not been easy to discover the truth, but I have persisted. Gradually the stories behind the stories have come clear" (ix). The opening of "The Voice of Love" suggests that people may think they know a story like the one about the little mermaid, but "they never know the whole of it" (60). Not only are the tales incomplete, they are also inaccurate: "And always, some of the details are wrong" (60). Her retelling of "Hansel and Gretel" goes even further, as it suggests in the first line that more than a few "details" of that story need correcting. Narrated in the first person by the witch who also becomes the children's stepmother in Galloway's version, "The Woodcutter's Wife" begins: "The story that I intended to eat them is a fabrication. People will make up anything" (107). Although the shift in focalization may bring to mind works like Jon Scieszka's *The True Story of the 3 Little Pigs!*, the purpose and effect of the technique is very different in Galloway's tale, which reminds us of Donna Jo Napoli's retelling of the same tale in *The Magic Circle*. Most stories in Galloway's collection do not begin with an allusion to the hypotext. Nor does the author use the traditional incipit of the fairy tale. On the contrary, she deliberately seeks to disconcert and disorient readers by immediately placing them on unfamiliar terrain. "The Good Mother" evokes a strange science fiction setting in the opening sentence: "The giant clams were the real danger . . ." (74).

"The Good Mother" is not the best tale in *Truly Grim Tales*, in part because it departs from the ancient, timeless fairy-tale atmosphere the author very effectively retains in "The Bed of Peas," a clever hybrid of "The Princess and the Pea" and "Rapunzel," or "The Name," a retelling of "Rumpelstiltskin." In "The Good Mother," as in "Blood and Bone," Galloway borrows elements from the science fiction genre. The story takes place in a post "Chem Wars" period when clams have become "mammoth bivalves" and humans or "smoothskins" as they are known by the other species, are subject to "beast attacks" and "infestations" (79, 76, 74). In the words of the beast: "fur, feather, fin made common cause against the smoothskins" (82). In her review of *Truly Grim Tales*, Cornelia Hoogland criticizes the "mish-mash of conflicting settings and times" in "The Good Mother" (Hoogland 1996, 86), but this is perhaps somewhat harsh, as the spatio-temporal setting remains, in fact, quite vague. Galloway's tale takes place somewhere by the sea, but no details allow the reader to situate it, nor is there anything distinctively Canadian about the setting. Viviane

Julien's *Bye Bye Chaperon rouge*, on the other hand, is set in an enchanted forest that could only be found in Quebec, with its autumn colours, early snowfall, long winter, wild berries, and streams that remains icy even in the summer (1989, 108, 26).

In "The Good Mother," traditional motifs are blended with new ones, only a couple of which are truly futuristic. The forest is replaced by an ocean setting, as Ruby sets out to "Grandma's island" (Galloway 1995, 74). Galloway's new Little Red Riding Hood cannot imagine her grandmother living anywhere else, but the image she paints of her in her unconventional setting is, paradoxically, quite traditional: "Grandma belonged in her rocking chair in the living room of the little brown house, or nestled in the quilts of her big carved bed" (75). The familiar image of the grandmother in her bed is altered by the addition of one modern detail that provides perhaps the only slightly humorous moment in the story: the old lady's illness forces her to wear an oxygen mask, and the beast later dons the badly-fitting and very uncomfortable "face" to "trick the little smoothskin"(83). The fact that the elderly woman will not leave her home and move in with them is a source of concern for Ruby's mother, just as it is for Sara's in Martín Gaite's *Caperucita en Manhattan*. Medicine and muffins replace the cake and wine in Ruby's wicker basket. The cautionary scene of the Grimms' version is retained, but with variations: Ruby's mother warns her not to stop on the way, but also to wear her boots, to take her stick, to give her grandmother a dose of medicine, not to burn herself making tea, and so forth. Like her predecessor, Ruby ignores her mother's warning, "dawdling" and stooping to pick wildflowers for her grandmother.

Female ancestry and matriarchal bonds are often accentuated in the retellings by women. In the Québécois novel *Bye Bye Chaperon rouge*, Viviane Julien tells the story of "a little girl, her mother, her grandmother, her great-grandmother and . . . a wolf" (1989, 9). Knowledge is passed on from one generation of women to the next. Each of the women in *Bye Bye Chaperon rouge* is responsible for a different aspect of Fanny's education, but there is a particularly strong bond between the young heroine and her very old and very wise great-grandmother. In "The Good Mother," Ruby looks to her grandmother for counsel and direction, even when the old lady lies "like a broken doll against the cottage" where she fell after the beast swatted the pistol from her hand (Galloway, 1995, 92). Holding the

injured beast's wailing cub over the cliff, Ruby seeks her advice: "It's so little, Grandma. What should I do?" (92). Her grandmother calmly instructs
her to go to the cave and bring the other cubs back to the house in the basket. Unlike the many humorous versions that portray the grandmother as
senile, cantankerous, or belligerent, Galloway's grandmother is presented
as a wise woman, who realizes that the beasts are reasoning, talking, feeling
beings, and that lack of food is the sole reason for their attacks on humans.

The role of the grandmother or great-grandmother as storyteller is
often emphasized in retellings by women. This is a common theme even
in the parodic versions, but there it tends to become just another humor-
istic device, as, for example, in *L'étrange monsieur Garou*, where Sonia's
grandmother is an "extraordinary storyteller" with a troubling penchant
for "wolf stories" (Rocard 1997, 27–28). In the more serious versions, on
the other hand, the emphasis is generally on the importance of the female
storytelling tradition. In "The Good Mother," Ruby's grandmother tells
her stories about the time "when Great-grandma was [her] age" (Galloway
1995, 79). She tells stories about beasts that talk, but these talking animals no longer belong to a bygone era of fairy tales, but are a reality in
Galloway's futuristic tale. However, Ruby's grandmother also tells her stories about once upon a time (perhaps back in the twentieth century) when
beasts couldn't talk and little creatures were not yet extinct.

Galloway's title, "The Good Mother," suggests a shift in focus to
the maternal figure. The reader may anticipate a reversal of the image of
the "bad mother" in Perrault's version, who has been accused of irrespon-
sibly sending her daughter into the woods without even a word of warning. In Claverie's somewhat feminist retelling, it is Mamma Gina, the
"great-great-granddaughter of a woodcutter," who rescues her daughter by
threatening the wolf with the axe she uses to chop firewood for her pizzas
and forcing him to regurgitate Little Red Riding Hood and her grandmother. Ruby's mother has always accompanied her to Grandma's house
and the first page emphasizes the regular trips made by "woman and
child," during which the mother was always armed, not with an axe, but
with a rifle "in case of beasts" (74). On one occasion, she had to cut
Ruby's crimson velvet cape from a giant clam and the traumatic incident
had resulted in months of nightmares. However, the "good mother"
referred to in Galloway's title is not Ruby's mother. Although she is reluctant to let Ruby take the life-saving medicine to her grandmother all

alone, she does allow it in the end despite the grave danger. In modern retellings, Little Red Riding Hood's mother often has a career outside of the home. In *Bye Bye Chaperon rouge*, Fanny is left to her own devices because her divorced mother is busy operating a meteorological observation post in the forest. Ruby's mother, who may also be a single parent as there is no mention of Ruby's father, is a radio operator who alerts hunters about beast attacks. "Mum's work saved lives," says Ruby, but the statement is somewhat ironic because it is that work that prevents her from accompanying Ruby to her grandmother's, and so puts the lives of both her mother and her daughter in danger (76).

Like so many modern retellings, Galloway questions the main binary opposition: Little Red Riding Hood/the wolf. But she does not simply reverse the roles by presenting a wolf that is the unfortunate victim of a cunning, and sometimes callous, little girl, as do Dahl, Cami, and Dumas. Galloway's inversion involves a gender change, which allows her to add another female dimension to her retelling. We are so conditioned by our previous readings of the tale that we are completely taken off guard when the feminine possessive adjective is used for the beast that squeezes its monstrous body through the narrow door of the grandmother's house. The "good mother" of the title is, in fact, the beast that attacks Ruby and her grandmother in order to feed her hungry cubs which cannot survive without the blood and flesh of "smoothskins." When Ruby taps lightly at the door and calls out in her tiny voice, the beast's maternal instincts are aroused: "A strange warmth tugged at the huge creature inside the cottage, akin somehow to the fierce love she felt for her own little ones" (84). Little Red Riding Hood herself is assimilated with the "good mother" because when the beast's injury prevents her from attending to the needs of her cubs, Ruby becomes a surrogate mother, rescuing the little creatures and feeding them soybean milk out of a baby bottle (cows have been extinct since the grandmother was Ruby's age). The female "smoothskins" and the female beast are able to show compassion for one another, resolve their conflict, and come to a mutually beneficial arrangement: the beast will protect the humans from the giant clams and in exchange the humans will prepare the clams as food for the beast and its young. The arrival of the male hunters with their "fire sticks" (90) threatens to destroy the newfound peace. Like Broumas, Galloway "deconstructs the myth of female identification with the protective male, Grimms's hunter, and constructs a female community that defies the constructs of a repressive society and the impositions of convention" (Hoogland 1996, 15). The tale ends with Ruby looking up at the beast who holds her after she has been accidentally shot by a hunter as she attempted to screen the beast from their guns. Galloway's subtle inversion of the familiar dialogue of the tale is typical of the way in which she adapts traditional motifs and language to convey another message: "From this angle, the creature's eyes and ears weren't big at all. Nor were its teeth"(Galloway 1995, 96).

Virtually all contemporary retellings posit an active and courageous heroine, one who is no longer naive but quite capable of looking after herself. However, whereas some authors carry this to its absurd extreme by having Little Red Riding Hood not only outwit the wolf, but shoot it or even eat it, authors like Priscilla Galloway present a heroine whose bravery is the result of altruistic concern and brings about social change. Galloway's Little Red Riding Hood does not conquer her wolf, but overcomes her fear to befriend and help the beast.

Priscilla Galloway adds a Canadian voice to the literary dialogue that Perrault started more than three hundred years ago with the publication of "Le Petit Chaperon Rouge." She takes her place among many women authors around the world whose appropriation of the tale and its mythic content is revisionist. By breathing new life into the archetypes, characters, motifs, images, and narrative structures of the traditional tale, contemporary authors like Priscilla Galloway ensure that Little Red Riding Hood will celebrate many more birthdays.

NOTES

1.   I have completed a study that includes a much larger international corpus of retellings of Little Red Riding Hood.

2.   *Jeremiah and Mrs. Ming* is not paginated; the author has added a page number in square brackets for easy reference. Editor's note.

3. The reverse phenomenon occurs in Anthony Browne's *Willy the Dreamer,* where Willy's dream of becoming "a famous writer" is a wonderful parody of characters and scenes from Carroll's *Alice* books, while at the same time cleverly alluding to Browne's own version of *Wonderland.*

74

4.   Of the thirty-one versions written between 1697 and 1979 that Jack Zipes includes in *The Trials and Tribulations of Little Red Riding Hood*, only seven are by women authors.

WORKS CITED

Ahlberg, Allan. *Ten in a Bed.* Illus. by André Amstutz. London: Granada, 1983.

Anno, Mitsumasa. *Anno's Journey.* New York and Cleveland: Collins & World, 1978.

Aymé, Marcel. "Le Loup." In *Les contes bleus du chat perché.* Folio Junior. Paris: Gallimard, 1987.

Beckett, Sandra L. "Le Petit Chaperon rouge globe-trotter." In *Tricentenaire Charles Perrault: les grands contes du XVIIe siècle et leur fortune littéraire.* Ed. Jean Perrot. Paris: In Press Editions, 1998.

Biegel, Paul. *Wie je droomt ben je zelf.* Illus. by Carl Hollander. Haarlem: Uitg. Mij Holland, 1977.

Broumas, Olga. *Beginning with O.* New York: Yale University Press, 1977.

Browne, Anthony. *The Tunnel.* New York: Knopf, 1989.

———. *Willy the Dreamer.* Cambridge, MA: Candlewick Press, 1998.

Cami. *Le Petit Chaperon vert.* Illus. by Chantal Cazin. Paris: Père Castor Flammarion, 1996 [1972 for the text].

Cano, Carles. *¡Te pillé, Caperucita!* Illus. by Gusti. Madrid: Bruño, 1995.

———. *Caperucita de colores.* Illus. by Violeta Monreal. Madrid: Bruño, 1996.

Claverie, Jean. *Le Petit Chaperon rouge.* Paris: Albin Michel Jeunesse, 1994.

Company, Mercè. *Las Tres Mellizas y Caperucita Roja.* Illus. by R. Capdevila. Barcelona: Arin, 1985.

Corentin, Philippe. *Mademoiselle Sauve-qui-peut.* Paris: L'École des loisirs, 1996.

Craipeau, Jean-Loup. *Le Petit Chaperon bouge.* Illus. by Clément Oubrerie. Paris: Hachette, 1997.

Cross, Gillian. *Wolf.* London: Puffin, 1990.

Dahl, Roald. "Little Red Riding Hood and the Wolf." In *Revolting Rhymes.* New York: Knopf, 1982.

Del Arno, Álvaro. *Caperucita cuenta "Caperucita."* Illus. by Juan Ramon Alonso. Zaragoza: Edelvives, 1989.

Devernois, Elsa. *Grosse peur pour bébé loup.* Illus. by Savine Pied. Chanteloup. Paris: Père Castor Flammarion, 1997.

Dubé, Jasmine. *Le Petit Capuchon rouge.* Illus. by Doris Barrette. St-Hubert: Les éditions du Raton Laveur, 1992.

Dumas, Philippe. "Le Petit Chaperon Bleu Marine." In *Contes à l'envers.* Illus. by Boris Moissard. Paris: L'école des loisirs, 1977.

Fagerli, Elise. *Ulvehunger.* [Oslo]: Cappelen, 1990.

Fleutiaux, Pierrette. "Petit Pantalon Rouge, Barbe-Bleue et Notules." In *Métamorphoses de la reine.* Folio. Paris: Gallimard, 1984.

Galloway, Priscilla. *Truly Grim Tales.* Toronto: Lester Publishing Ltd., 1995.

García Sánchez, José Luis. *El Último Lobo y Caperucita.* Illus. by Miguel Angel Pacheco. Barcelona: Labor, 1975.

Gotlib, Marcel. "La Triste Histoire du loup végétarien marqué par son hérédité." In *Rubrique-à-brac.* Paris: Dargaud, Pocket BD, 1989.

Hoogland, Cornelia. "Galloway's Grim Tales." Rev. of *Truly Grim Tales*, by Priscilla Galloway. *Canadian Children's Literature* 82 (1996): 85–87.

————. "Real 'wolves in those bushes:' readers take dangerous journeys with *Little Red Riding Hood.*" *Canadian Children's Literature* 73 (1994): 7–21.

Janosch. "Das elektrische Rotkäppchen." In *Janosch erzählt Grimm's Märchen.* Weinheim: Beltz & Gelberg, 1972. 102–107.

Jennings, Sharon. *Jeremiah and Mrs. Ming.* Illus. by Mireille Levert. Toronto: Annick Press, 1990.

Joiret, Patricia. *Mina je t'aime.* Paris: L'école des loisirs, 1991.

Julien, Viviane. *Bye Bye Chaperon rouge.* Montréal: Québec/Amérique,1989.

Levert, Mireille. *Le Petit Chaperon rouge.* Toronto: Groundwood Books, 1995.

Lypp, Maria. "The Origin and Function of Laughter in Children's Literature." In *Aspects and Issues in the History of Children's Literature.* Ed. Maria Nikolajeva. Westport, Conn.: Greenwood Press, 1995.

Marshall, James. *Red Riding Hood.* New York: Dial Books for Young Readers, 1987.

Martín Gaite, Carmen. *Caperucita en Manhattan.* Madrid: Siruela, 1990.

Munari, Bruno. *Cappuccetto Rosso Verde Giallo Blu e Bianco.* Trieste: Einaudi Ragazzi, 1993.

Napoli, Donna Jo. *The Magic Circle.* New York: Dutton Children's Books, 1993.

Nodelman, Perry. "'Little Red Riding Hood' as a Canadian Fairy Tale." *Canadian Children's Literature* 20 (1980): 17–27.

Perrault, Charles. *Contes.* Le Livre de Poche. Paris: Hachette Jeunesse, 1989.

Perrot, Jean. "L'ogre de l'altérité ou l'émergence d'Artémis." In *La littérature de jeunesse au croisement des cultures.* Eds. Jean Perrot and Pierre Bruno. Paris: CRDP de l'Académie de Créteil, 1993.

Pescetti, Luis María. *Caperucita Roja (tal como se lo contaron a Jorge).* Buenos Aires: Alfaguara, 1996.

Pommaux, Yvan. *John Chatterton détective.* Paris: L'école des loisirs, 1993.

Quentin, Sophie. "De la tradition orale aux adaptations modems: 'Le Petit Chaperon rouge' ou le carrefour des Écritures . . . " In *Écriture féminine et lit-*

térature de jeunesse. Eds. Jean Perrot and Véronique Hadengue. Paris: La Nacelle/Institut Charles Perrault, 1995. 203–17.

Rayner, Mary. *The Small Good Wolf.* London: Macmillan, 1997.

Rocard, Ann. *L'étrange monsieur Garou.* Paris: Père Castor Flammarion, 1997.

Rodari, Gianni. *The Grammar of Fantasy.* 1973. Trans. by Jack Zipes. New York: Teachers & Writers Collaborative, 1996.

———. "Little Green Riding Hood." In *Telephone Tales.* George G. Harrap & Co. Trans. of "A sbagliare storie." In *Favole al telefono.* Turin: Giulio Einaudi, 1962 and 1971. (Reprinted in *Cricket* 1 (September 1973): 19-21.)

Rodríguez Castello, Hernán. *Caperucito Azul.* Illus. by Jaáme Villa. 5th ed. Serie de divulgación popular. Quito: Talleres Heredia, 1989.

Ross, Tony. *Little Red Riding Hood.* London: Andersen Press, 1978.

Scieszka, Jon. *The Stinky Cheese Man and Other Fairly Stupid Tales.* Illus. Lane Smith. New York: Viking, 1992.

———. *The True Story of the 3 Little Pigs!* Illus. by Lane Smith. New York: Viking Kestrel, 1989.

Solotareff, Grégoire. *Le Petit Chaperon vert.* Illus. Nadja. Paris: L'École des loisirs, 1989.

Storr, Catherine. "Little Polly Riding Hood." In *Clever Polly and the Stupid Wolf.* Harmondsworth: Puffin Books, 1967.

Ungerer, Tomi. "Little Red Riding Hood." In *A Story Book.* New York: Franklin Watts, 1974.

Wijs, Ivo de. *Roodkapje en de zeven geitjes.* Illus. by Alfons van Heusden. Amsterdam: Leopold, 1994.

Zipes, Jack. *Fairy Tales and the Art of Subversion.* 1983. New York: Routledge, 1991.

———. *The Trials and Tribulations of Little Red Riding Hood: Versions of the Tale in Sociocultural Context.* South Hadley: Bergin & Garvey, 1983.

Zor, Marion. *La Terrible Bande à Charly P.* Illus. by Yan Thomas. Paris: Rue du monde, 1997.

Secrecy and Space: Glenn Gould and Tim Wynne-Jones's *The Maestro*

ALAN WEST and LEE HARRIS

THE IMAGINARY WORLD OF NEVERLAND created by children, with its opportunities for escape into secret spaces, is one which, according to J. M. Barrie, adults can recall but not inhabit: "We too have been there; we can still hear the sound of the surf, though we shall land no more" (Barrie 1911, 14). Barrie's island of juvenile make-believe is therefore one within which only children can live completely comfortably. Neverland, however, is far from unique in children's fiction as a challenging space in which young subjects find themselves and, often, find *themselves*. For in coping with a new and often alien environment the fictional child or child surrogate explores both it and, in effect, her or his self. In crossing a threshold into this new and often secret place, s/he moves toward a more integrated sense of identity and, at some level, a new understanding of life. The Misselthwaite of Frances Hodgson Burnett's *The Secret Garden,* the lost garden in Philippa Pearce's *Tom's Midnight Garden,* Civil War America in Janet Lunn's *The Root Cellar,* Nathaniel Gow's pyramidal shack in Tim Wynne-Jones's *The Maestro*—all provide opportunities for transplanted young protagonists to grow as the result of being in a new or defamiliarized environment, distanced in space and/or time from the character's home.[1] In part this prepares the child protagonist for the adult world which lies ahead for both character[2] and child reader, even for archetypal children like A. A. Milne's Christopher Robin.[3] Moreover the protagonists of these texts often tend to start the novel as incomplete, the result of a sense of lack which stems from familial figures being deceased, absent, flawed, or ineffectual in some way. The consequent tendency towards introversion or solipsism is usually not negated or reversed by the individual child alone, but through the assistance or agency of guides, such as Dickon and Mrs. Sowerby in *The Secret Garden*, Susan in *The Root Cellar*, and, more ambiguously, Gow in *The Maestro*. The combination of the guide and the unfamiliar—or defamiliarized—physical space within which he or she operates, opens up the stunted potential of the protagonist to a new possibility of growth. This present paper examines *The Maestro*, a novel in which the Glenn Gould-like figure of Gow is important to the progress of the hero (Burl) away from an unhealthy introversion—the stagnant confinement of secrecy—towards a more vigorous openness—a vital new psychological space.[4] Consequently we will discuss how Gow operates in the text in the light of Gould's own philosophy.

Gow serves as a guide to Burl in his journey towards artistic as well as self understanding. What is also compelling about Gow and Burl is that their relationship sounds the depths of the archetypal pattern found in the relationship between guide and hero in many myths, legends, fairy tales, and children's fiction, a pattern explored in Joseph Campbell's classic study of archetypal motifs *The Hero With a Thousand Faces*.

That Wynne-Jones's character Gow is modelled on Glenn Gould is quite obvious early in the novel in the initial depiction of the eccentric and reclusive virtuoso pianist clad in "a heavy grey coat, a scarf, and a flat hat" with fingerless gloves (Wynne-Jones 1995, 36). What is perhaps less obvious than Gow as a fictional and physical manifestation of the Gould persona is the way in which Gould's philosophy agrees with, and offers insight into, Wynne-Jones's text. The story of Burl Crow—an adolescent coming of age against a backdrop of parental abuse and an unforgiving northern landscape—manages to go to the heart of the issues that occupied the Canadian pianist.

Briefly, Gould's thought was process oriented: he saw art not merely in terms of artefacts, but as a means of facilitating genuine psychological transformation. This opportunity for enhanced self-understanding, however, is critically dependent upon the manner in which one engages in the artistic process. Availing oneself of the *chance* of participation inevitably involves the adoption of risk.

A great deal of Gould's intellectual energy was directed to a critique of the social context of his profession, and its failure to promote a supportive environment conducive to the inner uncertainty that this risk constitutes. The immediate goal, then, was the creation of a psychological demilitarized zone, a space in which the mind can forge creative responses of which it is innately capable. In evolutionary terms, art could also be considered a human extension of the mammalian propensity for play, a game of semantic exploration conducted within the relative security of supportive constraints.

But where exactly was this "mythical" space situated? For Gould it lay in that ambiguous zone where the familiar opposition between nature and culture breaks down. The underpinnings were likely to be found in the concrete complexities of the human brain, but entrance into its wonders required the use of intuition. The Gouldian notions concerning the isolated north, hermetic nocturnal living, extreme privacy, negativity, recording studios, and lack of "live" performance, all were only attempts to create a viable space for genuine risk-taking to ensue. Without this genuine risk-taking, no real self-discovery would be possible. Of course, with this comes the possibility of failure, of returning to the everyday world with one's habitual vision intact, unaltered by the experience undergone, no matter how pleasurable or energizing its duration. Consequently, there had to be a corresponding commitment to ensure that the artistic "retreat" from the world became more than a frivolous exercise in escapism. The traditional religious maxim "in the world but not of the world" which occurs in Gould's radio portrait of a Mennonite community, *The Quiet in the Land* (1977), aptly conveys this idea of a detachment that is at once necessary and insufficient.

We would now like to apply this admittedly meagre tour of the Gouldian universe to the Wynne-Jones text, with some emphasis upon the relationship of secrecy and art. The prologue to *The Maestro* manages to condense many of the essential elements of this analysis. We first meet Cal, Burl's abusive father, at his secret fishing spot (1995, 7). The stealth concomitant with his secrecy, of course, is part of the natural order of things, the relationship between predator and prey. But Cal's expertise in this wild setting far exceeds the level of a purely biological sustenance. It is here he conducts his illicit sexual affairs, perpetrates violence with impunity, perpetuates a myth of manliness and dominance, and ultimately avoids contact with a world he both fears and holds in contempt. The abuser's actions—and indeed his natural environment—are all part of a complex semiotic system designed to gratify his ego, cover his insecurities, and continuously evade those genuine interactions that would serve to undermine his structured universe of meaning. As Burl eventually realizes, "the man had to put everything down. Not only Burl, but everyone . . . who crossed his path" (183). Secrecy in this context is thus, like Cal's put-downs, a function of control.

Yet we soon discover the moral ambivalence of the concept of secrecy. For fourteen-year-old Burl, even knowledge is "a thing to keep well hidden" from his father (14). As Roderick McGillis points out in "Huck Finn meets Glenn Gould: *The Maestro*," "[Burl] stores his inner life with secrets"(1996, 59). To the boy, seclusion means the opportunity to escape from physical violence, a sanctuary in which to indulge his active imagination, and, as well, a place from which to eavesdrop on an adult world he cannot otherwise safely observe. It is during just such a moment, albeit a failed one—Burl has been caught by his father and is about to receive a beating—when a watershed event occurs that saves him from violence and initiates the journey of self-discovery which will open up his severely circumscribed life. What erupts into this world of the densest secrecy is a grand piano, dangling incongruously from a helicopter as it sweeps across the bush, an emblem of the Maestro's own retreat from the city, and an omen of the meeting between boy and musician.

A number of important points are embodied here. It is the piano as a symbol of art that throws a sudden element of novelty into the characters' lives, disrupts their usual behavioural patterns and serves later to direct Burl's rebellious flight of self-assertion. But significantly, it is only Burl who can avail himself of the opportunity. Unlike his father, his attitude is not one of total domination, and his relation to the piano is not—pardon the pun—wholly instrumental. Instead, the boy harbours an intuitive attraction for the mysterious sight and its sounds. We read: "Burl had never seen a grand piano, but he knew that's what was hanging from the cable. Its shadow passed over him before it did" (Wynne-Jones 1995, 11). And a little later: "[I]t spoke to him. At the moment it was above him, even through the shattered air, he heard its song. The wind was playing that thing" (11).

Three further points are of significance in relation to the virtues of "secrecy" and "space." First, the solitude that the North provides has a concrete, functional role. Ironically, this is particularly obvious in Toronto, where Burl observes: "[t]here were too many signs in the city as far as he could tell. If you paid attention to all of them you'd go crazy" (140). It is therefore necessary to go beyond the act of so-called "critical analysis" with respect to urban chaos. If one cannot learn to *ignore* the veritable tangle of man-made, semiotic overgrowth, one's cognitive resources will be depleted by the burden of decoding that the urban chaos wishes to impose. Conversely, the singularities of the Northern bush may be "read": Burl notes that "[t]here were still paths and signs to follow and, beyond that, he had a pretty good store of wilderness knowledge" (27). But this is the environment decoded as a complex of signifiers on a basic survival level, the animal instinctually reacting to its environment; as far as a manufactured semiotic system, however, the natural environment is devoid, a negative. In Gould's view, art takes place in the ambiguous space between these; that is to say, between culture and nature. To be sure, Burl adopts various roles or selves in order to survive in the human world of power, but a greater freedom lies in his ability to listen and respond to a calling he had never heard before, the strains of the suspended piano's aeolian harp.

Finally, the crux of the issue is metaphorically embodied at the outset, when the airborne piano reminds Burl of an image he had seen on TV: "[a] flood; cattle being airlifted to safety, dumb with shock, leather straps around their fat bellies" (11). When art becomes too much of a sacred cow, it forfeits the element of risk discussed earlier, and consequently, its greatest utility. If *The Maestro* ends with the apocalyptic loss of both the deceased musician's beloved piano and the manuscript of his magnum opus, the gift of self-knowledge they impart to the boy is ample compensation in the Gouldian world-view. It is only by virtue of risk, of genuine "wilderness," that art becomes capable of fulfilling its mission. To this end, however, it must be experienced not simply as a ritual display of violated social conventions, but rather as a deeply disciplined descent into vulnerability.

However, Gould's utility to the text of *The Maestro* lies not only in the novel's concurrence with his philosophy. The Gouldian figure of Gow is part of the process by which Burl's descent into vulnerability and movement into an unfamiliar space results in the boy's individuation. That process also follows, in significant ways, the mythic pattern set out by Joseph Campbell in *The Hero with a Thousand Faces* (1949): "a separation from the world, a penetration to some source of power, and a life-enhancing return" in which "he comes back as one reborn" (Campbell 1949, 35-36). In Campbell's model the hero's entry to "the zone of magnified power" involves passing through or over a Threshold (77). Wynne-Jones himself discusses the importance of crossing boundaries for both characters and readers in the 1987 article "An Eye for Thresholds." In it, he suggests that the fictional Threshold, which, in its tangible form, is a "physical manifestation of change" (49), has a value in that it may make the less obvious— but nevertheless real—Thresholds crossed in his or her own life more apparent to the reader: it therefore "lends form to the chaos of living" (61). Wynne-Jones also states that "[e]very book is [itself] a Threshold" (60). We would suggest that this is particularly true of *The Maestro,* a text rich in potential for the reader.

Campbell's analysis of the journey of the hero identifies this pattern in myth and fairy tale, and the protagonist's quest typically begins with a "call to adventure" (Campbell 1949, 51); in Burl's case the call is heralded by the unlikely sight of an airborne grand piano. His adventure begins as a mere escape but evolves into a morally supportable quest emerging from the ashes of a more dubious one. Both quests fail in a material sense and are therefore, in a literal sense, unlike those typical of fairy tale and myth; there is no princess whose hand is won, nor any treasure as a reward. In fact Burl's path to the achievement of a new sense of self, while following the general pattern which Campbell identifies in traditional myth and fairy tale, is also reflected in the text's use of fairy-tale imagery itself. Wynne-Jones gives fairy tale two distinct, if complementary, values: it has the power to transform a bleak mental landscape, but it can be a realm of "useless ideas" if taken literally (1987, 33). Wynne-Jones, as storyteller, knows that the fantasy of fairy tale is important in children's lives, but must not become more dominant than reality. It takes personal effort— heroic effort—to effect change. Consequently Burl imagines his abusive egotistical ogre of a father, Cal, as "Koschei the Deathless" from Andrew Lang's *The Red Fairy Book* (Wynne-Jones 1995, 16), yet his eventual coming to terms with Cal and all the Crow familial baggage requires him to fall back on his own resources. Furthermore, while the text often employs fairy-tale imagery to connote positivity or a use as a coping mechanism, it balances that by also associating fairy tale with disappointment or delusion. At the text's end Burl's new-found sense of self—the "reborn" aspect referred to by Campbell (above)—is symbolized by the fairy-tale image of a "quite new" pair of shoes which have mysteriously appeared on Burl's feet and "fit him well" (223). Yet when Burl's false quest to Toronto claiming he is Gow's son founders at the possibility of DNA testing, we are told that "[t]he fairy tale was well and truly over" (159). The more morally viable quest to retrieve Gow's oratorio and thus acquire the cabin at Ghost Lake sounds to Burl "like a fairy tale" (175) and consequently does not unfold that way. Instead Burl literally wrestles with his problems in an apocalyptic struggle with a father who overshadows both Burl's past and, in the potential he recognizes in himself for Cal-like violence (165), his future.[5] However, the catalyst in the process by which Burl eventually achieves the rebirth that follows this apocalypse, is, in an oblique way, a "fairy godfather," Gow. It is Gow who enables Burl to transcend the constrictions imposed on the latter's inner life by Cal and to begin the process by which he will achieve a more complete identity. It is Gow who therefore stands at the threshold.

Campbell writes of the ambiguity of the "threshold guardian"(1949, 77). In Wynne-Jones's novel, Gow is the keeper of the "magic door" (1995, 50) by which Burl enters the new world of the cabin and beyond, a threshold guardian whose ambiguity is manifest in that, again in fairy-tale imagery, he is sometimes "a wizard, sometimes . . . an ogre" (51). With his riddles and word games, Gow is a guardian whose challenge must be met. Burl does so. However, their brief association is also symbiotic in that Gow provides food, shelter, and a little art in the shape of the four chords from "silence in Heaven" (55–56). Burl, for his part, scares off the bear that attacks the cabin (60–62).[6]

Towards the end of *The Hero with a Thousand Faces*, Campbell writes that the problem today, the problem facing each of us as hero or heroine as we negotiate the "crooked lanes of [our] own spiritual labyrinth" (1949, 101), is the difficulty of coming "to full human maturity through the conditions of contemporary life" (388). Campbell's concern here is with a contemporary society lacking either tribal myth or codified myth-as-religion. In *The Maestro* Tim Wynne-Jones depicts an adolescent whose own journey through the labyrinth of desire and despair ultimately results in a coming-to-terms with himself and his family, and a rebirth in the baptismal waters of his own hitherto-repressed tears (1995, 220). Gow, guardian of the outward threshold, had told him that achieving the results you want is often hard work: perfection "is really nothing more nor less than getting the results you desire" which "is never a simple business" (51). Toward the end of the text, Burl encounters a parallel figure to Gow at the threshold of his return. Japheth Starlight's advice to Burl, ostensibly regarding the burned-out cabin, is simple: "You made the mess—you clean it up. That's the way you become master of your own destiny, the way I see it" (221). The way to the integration of the self is through dealing with your problems, not in escaping them; it is not "a simple business."

It is the call of art that initially lures Burl, first unsuccessfully through *The Red Fairy Book* and then, more profoundly, in the form of the piano and its enigmatic owner. He is transported through the portal of secrecy, into a strange and dangerous solitude that leaves the world behind, and eventually, leaves behind his shadowy self. Yet if one is able to hear the call and is willing to enter, such a space can truly act as a chrysalis for the emergence of a more authentic relation to the world. Burl's journey really began with his simply escaping his circumstances by fleeing into the bush. It ends, after a geographical and psychological journey climaxing in an apocalyptic battle, with a return and a commitment: "He would clean up the mess" (222).

Escape can never be an end in itself. Aldous Huxley's protagonist Anthony Beavis comments in *Eyeless in Gaza* that "means determine ends" (1936, 325); applying this to Burl's case would suggest he would always be escaping from something or from himself if that was his sole *modus operandi* in dealing with the world. Just as fairy tale has value as a way of exercising the imagination but is no substitute for change effected by effort, so fleeing from a continuing problem can only be a short-term solution. In *The Maestro* Burl's flight into the bush is instrumental in bringing him to Gow and the threshold of his real journey. Beyond that threshold he is working toward something, not simply fleeing from it. Burl's quest, aided variously by Gow, the Agnews[7] and finally Japheth Starlight, is for identity, both as an individual and within a community. He journeys away from introversion and isolation and the egotism and solipsistic potential in them. Paradoxically, his flight into the daunting geographical space of the bush, in order to keep his self-preserving secrets, actually results in him freeing his self from that secrecy, propelling him into the pristine psychological space of his future.

The Maestro thus depicts the need for self-realization. The consequences of falling short of this goal can be seen in Cal's brutishness and

Gow's neuroses. The adolescent Burl needs the opportunity to develop fully, something equally true for the young reader. Tony Watkins writes, "The stories we offer our children can help them shape their sense of identity, help them find a home in the world" (Watkins 1992, 194). Burl escapes from a repressed and guarded introversion to the more positive form of secrecy afforded by Gow's pyramidal retreat and the opportunity it gives him to elude familial pressures, finally journeying to a resolution in which he actively takes control of his life. In depicting Burl's passage to selfhood, *The Maestro* suggests that there is always the possibility of hope, no matter how strong the feeling of alienation, no matter how great the sense of angst. Wynne-Jones's novel is an exemplification of the type of story to which Watkins refers, offering an important threshold to be crossed on the journey on which every child must be a hero, that of life.

NOTES

1.   There are many texts that conform to this model. Others include Kit Pearson's *A Handful of Time,* and Janet Lunn's *Shadow in Hawthorn Bay.* Arguably the "Golden Age" fantasies of Kenneth Grahame's *The Wind in the Willows* and James Barrie's *Peter Pan* also play with this concept; both Toad in the former and the Darling children in the latter mature (albeit somewhat problematically) having returned from their adventures. In J. R. R. Tolkien's *The Hobbit* the child surrogate Bilbo Baggins matures considerably after his long journey, while in the more recent and anthropomorphic *Redwall* by Brian Jacques part of Matthias's maturing into a warrior results from a journey into the unknown depths of the forest.

2.   With the notable exception of Peter Pan.

3.   ". . .When I'm—when—Pooh!"

"Yes, Christopher Robin?"

"I'm not going to do Nothing any more."

"Never again?"

"Well, not so much. They don't let you." (Milne 1928, 178)

4.   Wynne-Jones's utilization of aspects of Gould's persona also provides an opportunity to read the novel contrapuntally; that is, to explore the ways in which Gould's philosophy of art and his belief in the value of the Canadian North provide an independent "melody" which nevertheless harmonizes with Wynne-Jones's text. This process accords somewhat with Gould's own ideas, in that the resulting polyphony partially reflects Gould's accomplishment in the 1967 CBC radio broadcast *The Idea of North* in which multiple overlapping

voices on the same subject, i.e. the North, create a dialogic text with the potential for an exponential increase in the philosophical dimensions of the discourse(s) on that subject.

5.   Cal is, in a sense, the mythical "beast and . . . dragon and . . . antichrist" from Gow's oratorio (67).

6.   The bear has at least two levels of meaning. Its assault on the door is initially visualized by Burl as his father hacking his way in with an axe, and Burl's thwarting of it obviously foreshadows the eventual defeat of Cal at the same site. The bear also symbolizes the wildness and non-human quality of the North, the wilderness which paradoxically both draws Gow as an escape into solitude from the pressures of the Shadow (65), and repels him as the frightening and inscrutable Other.

7.   Natalie Agnew, Burl's teacher, and her husband. Ms Agnew takes a personal interest in Burl and the Agnews give him the opportunity to live with them.

WORKS CITED

Barrie, J. M. *Peter Pan*. 1911. London: Puffin, 1994.

Campbell, Joseph. *The Hero with a Thousand Faces*. New York: MJF Books, 1949.

Gould, Glenn. *The Idea of North*. Toronto, CBC, 1967.

———. *The Quiet in the Land*. Toronto, CBC, 1977.

Huxley, Aldous. *Eyeless in Gaza*. 1936. London: Chatto, 1939.

McGillis, Roderick. "Huck Finn meets Glenn Gould: *The Maestro*." *Canadian Children's Literature* 81 (1996): 58–59.

Milne, A. A. *The House at Pooh Corner*. 1928. Toronto: McClelland and Stewart, 1994.

Watkins, Tony. "Cultural Studies, New Historicism and Children's Literature." In *Literature for Children: Contemporary Criticism*. Ed. Peter Hunt. London: Routledge, 1992.

Wynne-Jones, Tim. "An Eye for Thresholds." *Canadian Children's Literature* 48 (1987). Rpt. in *Only Connect: Readings in Canadian Children's Literature*. Ed. Sheila Egoff et al. Toronto: Oxford University Press, 1996. 48–61.

———. *The Maestro*. A Groundwood Book. Vancouver/Toronto: Douglas & McIntyre, 1995.

Brian O'Connal and Emily Byrd Starr: The Inheritors of Wordsworth's "Gentle Breeze"

MARGARET STEFFLER

O there is a blessing in this gentle breeze
That blows from the green fields and from the clouds
And from the sky: it beats against my cheek,
And seems half conscious of the joy it gives (*The Prelude* I, 1-4).

WHEN W.O. MITCHELL DIED LAST YEAR I could not help but consider the pivotal role played by *Who Has Seen the Wind* in the development of my interest in Canadian literature dealing with the child and subsequently in Canadian children's literature. In Mitchell's novel I found a merging of a number of areas that interested me: the growth of the Romantic child, the sublimity of the Canadian landscape, and the effect of the child's consciousness on the rather staid and insular small town community. This was the book that turned my attention from the Romantic poets to the literature of our country, and thus W.O. Mitchell has always been a writer to whom I feel indebted. A member of the local news station visited one of my tutorials in Canadian literature at Trent University for thoughts about W.O. Mitchell the day after his death. When asked if I thought W.O. Mitchell's work would endure, I was able to say that my twelve-year-old daughter had just read *Who Has Seen the Wind* and was very moved by it. I then began to struggle once again with the rather artificial and arbitrary boundaries and divisions we seem to impose between literature concerned with the child and children's literature. Much of our literature dealing with the child, supposedly written for adults, is informed by and closely connected with our children's literature; to deal with the two areas separately is to lose important historical and comparative perspectives.

I have long been fascinated by the presence of the Wordsworthian child, in the tradition of *The Prelude*, in Canadian literature.[1] The most obvious and pure inheritor of a Wordsworthian temperament in Canadian children's literature is L. M. Montgomery's Emily Byrd Starr, who takes her place beside W.O. Mitchell's Brian O'Connal as our ideal of the Canadian Romantic child. The Wind Woman in *Emily of New Moon* and the Young Ben and prairie wind in *Who Has Seen the Wind* are the mysterious and animate forces of the universe, which, in the manner of Wordsworth's "gentle breeze," inspire a response from the receptive child. The fact that *Who Has Seen the Wind* is conventionally classified as literature for the mature reader and *Emily of New Moon* as children's literature reveals the limitations of such classifications. Elizabeth Waterston makes the point that *Who Has Seen the Wind*, "like many children's 'classics' . . . was not written for children. But children of ten or eleven, who find it in school or in the library tap into a book that serves deep needs" (Waterston 1992, 85–86). Mitchell, primarily viewed as a writer for adults in spite of his accessibility to younger readers, and Montgomery, automatically classified as a children's writer despite the popularity of her books with adults, seem to meet at this border of adult literature dealing with the child and children's literature. Brian and Emily inhabit the overlapping territory between the two genres. Examined together in this shadowy border area, they each cast light on the adjoining territory from which they should not—and perhaps *cannot*—be excluded.

Despite the obvious and strong influence of Wordsworth on both authors, Mitchell and Montgomery express frustration as well as admiration when referring to William Wordsworth. Montgomery, evaluating poets in her journal, says that Wordsworth "occasionally says something so vital and poignant that I am ready to cry out with the agony of it—and so I love him too, in spite of his much balderdash" (Montgomery 1985, 358). Mitchell's assessment is similarly mixed: "God wasted on him [Wordsworth] more perceptions than any goddamn, square conservative Anglican I've ever known . . . perceptions which he bitched up" (O'Rourke 1980–81, 152). The poignancy and the perceptions valued by Montgomery and Mitchell appear in their own work as celebrations of this Romantic temperament which originates in the Lake District and manages to work its way through the "balderdash" and "bitched-up perceptions" in order to root itself in the Canadian landscape.[2]

Montgomery's Emily and Mitchell's Brian are so closely related to the young Wordsworth of *The Prelude* that a reader familiar with the growth of that Romantic poet is repeatedly drawn back to the earlier place and character. The twentieth-century Canadian setting is thus emphasized because it provides a striking contrast to the scenery of the nineteenth-century Lake District. W.O. Mitchell and L. M. Montgomery have effectively transported the Romantic child from the Lake District to the receptive Canadian landscape of the prairies and the Maritime island. These Romantic children, on whom "the surface of the universal earth / With triumph, and delight and hope and fear, / Work like a sea" (*The Prelude* I, 473–475), flourish in the sublimity of the Canadian landscape. Present in some degree in earlier characters in Canadian children's literature such as Catharine Parr Traill's Catharine and Ernest Thompson Seton's Yan, the Romantic temperament is fully developed in Montgomery's Emily, who prefigures and matches the Wordsworthian intensity of Brian O'Connal. The question to be asked seems to be whether these writers use Wordsworthian children simply because they are familiar, convenient, and "ready-made," or whether the use of this established literary character deliberately comments on important differences found in the Canadian child, situation, and society. Although important and memorable as characters in themselves, Emily and Brian are used to comment on those around them. Assessments and evaluations of Canadian small-town society are derived from these children's insights into that world; as well, the treatment of these visionary and imaginative children by others provides a means to measure and often to judge the adult members of the families and communities.

The first sentence of Emily's "description"—"the hill called to me and something in me called back to it" (Montgomery 1923, 8)—recalls such basic Wordsworthian concepts as: "From nature largely he receives; nor so / Is satisfied, but largely gives again" (*The Prelude* II, 267–268), and "An auxiliar light / Came from my mind which on the setting sun / Bestow'd new splendour" (*The Prelude* II, 387–388).[3] The child's tempera-

ment is receptive and imaginative, responding to the impetus that originates in the external world. Emily does not make a conscious or cultivated
attempt to escape, transform, or transcend the real world, but does
respond to it in a way that facilitates such a transcendence. The active part
played by nature in *Emily of New Moon* is epitomized by the Wind
Woman, who anticipates W.O. Mitchell's wind and recalls Wordsworth's
breezes in her ability to inspire a response in the child—a response which
results in an escape from reality:

> Her [Emily's] soul suddenly escaped from the bondage of Aunt Elizabeth's
> stuffy feather-bed and gloomy canopy and sealed windows. She was out in
> the open with the Wind Woman and the other gypsies of the night—the
> fireflies, the moths, the brooks, the clouds. (Montgomery 1923, 62–63)

Emily, like the young Wordsworth, partially creates the activity and power
of the external world that results in her transcendence of it. Emily's "flash"
involves a process similar to Wordsworth's "spot of time." The active participation of the child is a prerequisite for the mystical moment, the landscape of Prince Edward Island being invested with the same type of
emotion and energy as the landscape of the Lake District.

The elements available in Mitchell's prairie landscape of the depression seem to constitute in themselves the powerful and overwhelming
forces required for the Romantic relationship between child and nature,
which Brian describes as the "feeling"—the equivalent of Wordsworth's
"spot of time" and Emily's "flash." The conditions required for a "spot of
time," particularly those of sublimity and power, are readily available to
Brian, and do not require the same amount of participation and projec-
tion of emotion onto the landscape as that demonstrated by Wordsworth[4]
and Emily. Brian, like Wordsworth, does invest the landscape with feelings and forces of power—his internal energy or guilt affects the external
world—which in turn works on the isolated and vulnerable child: "Brian
could feel its [the wind's] chill reaching for the very center of him, and he
hunched his shoulders as he felt the wincing of his very core against it"
(Mitchell 1947, 228). Brian exaggerates the terror of the landscape due to
his fear and guilt, and he is subsequently driven into himself, surrounded
and victimized by nature's powerful influence rather than continuing to
participate in the creation of its condition: "As the stook shadows length-

ened in the fields, his loneliness drove him more and more into his mind, there to seek the company of his thoughts and reassure himself in the face of all the frightening emptiness outside" (228). It is almost as if the prairie landscape does not require the embellishment of the mind in order to build it up into a force to be reckoned with; the elements of the scene— large, sublime, and threatening in themselves—do not need to be altered. Rather than using his energy to intensify the scene, the inherent power of the external world drains Brian O'Connal: "It was as though he listened to the drearing wind and in the spread darkness of the prairie night was being drained of his very self" (229). The reader of *Who Has Seen the Wind* is as impressed by the power of the natural world as by the power of the child's mind. The prairie itself is a central element to be reckoned with in the transcendental equation. The wind invigorates the prairie, which in turn impresses itself on the child. The sublimity of the prairie landscape is shaped in the reader's mind more through the child's response to its power than through the child's creation of its power.

Emily Byrd Starr, as a Romantic child, is definitely an outcast and an eccentric, as Ellen, the voice of proper society, makes clear: "The fact is, Emily Starr, you're queer, and folks don't care for queer children" (Montgomery 1923, 22). Emily's "queerness," or difference from others can be seen as positive or negative, depending on the viewpoint of the judgement: "Father says I am a genius, but Aunt Elizabeth says I'm just queer" (157). The most attractive explanation of Emily's isolation is provided by Dean Priest: "Stars are said to dwell apart, anyhow, sufficient unto themselves— ensphered in their own light" (280). This assessment of Emily recalls descriptions of the young Wordsworth, who "when rock and hill, / The woods, and distant Skiddaw's lofty height, / Were bronzed with deepest radiance, stood alone / Beneath the sky" (*Prelude* I, 294–297). Those who understand and love Emily are themselves not wholly accepted by society, and those who are antagonistic towards her conform to the narrowly defined and traditional values held by the majority. Montgomery's charac- terization is such that the reader automatically sides with the more attrac- tive outcasts, and condemns the insularity and limitations of the society, not to mention its lack of justice and tolerance, which are especially appar- ent to the child and the imaginative adult.

It is Emily, who, as a Romantic child at odds with society, exposes the faults and hypocrisy of that civilized and established world. Her effect on others is seen as beneficial, bringing out admirable qualities and values previously repressed by the strict standards of society. She has a "humanizing" effect on those around her, counteracting those conventional forces which stifle imaginative and creative activity. The effect and extent of her influence depend on the character of the recipient and range from amusement and diversion for Aunt Nancy to love and rejuvenation for Dean Priest. Both Mary Rubio and Muriel Whitaker stress the importance of the imagination not only in its contribution to the vitality of Montgomery's child characters, but also in its ability to influence the environment through these children (Rubio, 1975; Whitaker, 1975).[5] Opposed to the world of Emily's flash—the realm of dreams, visions, nature, and sensuous indulgences—is the oppressive world of society, reflected in Aunt Elizabeth's stuffy bed, the reaction of Miss Brownell to Emily's passionate enthusiasm, the taunting of the schoolchildren, and the critical appraisal of the Murray relatives. Emily's ability to escape from this realm takes little effort on her part; her temperament invites a transcendence of this oppression.[6]

The resolution of the novel optimistically suggests in its idyllic fashion that society will benefit from Emily's gifts and imagination. Indeed, certain characters, especially Aunt Elizabeth, have already been "humanized" by her influence: "Elizabeth Murray had learned an important lesson—that there was not one law of fairness for children and another for grown-ups" (Montgomery 1923, 337). More importantly, Emily's vision and mysticism restore the emotion of love to Dr. Burnley. The tendency of society to view Emily's vision as madness perpetuates its own mistakes and misunderstandings; the attempt to use and understand her unusual viewpoint results in some degree of truth and regeneration for society. Obviously implied is the idea that Emily's effect on other characters will be broadened and intensified in her future influence, as a writer, on her readers. The process has been gradual, beginning with the challenges at Aunt Nancy's and taking its most significant step in the long awaited confrontation and reconciliation with Aunt Elizabeth, in which both sides—the rigidity of social tradition and the passion of the Romantic child—relent and meet. Recognition and admission of guilt on both sides suggest the need for compromise and tolerance, as well as a union of the two stances in order for peaceful co-existence to be achieved. Significantly, Emily's reorganization of the values of society destroys "the sense of reality—nearness—of close communion" (Montgomery 1923, 325) with her father.

The ability to commune with an imaginary realm set apart from reality is outgrown at the moment Emily revises her letters with the explanatory footnotes demanded by the society represented by Aunt Elizabeth. Thus Emily will influence society, but not without being influenced and tamed herself to some extent by the judgements and expectations of that society.

Similarly, Brian O'Connal, in his decision to become a "dirt doctor," reflects the influence of society as he begins to channel his talents and energy towards a practical, community-oriented activity. While Brian O'Connal's response to the prairie is similar to the young Wordsworth's response to the English Lake District, Wordsworth's emphasis is on "the growth of the poet's mind" as indicated in *The Prelude's* title, whereas Mitchell's main concern seems to be the way in which the child's temperament and outlook can be used to comment on the society of the Canadian prairie during the depression of the thirties. Through Brian, the Romantic attributes and tendencies of the child expose the hypocrisy and lack of vision in his society.

Individuals associated with the prairie are outcasts in the extreme sense, often approaching madness, and Brian's association with Uncle Sean, the Young Ben and Saint Sammy have familiarized him with that group to which he is attracted and with which he shares many characteristics. Although an outcast to a certain degree, Brian does manage to conform to a reasonable extent and to participate in his community without relinquishing the idealism and sensitivity derived from his childhood prairie experiences. His decision to minister to the needs of the prairie combines the pragmatic approach of his father, Gerald, and the idealistic world of Uncle Sean. Brian plans to bring education and rationality to the land, while simultaneously upholding the ideal harmony and vitality associated with the prairie and the wind.

The Presbyterian practicality and puritanism of Brian's heritage prevent him from becoming a Saint Sammy or a Young Ben, outcasts separated from society. However, the mysticism and vision of the sensitive child, associated with the prairie wind, take Brian away from the society his father served to the environment that taught him about death, and thus about life:

> There was the prairie; there was a meadow lark, a baby pigeon, and a calf with two heads. In some haunting way the Ben was part of it. So was Mr. Digby. (Mitchell 1947, 292)

To combine Mr. Digby and the Young Ben is to take the nobility and intelligence of the town and combine it with the freedom and harmony of the prairie. Thus Brian's heritage and temperament demand a union of practicality and vision. To remain in the realm of the visionary at the expense of the practical would be indulgent and selfish on the Canadian prairie of the depression years. The experiences of the Romantic child can be put to use by providing vision and idealism to temper the limitations and intolerance of the Canadian prairie community, isolated and struggling against the drought and depression.

The balance which Brian finds between the prairie and town, or vision and practicality, is similar to the "innocence of experience," which Mitchell describes as "the artist's innocence, a sort of inner balance between spontaneity and discipline which must never tip too far in either direction" (Mitchell 1976, 37). Although no longer an "outcast" or Ben-like figure at the end of the novel, Brian does retain a degree of spontaneity which will affect those with whom he comes into contact. Like Emily, he conforms in that he is functioning within society, but he still manages to trail the transcendental and mystical moments behind him, bringing them to a society in need of such an influence. The desiccated town, like the dry landscape, will benefit from Brian's association with the prairie and the Young Ben. Eventually, the Mrs. Abercrombies of the town will feel the effects of the prairie wind that Brian seems to carry with him into his adulthood and his society.

Although the characters of Emily Byrd Starr and Brian O'Connal, along with the landscape with which they interact, are central to these novels, memorable, and successfully developed, the nature and changes of the communities or small towns seem to be just as important as these child figures. The contrast provided between the Wordsworthian child and the community in which he or she lives is resolved by the promise or at least the suggestion that the grown child functioning within that community will influence others, touching them with the imagination and intensity developed in the childhood relationship with nature. The Romantic child fits well in the Canadian landscape, the wind working on tree and prairie to initiate a "flash" or "feeling" at least as powerful as a Wordsworthian "spot of time." More importantly, however, the Romantic child provides a striking commentary on a society lacking imagination and vision, and through his or her influence provides a means to inspire and change the rather insular and judgemental Canadian community. Although interesting in themselves as familiar figures in a new landscape, Emily and Brian, along with the Wordsworthian children who precede and follow them, become instruments to measure, judge, and influence a society in need of the insight and inspiration of the "flash" and the "feeling." Wordsworth's concentration on the artistic and psychological "growth of the poet's mind" is replaced here in our literature by Montgomery's and Mitchell's more practical concerns of how the Canadian community can benefit from the powerful and idealistic experiences and temperaments of our Romantic children.

NOTES

1. Wordsworthian vocabulary and concepts appear in a number of works, such as Ernest Buckler's *The Mountain and the Valley*, Wallace Stegnor's *Wolf Willow*, and Hugh Hood's *A Swing in the Garden*, to name but a few. Wordsworthian philosophy and characters also inform our early children's literature, as seen in Catharine Parr Traill's *Canadian Crusoes: A Tale of the Rice Lake Plains*, Ernest Thompson Seton's *Two Little Savages*, and Ralph Connor's *Glengarry Schooldays*.
2. This "rooting" of the Romantic child in the Canadian landscape occurred with the help and earlier contributions of Traill, Seton, Connor, and others.
3. Elizabeth Waterston calls *Emily of New Moon* "an intriguing though unpretentious version of Wordworth's *Prelude.*" See Elizabeth Waterston, "Lucy Maud Montgomery," in *The Clear Spirit*, ed. Mary Quayle Innes, (Toronto: University of Toronto Press, 1966), 212.
4. Wordsworth, for example, in relating the scene of the pool, the beacon, and the girl in Book XI, makes the comment that "It was in truth, / An ordinary sight" (*The Prelude* XI, 308–309), suggesting that his state of mind and his own response to this scene are partially responsible for its power. In his second description of the scene, after he perceives a "visionary dreariness," he adds the words "lonely," "vexed," and "tossed," imbuing the scene with his own emotions and feelings, and thus participating in, and encouraging, albeit in an unconscious way, the transcendent experience that occurs.
5. Mary Rubio, discussing Anne, and Muriel Whitaker, referring to Anne and Emily, emphasize the ways in which these characters influence and change the world and adults around them.
6. The only evidence of an ability to encourage and train these visionary tendencies is seen in Emily's conscious attempts to "see the [wall]paper in the air"

(Montgomery 1923, 57). "This odd knack" (57) seems to be closely associated with the "flash," for it invites a removal from ordinary perception and reality. Aunt Elizabeth, of course, disapproves: "Don't do it again. It gives your face an unnatural expression" (57). The visionary, the mystical and the dreamy are all "unnatural," according to Aunt Elizabeth and the staid society of which she is an exemplary member.

WORKS CITED

Mitchell, W.O. "Debts of Innocence." *Saturday Night*. March 1976: 36–37.

Mitchell, W.O. *Who Has Seen the Wind*. 1947. Toronto: McClelland and Stewart Bantam-Seal, 1982.

Montgomery, L. M. *Emily of New Moon*. 1923. Toronto: McClelland and Stewart, 1973.

———. *The Selected Journals of L. M. Montgomery. Volume I: 1889–1910*. Eds. Mary Rubio and Elizabeth Waterston. Toronto: Oxford University Press, 1985.

O'Rourke, David. "An Interview with W.O. Mitchell." *Essays on Canadian Writing* 20 (1980–81): 149–159.

Rubio, Mary. "Satire, Realism and Imagination in *Anne of Green Gables*." *Canadian Children's Literature* 3 (1975): 27–36.

Waterston, Elizabeth. *Canadian Children's Literature*. New York: Twayne, 1992.

Whitaker, Muriel A. "'Queer Children': L. M. Montgomery's Heroines." *Canadian Children's Literature* 3 (1975): 50–59.

Wordsworth, William. *The Prelude or Growth of a Poet's Mind*. Ed. E. de Selincourt. 2nd ed. rev. Helen Darbishire. Oxford: Clarendon Press, 1959. All references to *The Prelude* are from the 1805 edition.

The Eros of Childhood and Early Adolescence in Girl Series: L. M. Montgomery's *Emily* Trilogy

IRENE GAMMEL

[T]he public and the publisher won't allow me to write of a young girl as she really is [. . .]. [Y]ou have to depict a sweet, insipid young thing— really a child grown older—to whom the basic realities of life and reactions to them are quite unknown. *Love* must scarcely be hinted at—yet young girls in their early teens often have some very vivid love affairs. A girl of "Emily's" type would.

— L. M. Montgomery, January 1924

[C]hildren's books may look sweet and innocent, but they cannot be— nor can their critics.

— Peter Hunt, 1991

$\mathbf{B}$OTH EPIGRAPHS INVITE US TO QUESTION the putative "innocence" of children's books, pointing to the complexity of the genre's ideological and political messages. Indeed, as theorists of children's literature and culture have documented only very recently, products for children ranging from literature to toys are rarely value-free or apolitical, for sexually charged Barbie Dolls and asexual Anne Dolls encode specific values and ideals.[1] Indeed, the issue of ideological advocacy and social value is heightened when it comes to representing the girl's body and her sexuality, or what Montgomery cautiously subsumes under the rubric of "the basic realities of life." Theorists of girl literature and culture have only just begun to study the girl's body in the larger scholarship of children's literature, itself a young discipline.[2] Children's literature theorist Sally Mitchell, in *The New Girl: Girls' Culture in England, 1880–1915*, situates sexuality outside of the realm of girlhood and makes the end of girlhood coincide with the emergence of the girl's sexual being; yet she also writes that the "age at which young people are seen as sexual beings is, quite evidently, not necessarily linked to puberty; both the gendering and the sexualizing of people in their second decade of life is subject to wide historical and cultural variation" (1995, 7). Yet how is sexuality configured or mapped on the girl's body in a literature produced for girls? What are the boundaries and conventions that determine the shape of such representations? And to what extent is the girl given agency over her body in her developmental journey? By exploring these questions from a feminist and historical approach, I propose not only to expand our understanding of the role the girl's body plays in children's literature, but also to provide insight into the sexual politics that underpin the genre, revealing children's literature to be deeply involved in political debates and historical structures.

I propose to take L. M. Montgomery at her word, using *Emily of New Moon* (1923) as my key text of examination. By the early 1920s Canada's beloved author of children's fiction had grown tired of the Anne series (Anne had become conventional as an adult woman) and longed to write a different character who was better equipped to maintain her autonomy in adulthood. With *Emily of New Moon* Montgomery presented her readers with a deeply subversive and unsettling novel featuring a girl-heroine endowed with a powerful drive to become a writer and with an equally keen sense of her developing body, a combination that would prove irresistible for twentieth-century Canadian women writers including Margaret Atwood, Alice Munro, P. K. Page, Jane Urquhart, and most recently Kit Pearson and Lillian Nattel, who have acknowledged their indebtedness to this novel. As well, the novel is a favourite amongst feminist Montgomery scholars (Gwyn 1997, 71–80) and has been widely consumed through television adaptation in the *Emily of New Moon* series and through follow-up reading. The text's unsettling quality is all the more tantalizing as the novel is based on Montgomery's own unusual bodily and artistic development from a precocious ten-year-old to a thirteen-year-old growing up surrounded by the breathtaking pastoral beauty of Prince Edward Island, while also experiencing first-hand its small town repressive and conformist social structures (cf. Rubio and Waterston 1995, 73). Montgomery successfully initiates her girl-protagonist into the "basic realities of life," while at the same time satisfying the publisher's demand for generic conformity and suitability for mass consumption in Canada and abroad. Yet the book's message is far from innocent, for Montgomery was a master in encoding decidedly subversive messages that speak of women's power and of girls' rights (Poe 1997, 15–35).[3]

While Emily's powerful struggle for an artistic voice in a repressive environment has been investigated by Marie Campbell (1994, 137–45), Elizabeth Epperly (1992, 149–67), and Judith Miller (1984, 158–68), Emily's developing body-self remains to be analysed for a complete picture of Montgomery's claiming of the sexual realities for her girl protagonist. In my earlier work on Montgomery's *Emily*, I examined the role of female autoerotic fantasies, arguing that Montgomery thoroughly subverts a cultural norm that teaches girls and women that their function is to provide pleasures for others, not for themselves; most notably, Montgomery strategically eroticises Emily's vocation as a writer, thus defying a cultural norm that associates women's writing with unhealthy isolation and lack of attractiveness (Gammel 1999). Building on this earlier argument, I now shift my focus to Montgomery's so far unexplored representations of *female embodiment*; more specifically, I propose to show that *Emily of New Moon* advocates the female body as a locus for girl experiment and pleasure, while also presenting it as a privileged social battleground similar to the adolescent female body Brenda Boudreau has traced in contemporary fiction by women (1998, 43–56). It is through her body, I argue, that Montgomery's girl claims agency for herself by actively negotiating the socialization and normalization requested from her body in its developmental journey from child to early adolescent.[4]

To understand Montgomery's feminist advocacy for girls' body pleasure and agency it is important to place this work within its historical context. Montgomery was writing *Emily of New Moon* in 1921–22, when the girl's body had just undergone significant changes in cultural and popular perception. As Rhona Justice-Malloy has documented in her recent American study of girl representations in the popular *Sears Catalog* from

1906–1927, girls were associated with much greater freedom of movement after the war than before, with advertisements now reflecting a new visual preference for girl mobility and action: "Girls were no longer floating within their spheres. They were on the move at home and in public" (Justice-Malloy 1998, 121). Popular notions of sexuality were changing dramatically as witnessed in Margaret Sanger's courageous birth control movement in the United States starting in 1912: "Margaret's graphic descriptions of the reproductive process and of sexuality in childhood, adolescence, and adulthood, presented in 1912 and 1913 under the column head 'What Every Girl Should Know,' aroused a furor," writes Sanger biographer Ellen Chesler (1992, 65).[5] While these new representations were highly contentious in both the United States and Canada, and while Montgomery was adamantly set against the craze for new "'sex' novels" (Montgomery 1992, 387), she used the new freedoms and the spirit of experimentation for working through her own developmental history as a girl growing up in late nineteenth-century Canada.

Montgomery, then, was writing about a body she knew intimately well: her own. Emily is Montgomery's most autobiographical novel, written in only six months time, and providing the author with "intense pleasure in writing it" (Montgomery 1992, 39), the pleasure perhaps resulting from what is ultimately a *revisionary* history of her *body-self*. Retrospective writing allowed Montgomery to advocate a decidedly 1920s sensibility of girl freedom, mobility, and vocation in her (re)writing of her late nineteenth-century girl character. Emily's relationship with her body and the emerging girl subjectivity, as we shall see, are 1920s in their outlook and focus, granting much greater status to the forces of sexuality than the 1908 *Anne of Green Gables*. It is, at the same time, a much more disturbing book, one that reveals Montgomery's own wrestling with the dangers and powers of sexuality and in some areas it risks exploding the borders of the genre. Indeed so crucial was Montgomery's focus on the body and the girl's agency that she was willing to push the boundaries of the genre to its very limit in order to accommodate her vision of a girl who was both aware of her bodily realities and who was an active agent in shaping her body. As a result *Emily of New Moon* is so transgressive that it ultimately raises questions about the boundaries of children's literature itself.

To document Montgomery's political advocacy of bodily pleasure and agency for her girl heroine, I will begin by situating *Emily of New*

Moon within the context of modern feminist body theory; I will then move on to examine her focus on Eros and sexuality as inscribed on the girl's body, while also drawing attention to some of the ideological contradictions of this enterprise; and I will finally reflect on the complex translation of Montgomery's idea of body pleasure and agency in the recent television adaptation. I ultimately propose a *feminist model of body and pleasure reading*, that is, a process that confers body agency and body control for the girl reader, while also drawing attention to the body as a complex zone of social pressures and norms. This feminist and historical approach asserts that in her "thinking through the body," Montgomery directly links the girl's healthy development to her experience of pleasure and agency in relation to her body.

Body-Theory and Emily-in-the-Glass

During the 1970s and 1980s, the French historian of sexuality Michel Foucault has powerfully shown that the body presents a surface for the inscription of cultural history: the body is not biologically determined but is a locus of social control, shaped as a "docile" body according to specific cultural norms and regulations, which begin with such simple activities as toilet training and end in a person's voluntary subjection to the demands of fashion. In the wake of Foucault's influential *The History of Sexuality* (1976), feminist body theorist Elizabeth Grosz theorized the body as a "hinge" and "interface" situated somewhere between nature and culture (Grosz 1994), while feminist philosopher Susan Bordo, in her compelling examination of female body pathologies including anorexia, agoraphobia, and hysteria, has documented that the female body is a privileged "locus of practical cultural control" (Bordo 1997, 104).[6] Yet if the body is a locus for social control, it can also act as a "subversive body," as the American gender theorist Judith Butler has documented in *Gender Trouble* (1990) by arguing that women often reiterate the social norms they are asked to play, but do so with a significant difference, subverting the gender roles in place. In alignment with this focus on the body's constructedness, I use the term *body-self* to refer to the complex and dynamic image the girl constructs of her changing body within the social context, a representation that is intimately linked to her sense of self, as we shall see. Her sense of agency emerges in her active negotiation of social, psychological, and biological realities that impinge on her body.

On 21 August 1921 Montgomery begins recreating in fiction the memory of her youthful body-selves, after having burnt her childhood diary at age fourteen. While some memories focus on repressions and humiliations, on rebellion and bitterness (Montgomery 1992, 21), she takes pains in giving Emily a sense of agency and control over her body development by putting the ten-year-old in touch with body pleasure. In the first chapter of *Emily of New Moon*, we see Emily looking at herself, delighting in the spectatorial desire of her mirror-self: "'We've been friends *always*, haven't we?' With a blown kiss to little Emily-in-the-glass, Emily out-of-the-glass was off" (Montgomery 1923, 13). This unmitigated enjoyment of an extended mirror stage reflects Emily-in-the-glass as an ideal object of love and admiration, for she is surrounded by an all-loving (though dying) father and by her imaginary maternal friend, the Wind Woman, whose erotic potential is tremendous (cf. Gammel 1999). Emily's sense of self, and her awareness of being in the world, is connected with the mirrored body-self. This also suggests a split: the mirrored self is also the "other," that is, an object for intersubjective engagement in the diary, which contains "all her fancies about the Wind Woman, and Emily-in-the-glass—all her little cat dialogues" (Montgomery 1923, 57). Emily takes ownership of her body-self's development in language by recording and mythologizing it. The body-self thus produced as a representation suggests not the blindness of narcissism, but active exploration of self leading to the proud realization that she is "important to [her]self" (30) and will be "a famous *authoress*" (47). The self-representational moment, the claiming of the embodied self in language, marks the child as an important agent in her own development.

As a child agent Emily triumphantly rules the realm of Eros, the realm of bodily and imaginary pleasure that allows her to multiply moments of pleasure for herself. This agency is perhaps best illustrated through Emily's dramatic *flash*, the intensive, climactic moment of pleasure that always fills her with supreme rapture and delight, and which she receives and cultivates as a gift (e.g. 9, 15). Intimately intertwined with her concept of body-self, the flash is a touchstone to which Emily/Montgomery return, not as an ultimate essence but as a base for instantiating an embodied self for the girl-protagonist. It is significant to note that the focus on Emily's body-awareness is not based on intuitive knowledge of the body, what philosophers and psychologists call *proprioception* (that is, a personal awareness of the body's empirical location in space and time) (Eilan et al. 1998, 1–28); often Emily is lost in thought and reverie, getting into scrapes because she forgets where she put her shoes, or she is oblivious to the bodily dangers that surround her. Rather, Montgomery instantiates the girl's authority over her *body-imaging* in erotic moments.

In "The Uses of the Erotic," the American feminist writer Audre Lorde writes that the "very word 'erotic' comes from the Greek word *eros*, the personification of love in all its aspects—born of Chaos, and personifying creative power and harmony" (1997, 279), thus providing a description of Eros that nicely encapsulates Montgomery's use of it. Emily's pleasure is sensory based, as visual, olfactory, and most frequently haptic experience, as when she walks in nature, with intensive awareness that "the brown, frosted grasses under her feet were velvet piles" (Montgomery 1923, 14), the body perception already translated into erotic language. Thus sensory based body pleasure is autoerotically enhanced through fantasy and language, creating an erotic body mythology.[7] Montgomery dramatizes the development of the girl's body at the complex intersection of the biological, the social, the psychological, and the mythological, whereby the girl asserts her agency in accommodating and actively negotiating the inscription of these different discourses. The emerging selves come to be represented by the word *queer*, first brought to Emily's consciousness by the mean-spirited housekeeper Ellen Greene: "You talk queer—and you act queer—and at times you look queer" (30). This epithet more positively denotes her self-construction in opposition to cultural norms, her holding on to a creative configuring of self in moments of pleasure and rapture.[8] Yet the "queerness" of her self also prepares the reader for the conflicts that will be the topic for the rest of the novel, as Montgomery sets in motion a conflictual plot pattern drawing attention to the social pressures that require *active* negotiation.

Conflicting Body Selves

Just as body theorists focus on the cultural inscription of the body, so Montgomery powerfully documents that the girl's body becomes a locus for social inscriptions of identity. Emily makes her entry into "society" when her father dies. As an orphan at the mercy of her extended family, she is reluctantly adopted into the proud Murray clan, and for the first time goes to school and church, and becomes part of the social institutions. Significantly, her body-self is now refracted through the social mirror that powerfully fragments the body into body parts, brilliantly dramatized by Montgomery when the family members arrive for Douglas Starr's funeral and proceed to read the girl's body, tracing, deciphering, and verifying her family alliance like genealogical detectives: she has her "grandmother's hair and eyes" (Uncle Oliver), "old George Byrd's nose" (Aunt Ruth), "her father's forehead" (Aunt Eva), "her mother's smile" (Aunt Laura), and "Juliet's long lashes" (Aunt Addie). Refusing to be thus de-composed to be absorbed in bits and pieces into the family lineage, Emily is indignant, "You make me feel as if I am made of scraps and patches" (38).

In *Emily of New Moon*, girl agency over self-representation is under siege, contested by autocratic adults, just as Montgomery's was. Immediately following Emily's adoption by the puritanical and insensitive Elizabeth Murray, her new guardian takes ownership of Emily's diary thus provoking the first of many battles: "Emily sprang across the floor and snatched the book. 'You mustn't read that, Aunt Elizabeth,' she cried indignantly, 'that's mine—my own *private property*'"(56). Emily claims her body-self as her property in a language of rights using powerful *legal* and *moral* terms ("'I'm *not* ashamed of it,' cried Emily, backing away, hugging her precious book to her breast" [56]), arguing for the girl's agency in representing herself. Yet her efforts to rescue this body-self from violation by a more powerful adult also requires that she sacrifice it: Emily burns the diary in the fire to prevent her aunt from reading and ridiculing it, an act that will be repeated later in the novel with the autocratic teacher, Miss Brownell, revealing the limits of the girl's rights over self-representation.

Montgomery argues against the autocratic adult who refuses to respect the girl's body agency and the reader's sympathy is with Emily; in fact, the reader's pleasure consists in participating in Emily's subversive reclaiming of *self-representational* agency as in the example of the photography specially commissioned for Aunt Nancy Priest (née Murray) in Shrewsbury and designed to align Emily in the history of the Murrays. Emily looks sulky and hates the pictures of herself ("They made her look hideous. Her face seemed to be *all* forehead" [240]), yet Elizabeth Murray likes them precisely because this expression highlights Emily's Murray likeness. Emily subversively reclaims her body-self, when she sends Aunt Nancy a more satisfactory second picture, namely, Teddy's artistic picture of her: "I'm smiling and have a bang"(240). The repressive adult's power has been checked, while the girl emerges a true heroine through her wrestling with shaping her body-self. This struggle for authority and dominance provides the comic matrix of this novel, notwithstanding the fact that Elizabeth is also a strong role model as an independent woman who occupies the male position as head of the household. In fact, the conflict will intensify, as the girl's body-self slips from the domain of the erotic into the more specifically sexual.

In her influential work *Female Sexualization* (1987), the German feminist Frigga Haug has theorized the complex ways in which seemingly "innocent" body parts (hair, breast, legs, etc.) become sexual in the process of the girl's socialization, preparing her for (hetero)sexual union. Each culture, of course, features different sexual signifiers, which are inscribed on bodies "through a repertoire of camouflage, concealment, intonations, flattery" (Haug 129). Through strategic narrative repetition Montgomery exposes seemingly innocent activities as sexually charged.

In light of Frigga Haug's analysis, it comes as no surprise that Emily's hair is the bodily conflict zone on which the wills of Emily and Elizabeth most fiercely wrestle for control. "Trial by Fire" is the appropriately titled chapter in which Emily starts school and is exposed to new body images (in fact, the girls are identified through their bodies as in "Black-eyes," "Chestnut-curls," "Piggy-eyes," and "Freckled-one" [Montgomery 1923, 89–92], before we learn their proper names), and Emily develops a wicked crush on the pretty Rhoda Stuart. With her ribbons and flattery Rhoda is already an expert of seductive femininity and advises Emily to reach her own feminine-seductive potential: "*You* ought to have a bang, Emily. They're all the rage and you'd look well with one because you've such a high forehead. It would make a real beauty of you" (95). Of course, the bang idea, with its sexual lure, is immediately countered by Aunt Elizabeth's "We will not have bangs at New Moon—except on the Molly cows" (97). Yet the bang becomes Emily's body fetish, the *one* absent signifier that will guarantee her physical beauty, even after the affair with Rhoda is over. The hair itself is a bodily war zone on which Emily and her aunt keenly register victories and defeats. When Emily loses her appetite, her guardian immediately zooms in on the hair as the bodily culprit, concluding that "Emily's heavy masses of hair 'took from her strength' and that she would be much stronger and better if it were cut off" (116). The taming of hair, as we recall from Maggie Tulliver's stubborn hair in Eliot's tale, is also a trope for initiation into docile Victorian femininity, and when faced with such aggressive scissors, Emily for the first time deploys her powerful "Murray look" (the mask of the male family tyrant) that makes Elizabeth flee in terror.

In *Emily of New Moon*, the socially sexualized parts of the body are the *hair* (as the privileged sexual signifier and the most contested conflictual locus in the novel), the *eyes* (in particular Emily's long lashes), the *hands*, and the *ankles*, the body "cluster" of Victorian femininity. This sexual body map is first provided by Rhoda,[9] but is structurally repeated in the novel, when Emily encounters more overtly sexual teasing in Aunt Nancy's Shrewsbury household, where amongst sexual innuendo and boasting of her youthful sexual exploits, Emily's sexual potential is expertly analysed in a reading of her body: her hands ("As pretty as mine when I was young"), eyes ("The Murrays have keep-your-distance-eyes" but they are contradicted by Emily's long lashes and "Men go by contraries oftener than not"), and, most notably, her ankles are inspected and approved for their sexual potential (256–257). Suspicious of such overt sexualization, Emily realizes that it signifies the fast-track into marriage: for the first time she yearns for none other than Aunt Elizabeth. Emily asserts her agency in negotiating the different sexual subjectivities that are offered as social realities: sexually seductive femininity (and its marital focus) or self-reliant asexuality (and its autonomous focus). No one woman in the trilogy will become *the* role model for Emily, for she has to negotiate actively her path amongst the positions offered by Elizabeth Murray, Nancy Priest, and others including the writer Janet Royal later in the trilogy.

Although her protagonist is only twelve years old, Montgomery seems as determined as Aunt Nancy to initiate her into sexual politics. Documenting Elizabeth Grosz's point that the body is a hinge or interface between culture and biology, Emily is soon confronted with decidedly material body realities, namely, biological changes that require social, psychological, and mythological adjustments. In chapter twenty-one, just before leaving for Shrewsbury, Emily is reading an anatomy book she finds in Dr. Burnley's house, claiming her biological body against her

guardian's opposition: "I *have* a liver, haven't I —and heart and lungs—
and stomach—and— " (238). At stake is precisely what Emily relegates
into the ellipsis, and Elizabeth Murray's sharp "That will do, Emily. Not
another word." (238) puts a stop to this biological mapping that may
include tabooed body realities. In an 11 January 1924 journal entry, just
finishing up the writing of "Emily II," Montgomery reminisces about her
own experiences with such a book, as she is teaching her son Chester the
basics of sexual knowledge:

> A certain "doctor's book" in the house, a clean, sensible volume, where sex
> was explained excellently, was forbidden to me sternly. It should have been
> put into my hands. Of course I read it by stealth and I have never felt that
> I did wrong to do so. I know I learned things that safeguarded me and
> saved me in many situations of after life and spared me many a worry.
> (Montgomery 1992, 157)

Montgomery finished writing *Emily of New Moon* on 15 February
1922, and a week later complained in her journal that the sex reality "is so
overlaid with conventions, inhibitions, and taboos that it is almost impos-
sible for anyone to see it as it really is" (39).

Yet in Wyther Grange she does tell the drama of bodily changes,
and Montgomery wrestles with ghosts of taboos trying to give aesthetic
form to unrepresentable realities. The chapter "Deals with Ghosts" is
remarkably bodily in its focus, exploiting Gothic conventions for Montgomery's story of girl initiation. Emily for the first time sleeps alone in the
Pink Room—that marks her as *feminine*. Frightened by uncanny noises in
her first night, she sleeps so badly that she gets up with pale, black-ringed
eyes, "so unstrung nervously" that her crying "left but little of hysterics"
(Montgomery 1923, 262), the wording drawing attention to the *hysterical
womb* that marks her as biologically *female*; moreover, she is fascinated by
the "pickled snake in the glass jar," and though repulsed by it, returns to
watch it every day (249). Montgomery's writing of the sexual hovers on
the edge of the genre in that the semi-transparent veil of metaphors and
symbolism reveals a decidedly genital and reproductive focus. Critics pre-
occupied with the intertextual allusions to Gothic romance and the resulting panicky *frisson* of Emily's imaginary wandering through subterranean
dungeon spaces have been remarkably blind to the fact that behind the

seemingly irrational fears lies the material reality of menstrual and pre-
menstrual symptoms. In a 22 October 1924 journal entry Montgomery
discusses *menstruation* in terms that directly relate to Emily's *hysteria* in
the Pink Room at Wyther Grange. Indeed, Emily's imaginary and self-
inflicted fears correspond to the "spiritual, vicarious self-flagellation" that
Montgomery diagnoses in Charlotte Brontë and that she links to her own
experience of the menstrual cycle, claiming this "masochistic" strain for
herself:

> [A]ll through the years of my sex life there was always one day or two
> every month when I became very nervous and somewhat depressed. Dur-
> ing this time a mental masochistic tendency made its appearance in me.
> (Montgomery 1992, 205)

She links this "masochism" in turn to the Rochester figure in Charlotte Brontë, "exactly the tyrant a woman with such a strain in her would
have loved" (205). Since Dean Priest is a Byronic Rochester figure, as Elizabeth Epperly has nicely documented in her comparative study of the two
novels (1992, 155-59), Montgomery also provides us with a critical key to
unlocking one of the most troubling figures in the novel, whose presence
will soon push the novel to the very boundary of the children's genre.
Montgomery's desire to claim material bodily realities for her protagonist
is real. Menstruation is so central to Montgomery's project that she alludes
to it in the novel's title: the moon, representing the twenty-eight day cycle,
is linked to Emily's name. It is remarkable that through her bodily references, Montgomery's spoof of the Gothic ghost story powerfully exposes
the ghosts of reticence that have silenced this topic. Yet Montgomery's
claiming of sexual agency for her heroine does not stop here; so crucial is
this issue that she is willing to push the genre to its very limits, as we shall
now see.

Dangerous Fantasies and Sexual Realities: Enter Dean Priest

In "The Vow of Emily," readers are startled when Emily's now sexually
charged body-self is promptly courted by the magnetic and seductive
Dean Priest, a man in his mid-thirties, a figure of flesh and blood, "the

nearest that L. M. Montgomery ever got to creating a plausible lover," according to Canadian writer Alice Munro whose knack for writing explicitly about female sexuality is well known (Munro 1989, 358). Montgomery introduces her twelve-year-old girl-protagonist and her girl readers to erotically charged sexual dangers so powerful that *Emily-in-the-glass* has been entirely displaced by Dean Priest's "enchanted mirror where her own dreams and secret hopes were reflected back to her with added charm" (Montgomery 1923, 289). In dramatizing her twelve-year-old heroine's precocious erotic and sexual life, Montgomery does more than enact the conventional girl's crush on an actor: she presents her girl readers with the potent mixture of desire and danger that feminists have described for adult women's experience of the sexual act (cf. Vance). Dean (Jarback) Priest's desire is real and all the more disturbing in a children's novel as Emily is receptive to his magnetic charm. Their bond lies in their common "queerness," for Jarback is a lame Hephaestus figure, deformed and exiled, yet able to win the heart of a beautiful woman by dressing and caressing her body with artful verbal webs and chains:

> "Emily, you have been a priestess of Pasht—an adorable, slim, brown, creature with a fillet of gold around your black hair and bands of silver on those ankles Aunt Nancy admires, with dozens of sacred little godlings frisking around you under the palms of the temple courts."
> "Oh," gasped Emily rapturously, "that just gave me *the flash.*" (291)

The fantasy of Emily as Priest's Egyptian *priestess*, with seductive chains of silver around the sexualized ankle, and gold around the hair, is remarkably physical and marks a decided slippage of Montgomery's novel into the Lolita plot. It is not surprising, then, that just two short paragraphs after this sexually charged scene, of which "Aunt Elizabeth would not approve" (291), the permissive Aunt Nancy "suddenly" decides to send Emily home. Possibly Aunt Nancy, like Montgomery herself, did not quite know how to deal with the new complexities arising from this decidedly transgressive twist in Emily's story, who returns home "no longer wholly the child" (297).

The situation is rendered even more complex by the fact that Dean Priest is a father figure (he knew Douglas Starr as a friend), and the adult reader cannot help but establish links amongst the father figures that populate this text including Father Cassidy, the Catholic priest, and Mr. Carpenter, the teacher. With all of them Emily has a "special" relationship which has to be kept secret from Aunt Elizabeth. The father figures in the novel are of strong physicality or have a strong physical presence in Emily's life (Douglas Starr sleeps in her room, holds her in his arms; Father Cassidy looks like "just like a big nut—a big, brown, wholesome nut" and talks in "a mellow, throaty voice" persistently commenting on Emily's body [206]; Mr. Carpenter only recognizes Emily's literary talent when she turns her attention to his body, describing him in a sketch, after which he exclaims, "by gad, it's literature" [354]). Both Father Cassidy and Dean Priest not only indulge but encourage and enjoy the titillation of speaking with Emily the "lover's talk" of her fiction. And Montgomery, like the permissive Aunt Nancy, is complicitous in allowing a pattern that will disturb the late-twentieth-century reader sensitized to detecting patterns of child sexual abuse. What, the reader asks, is the contract governing Montgomery's sexual representations?

Clearly, Montgomery is not naive with respect to sexual dangers. Sexual knowledge affects Emily in traumatic ways as in the deeply misogynistic accusations launched against Beatrice Burnley, her friend Ilse's mother, who is maligned as an adulteress. Emily cannot rest until she has proven these accusations wrong. Sexual knowledge comes with a price, for Emily almost dies after the Wyther Grange experience, haunted by her new knowledge in delirious fevers, yet also gaining new insights. Yet, in the face of these dangers, Montgomery also reaffirms her contract with the reader, drawing careful attention to the boundaries in her fiction, and carefully refocuses the reader's attention to Emily's agency over her body. Montgomery trusts Emily as an agent to set boundaries that will protect her autonomy. While Emily yields to the sexual fantasy, she rebels against the notion that she is bound to Priest, when she demonstratively destroys the aster that represents her life's bond with him. Montgomery's point is simple but forceful: a healthy girl, in touch with her pleasure and trained in body agency, will know when to say "no," refusing to yield to the ultimate danger of emotional dependency.

Similarly, Montgomery as a writer insists on generic boundaries: the cross-generational sex act is taboo in a children's book, just as incestuous sexuality is unimaginable. Montgomery the writer ensures that the idealized fathers who act as pseudo-lovers are all left behind (Douglas Starr dies of consumption, Mr. Carpenter of alcoholism (in volume two), Father Cassidy disappears from the novel, and Dean Priest is travelling off and on and finally rejected as a lover in book three). Also Montgomery's clear advocation of boundaries is highlighted in her shocked response when reading Valentine Dobrée's novel *Your Cuckoo Sings by Kind* (1927), which describes the rape of Christina (a girl of Emily's age) by her brother and his friends. Calling the rape "the vilest thing I ever read in a book," she burns the book: "Nothing but fire could purify it" (Montgomery 1992, 359). Montgomery's repulsion speaks volumes. Dobrée, as Montgomery sees it, had violated the reader's sacred trust, by presenting her reader with an incestuous rape in the midst of "a simple little story about a child" (359). And yet, Montgomery brought her girl protagonist and reader in close proximity of sexual dangers, a contradiction that is sidestepped but not entirely resolved. At the end of the novel, Emily retreats into auto-erotic writing of self, which significantly closes this novel: "I am going to write a diary, that it may be published when I die" (Montgomery 1923, 355).

Montgomery's Sexual Realities in the 1990s

How, then, does the late-twentieth-century girl reader respond to some of these complexities and how do we translate Emily for the contemporary television viewership? Filmed on Prince Edward Island, presenting the viewer with the spectacular sea shores and dunes that inspired Montgomery's writing, the television mini-series launched in 1998 promised a more authentic view of Montgomery, one that moved beyond the veiled pastoral of the popular *The Road to Avonlea* television series. Influenced by the publication of the *Selected Journals*, the filmmakers were intent on foregrounding a less romantic and a more realistic Montgomery, as *Emily of New Moon* scriptwriter Marlene Matthew explained in a 1998 lecture at the University of Prince Edward Island. It is interesting, though, that in this realistic version, the troubling figure of Dean Priest was thoroughly tamed and contained. Rejuvenated by at least ten years, he has become more central as a mentor to Emily's life, much like Gilbert Blythe in the televised mini-series of *Anne of Green Gables*. Given the modern audience's increased sensibilities to issues of child sexual abuse, the series sidestepped this thorniest and most controversial issue in Montgomery's text.

At the same time, sexual reality explodes onto the television screen so powerfully that it sometimes threatens to overwhelm the erotic pleasure Montgomery readers cherish. Consider episode seven titled "Falling Angels," which is not contained in the original book. Here a teenaged Maida Flynn, an outcast from society, finds herself pregnant and abandoned; Emily and her friends shelter her in the Disappointed House, providing her with food and support. When Maida suddenly goes into labour, the children not only become witnesses of the birth of the child but are called upon to act as competent midwives. The birth scene is enacted with brilliant realism by the same actress Canadian viewers witnessed just weeks before in the first airing of the television adaptation of *Nights Below Station Street,* David Adams Richards's New Brunswick novel (1988). This coincidence suggests that this episode has perhaps more to do with the 1990s preoccupation with teenage pregnancies than with Montgomery's *Emily of New Moon.* To what extent, the viewer may ask, is "Falling Angels" true to Montgomery's spirit?

This question goes to the heart of Montgomery's wrestling with sexual representation. Wrestling with giving voice to the "basic realities of life" within the context of her children's literature, Montgomery introduces fertility and reproduction in episodes focusing on Emily's beloved cat Saucy Sal, whose reproductive powers inscribe an important subtext in the novel. "Better take the Tom," advises Cousin Jimmy early in the novel, when Emily is forced to choose between her two cats, for "the Tom" means "not so much bother with the kittens" (Montgomery 1923, 56). Yet Emily takes Sal and throughout the novel carefully monitors the cat's reproduction, querying why Sal "will not have kittens" (105); the kittens' arrival coincides with Emily's visit at Wyther Grange, and as Ilse Burnley informs Emily, her "old barn cat is its father," thus provoking the wrath of Elizabeth Murray "by discussing tabooed subjects" (295). That Emily's Wyther Grange experience should be thus framed by the cat episodes inscribes a subtext about sexuality and reproduction that makes this novel highly political indeed, for it situates it within current Canadian debates about women's reproductive roles and obligations.[10] What is more, Montgomery inscribes a mythological subtext, for according to Barbara Walker's *The Woman's Encyclopedia of Myths and Secrets*, the cat is the primary lunar animal, intimately connected with the moon through her fertility (according to myth, the cat produces twenty-eight kittens in her lifetime).[11] Thus the cat is mythologically connected with the moon that gives the novel its title, a connection that remains partly veiled for the girl reader.

In an article titled "Can Anne Shirley Help 'Revive Ophelia'? Listening to Girl Readers," Angela Hubler discusses girls' active reading strategies in terms of "liberatory reading." She found that the girl readers in her study "commonly focused on aspects of texts that confirmed female behaviour they found desirable, while ignoring or forgetting aspects that undermined those behaviors" (1998, 270). Montgomery was an expert at providing her girl readers with such liberatory moments that they could remember. On the basis of my approach, I would conjecture that, even for modern-day girl readers, the reproductive focus in *Emily of New Moon* is secondary, while her legitimizing of girl Eros and pleasure is seen as primary. The novel abounds in scenes in which Emily's enjoyment of the cat's touch ("the feel of soft fur and round velvety head" [Montgomery 1923, 19]) provides the opportunity for experiencing and verbalizing erotic pleasure in her writing. In a crucial scene, "Emily gathered Sal up in her arms and kissed her joyously, to the horror of Aunt Elizabeth" (72). In order to dissuade Elizabeth Murray from the harsh prohibition against kissing cats that follows, Emily defends herself: "I didn't kiss her on the mouth, *of course*. I just kissed her between her ears. It's nice—won't you just try it for once and see for yourself?" (72), giving Aunt Elizabeth lessons on the haptic pleasures that can be drawn from cats. It is those pleasures that form the cornerstone of Montgomery's appeal.

In contrast to this eroticized focus, "Falling Angels" is powerfully social and anatomical, and girl readers used to deriving pleasure from Montgomery may resist the naturalistic focus imposed on a writer they associate with eroticised pleasure. While in a future study Hubler's methodologies could be fruitfully applied to *Emily of New Moon,* the novel as well as the television series, I would conjecture that even modern-day girl readers will remember the powerfully imaginary scenes with Wind Woman, which document the girl's connection with Eros and creativity. Modern-day girls, who are valiantly as ever struggling for body agency like their Victorian counterparts, are likely to be attracted to the drama surrounding the bang and the cutting of the hair. And I would even conjecture that Montgomery's focus on Dean Priest, the problematic wrestling with the idealized father-lover remains a topic of fascination and critical examination.

In this essay I have argued for a *feminist model of body and pleasure reading* as an appropriate entry point for discussing Montgomery's popular appeal for girls. Through pleasure writing, Montgomery advocated political messages even in seemingly simple passages, as one last example will illustrate. In her study *The Flesh Made Word* (1987), Helena Mitchie describes the representational taboo that existed against depicting Victorian women eating: the proper Victorian woman generally eats off-stage, and she eats little and delicately, for eating is associated with sexual hunger. Emily, with the exception of her grieving period, after her father dies, is fond of good eating: in fact, she delights in the sweet desserts, including ice cream, pedigreed apples, and cream puffs, and her fantasy of living with Teddy Kent includes not a gorgeous wedding celebration, but a breakfast with toast and bacon and marmalade. These descriptions are innocent and yet they encode her political claim that a girl should be in touch with her body pleasures and should exert agency in claiming these pleasures even if they are socially taboo. This is a timely reading model if we consider the anorexic girls and women discussed earlier by Susan Bordo.

Montgomery's epigraph indicates that she was dissatisfied with the asexual girl representation expected of her fiction, and, as I have argued, she powerfully subverted this convention, claiming passion and body agency for her girl readers—to the point that they risked overstepping the boundaries of the genre. While her wrestling with erotic pleasure, female autonomy, and the demands of reproduction were by no means easy or unresolved, Montgomery was crystal clear on one point: that the girl is always an agent in her fate. Montgomery's fiction articulates the desires and pleasures of a healthy and strong Canadian girl, imbuing her body with pleasure and putting her in touch with her own desire, while also making possible a "thinking through the body" that remains decidedly modern.

NOTES

1.   In addition to Peter Hunt's *Criticism, Theory and Children's Literature* (1991), see, for example, Sherrie Inness's compelling study on "Anti-Barbies: The American Girls Collection and Political Ideologies."

2.   Over the past two decades girls' literature and culture has come into its own thanks mostly to some pioneering studies by Jerry Griswold, Sherrie Inness, Sally Mitchell, and others in the United States, with some of these studies documenting the agency girls assume in shaping their own distinctive cultures. In Canada, see, for example, Elizabeth Waterston and Mary Rubio, the founding editors of *Canadian Children's Literature*.

3.   Although Montgomery was dismissed by scholars during her lifetime as a scribbler of children's fiction not worthy of scholarly attention, she has come into her own over the past fifteen years in the wake of gender studies and popular culture studies in academe which have propelled Montgomery into the mainstream of literary and cultural scholarship. Thanks to pioneering scholarship, Montgomery is now considered a sophisticated writer of children's fiction (Rubio and Waterston), a feminist writer (Åhmansson, Epperly), a political writer (Rubio), and, most recently, she has been discussed as a crucial touchstone for Canadian culture (Gammel and Epperly). The L. M. Montgomery Institute at the University of Prince Edward Island hosts biennial conferences on Montgomery.

4.   The definition of what makes a girl is contested. Some theorists see the girl as a prepubescent female only; for the purposes of this argument I follow Sherrie Inness's argument that such a boundary between preteenage girls and older girls is artificial in that both groups share many common features including their lack of rights and powers and their dependency on parents (Inness 1998, 3).

5.   The sexual culture was also marked by the publication of the sexually contentious *Ulysses* in *The Little Review* in 1918, while the new sexual freedom was reflected in the frolicking female nudes decorating the covers of the immensely popular *Vanity Fair* magazine from 1914 on.

6.   Bordo demands of feminists an increased awareness of "the often contradictory relations between image and practice, between rhetoric and reality. Popular representation . . . may forcefully employ the rhetoric and symbolism of empowerment, personal freedom, 'having it all.' Yet female bodies, pursuing these ideals, may find themselves as distracted, depressed, and physically ill as female bodies in the nineteenth century were made when pursuing a feminine ideal of dependency, domesticity, and delicacy" (105).

7.   Within the psycho-analytic context, Eros refers to the life instincts (as opposed to the death instincts in Freudian theory), while the autoerotic realm is linked to early infantile behaviour (Laplanche and Pontalis 1973, 45–47).

8.   "Queer" is also the linguistic marker for Ilse Burnley, Emily's tomboy friend, once she enters school. I discuss this crucial relationship between the two girls in detail in "My Secret Garden."

9.   Rhoda Stewart introduces this cluster: "My, but you have lovely hair, and

116

your hands are just lovely. All the Murrays have pretty hands. And you have the *sweetest* eyes, Emily" (Montgomery 1923, 95).

10.   Female reproduction was a topic on which Montgomery held strong views during a time that witnessed important debates regarding women's reproductive functions and obligations. While the birth control movement has gained momentum in both Canada and the United States since the early teens, the backlash was equally strong as reflected in such works as Hallyday Sutherland's *Birth Control Exposed* (1925) or the columns of Canadian newspapers, which admonished women to do their duty to their nation's health.

11.   "Its activity in the night, and the peculiar circumstances which attend its fecundity making it a proper emblem of that body. For it is reported that this creature, that it first brings forth one, then two, afterwards three, and so goes on adding to each former birth till it comes to seven; so that she brings forth twenty-eight in all, corresponding as it were to the several degrees of light, which appear during the moon's revolutions" (in Walker 1983, 148).

WORKS CITED

Åhmansson, Gabriella. *A Life and Its Mirror: A Feminist Reading of L. M. Montgomery's Fiction Vol. 1*. Stockholm: Uppsala, 1991.

Bordo, Susan. "The Body and the Reproduction of Femininity." In *Writing on the Body: Female Embodiment and Feminist Theory*. Ed. Katie Conboy et al. New York: Columbia University Press, 1997.

Boudreau, Brenda. "The Battleground of the Adolescent Girl's Body." In *The Girl: Constructions of the Girl in Contemporary Fiction by Women*. Ed. Ruth O. Saxton. New York: St. Martin's Press, 1998.

Butler, Judith. *Gender Trouble: Feminism and the Subversion of Identity*. New York: Routledge, 1990.

Campbell, Marie. "Wedding Bells and Death Knells: The Writer as Bride in the Emily Trilogy." In *Harvesting Thistles: The Textual Garden of L. M. Montgomery*. Ed. Mary Rubio. Guelph: Canadian Children's Press, 1994.

Chesler, Ellen. *Woman of Valor: Margaret Sanger and the Birth Control Movement in America*. New York: Simon and Schuster, 1992.

Conboy, Katie, Nadia Medina, and Sarah Stanbury, eds. *Writing on the Body: Female Embodiment and Feminist Theory*. New York: Columbia University Press, 1997.

Dobrée, Valentine. *Your Cuckoo Sings by Kind*. London and New York: Alfred A. Knopf, 1927.

Eilan, Naomi, Anthony Marcel, and José Luis Bermúdez. "Self-Consciousness

117

and the Body: An Interdisciplinary Introduction." In *The Body and the Self.* Ed. José Luis Bermúdez et al. Cambridge, Mass.: MIT Press, 1998.

Epperly, Elizabeth Rollins. *The Fragrance of Sweet-Grass: L. M. Montgomery's Heroines and the Pursuit of Romance.* Toronto: University of Toronto Press, 1992.

Foucault, Michel. *The History of Sexuality, Volume 1: An Introduction.* 1976. Trans. Robert Hurley. New York Vintage Books, 1980.

Gammel, Irene. "'My Secret Garden': Dis/Pleasure in L. M. Montgomery and F. P. Grove." *English Studies in Canada.* 25 (1999): 39–65.

Gammel, Irene and Elizabeth Epperly, eds. *Lucy Maud Montgomery and Canadian Culture.* Toronto: University of Toronto Press., 1999.

Griswold, Jerry. *Audacious Kids: Coming of Age in America's Classic Children's Books.* New York: Oxford University Press, 1992.

Grosz, Elizabeth. *Volatile Bodies: Toward a Corporeal Feminism.* Bloomington: Indiana University Press, 1994.

Gwyn, Sandra. "The Emily Effect." *Elm Street* (November/December 1997): 71–80.

Hubler, Angela E. "Can Anne Shirley Help 'Revive Ophelia'? Listening to Girl Readers." In *Delinquents and Debutantes: Twentieth-Century American Girls' Cultures.* Ed. Sherrie Inness. New York: New York University Press, 1998.

Inness, Sherrie A. "'Anti-Barbies': The American Girls Collection and Political Ideologies." In *Delinquents and Debutants: Twentieth-Century American Girls' Cultures.* Ed. Sherrie A. Inness. New York: New York University Press, 1998.

———, ed. *Delinquents and Debutantes: Twentieth-Century American Girls' Cultures.* New York: New York University Press, 1998.

Haug, Frigga. *Female Sexualization: A Collective Work of Memory.* 1987. London: Verso, 1992.

Hunt, Peter. *Criticism, Theory, and Children's Literature.* Cambridge: Basil Blackwell, 1991.

Justice-Malloy, Rhona. "Little Girls Bound: Costume and Coming of Age in the 'Sears Catalog' 1906-1927." In *Delinquents and Debutantes: Twentieth-Century American Girls' Cultures.* Ed. Sherrie Inness. New York: New York University Press, 1998.

Laplanche, J. and J.-B. Pontalis. *The Language of Psycho-Analysis.* New York: Norton, 1973.

Lorde, Audre. "Uses of the Erotic: The Erotic as Power." In *Writing on the Body: Female Embodiment and Feminist Theory.* Ed. Katie Conboy et al. New York: Columbia University Press, 1997.

118

Miller, Judith. "Montgomery's Emily: Voices and Silences." *Studies in Canadian Literature* 1.2 (1984): 158–168.

Mitchell, Sally. *The New Girl: Girls' Culture in England, 1880-1915.* New York: Columbia University Press, 1995.

Mitchie, Helena. *The Flesh Made Word.* New York: Oxford University Press, 1987.

Montgomery, Lucy Maud. *Anne of Green Gables.* 1908. Toronto: McClelland and Stewart, 1992.

———. *Emily of New Moon.* 1923. Toronto: McClelland and Stewart, 1989.

———. *The Selected Journals of L. M. Montgomery, Volume 3: 1921–1929.* Ed. Mary Rubio and Elizabeth Waterston. Toronto: Oxford University Press, 1992.

Munro, Alice. Afterword. *Emily of New Moon.* L. M. Montgomery. 1923. Toronto: McClelland and Stewart, 1989.

Poe, K. L. "The Whole of the Moon: L. M. Montgomery's *Anne of Green Gables* Series." In *Nancy Drew and Company: Culture, Gender, and Girls' Series.* Ed. Sherrie A. Inness. Bowling Green: Bowling Green State University Popular Press, 1997.

Rubio, Mary. Introduction. *Harvesting Thistles: The Textual Garden of L. M. Montgomery.* Ed. Mary Rubio. Guelph: Canadian Children's Press, 1994.

Rubio, Mary and Elizabeth Waterston. *Writing a Life: L. M. Montgomery.* Toronto: ECW Press, 1995.

Vance, Carole S., ed. *Pleasure and Danger: Exploring Female Sexuality.* London: Routledge and Kegan Paul, 1998.

Walker, Barbara. *The Woman's Encyclopedia of Myths and Secrets.* San Francisco: Harper and Row, 1983.

ADDITIONAL REFERENCES

Montgomery, Lucy Maud. *Emily Climbs.* 1925. Toronto: McClelland and Stewart, 1989.

———. *Emily's Quest.* 1927. Toronto: McClelland and Stewart, 1989.

———. *The Selected Journals of L. M. Montgomery, Volume 1: 1889–1910.* Ed. Mary Rubio and Elizabeth Waterston. Toronto: Oxford University Press, 1985.

"not one of those dreadful new women": Anne Shirley and the culture of imperial motherhood

CECILY DEVEREUX

In *Anne of Windy Poplars*, first of the two supplements reluctantly made to the popular "Anne" series by Lucy Maud Montgomery in the 1930s, a distraught Hazel Marr tells her once adored "Miss Shirley" "I'm not a bit ambitious . . . I'm not one of those dreadful new women. *My* highest ambition was to be a happy wife and make a happy home for my husband" (1936, 187). Hazel's self-referential italics convey the implication that Anne Shirley, principal of Summerside High School, *is* "one of those dreadful new women." Anne, after all, does seem to have "ambition": by this stage, she has obtained her teacher's certificate and her B.A., and has taken a position of authority for which there were other more mature candidates. She is known to "write," and has made money by her pen. After only a short time in Summerside, she has, moreover, conquered the Pringle family who resented her appointment as principal, and brought the embittered Katherine Brooke to happiness and productivity. Despite Hazel's tearful accusations, however, Anne is not "one of those dreadful new women." Indeed, although this novel recounts Anne's three-year period as principal, and focuses on her experiences and on the changes she produces in her environment through her teaching and influence, and although it is the only "Anne" novel in which the heroine tells much of her own story (in letters), in terms of the eight-part narrative as a whole, it does little more than fill in the gap which Montgomery initially left between Anne's engagement to Gilbert Blythe at the end of *Anne of the Island* (1915) and their marriage at the beginning of *Anne's House of Dreams* (1917b).

Readers of the six "Anne" novels published before Anne of Windy Poplars would already know that the heroine's "ambition" is not to be a teacher or a principal or a writer—at least, a writer of more than what she herself describes as "pretty, fanciful little sketches that children love and editors send welcome cheques for" (1917b, 19). Anne's "ambition," as it is staged in the original six-part narrative, is not very far from Hazel's. In what Gillian Thomas has described as the "[d]ecline of Anne" through five "progressively unsatisfactory . . . sequels" (Thomas 1992, 23), we see that the "dreams" of the heroine of Green Gables lead not to the literary fame for which Anne's celebrated imagination and her experiments with writing in the first three novels seem to establish a foundation, but to motherhood. That is, the first three novels of the series follow Anne's growth and education from the time she arrives at Green Gables to the completion of her B.A. at Redmond College, but by the fourth—*Anne's House of Dreams*—it has become clear towards what this "progress" has tended.

By the third page of *Anne's House of Dreams*, Anne's "dreams" have already been given an explicitly maternal outline. It is a month before her marriage to Gilbert, and Anne is watching Diana Wright with her baby. Diana, we are told, "cuddl[es] small Cordelia with the inimitable gesture of motherhood which always sent through Anne's heart, filled with sweet, unuttered dreams and hopes, a thrill that was half pure pleasure and half a strange, ethereal pain" (1917b, 3). A few chapters later, when Miss Cordelia tells Anne about a recent local birth, "I must go see it," Anne says, "I just love babies" (88). At this point, Anne is waiting for her own baby, still in the realm of "unuttered dreams," and she "smil[es] to herself over a thought too dear and sacred to be put into words" (88). But this thought—the desire for a child— will be "put into words" before the novel ends: when Anne's second child is born she tells Marilla, "The best dream of all has come true" (245). With this fourth novel, then, the series finally and uncompromisingly takes Anne from the career paths which she had seemed to be pursuing, and situates her romantic conclusion in the domestic image of the "house of dreams," where, we are to see, the highest "womanly" ambition is realized in motherhood.

Nancy Huse has suggested that Anne's story effectively ends with "her marriage to the man who had 'spoiled her pen-nib,' on the day they met" (Huse 1992, 137); and, if we regard Anne's story as the narrative of her literary "progress," it *does* end there, since, for Anne, wifedom and motherhood displace the literary dream she had appeared to cherish. It is Anne who draws our attention in this book to the fact that she "[hasn't] done much [writing] since [she] was married [and has, we see at last] no designs on a great Canadian novel" (Montgomery 1917b, 176). These "ambitions," it seems evident, are to be categorized with all her "old"— and, if implicit, adolescent—desires: "Oh, I once dreamed of a palace, too," she tells Leslie Moore, shortly after moving to Four Winds, "I suppose all girls do. And then we settle down contentedly in eight-room houses that seem to fulfil all the desires of our hearts—because our prince is there" (84).

While, however, as Huse and Thomas both indicate, Anne's motherhood is represented as an end, it is also shown to be the inevitable conclusion of the romantic dreams which are given so much attention in the first three novels, dreams which, we are now to see, have been moving Anne in this direction all along. Anne's maternity in the fourth novel is positioned not as the moment at which she relinquishes her "dreams," but as the high point in the story of her "progress." "[H]er pale face," we are told after her first baby is born, was "blanched with its baptism of pain, her eyes aglow with the holy passion of motherhood" (Montgomery 1917b, 147). The implications of this "holy . . . motherhood" as the zenith of her existence are reinforced in the response of childless Leslie Moore after the death of the baby: "'I envy Anne,' says Leslie, 'and I'd envy her even if she had died! She was a mother for one beautiful day. I'd gladly give my life for that!'" (150). In effect, as Anne so clearly demonstrates when she arrives at the "house of dreams" which, after all, she herself has constructed, it is precisely towards this domestic ideal that Anne's story has been directed: motherhood is her ambition, and reaching it is her story.

That the narrative of Anne's "progress" and all of her "dreams" concludes with the realization of this ambition is emphasized in the two final novels of the original six—*Rainbow Valley* (1919) and *Rilla of Ingleside* (1920). Both are about Anne's children, and, while Anne figures in the background, dispensing caresses and benevolent instruction, she does not figure in any significant way in these two books. Moreover, when Montgomery returned to Anne's story with *Anne of Windy Poplars* in 1936 and *Anne of Ingleside* in 1939, it was to reaffirm that maternity—pending in the former and in process in the latter—had unquestionably become the heroine's defining feature. The culmination of Anne's "progress" in motherhood should not, however, be as surprising and disappointing as so many critics have found it to be, for such an end to Anne's "romance" is signalled long before the fourth novel. The foundation for the construction of Anne's "house of dreams" is quietly but unmistakably established in the first three novels; and even *Anne of Green Gables* (1908), the first book and the one which appears most compellingly to foreground and to promote Anne's literary ambition, does not actually direct its heroine towards a career and "new womanhood," but serves rather to entrench her story within the maternalism that comes to dominate the series.

Eve Kornfield and Susan Jackson have pointed out that the first Anne novel ends with Anne's decision to turn back the scholarship which would have enabled her to go to college, and to remain instead at home with Marilla after Matthew's death, teaching in Avonlea school (Kornfield and Jackson 1992, 150). Although Montgomery did comment in *The Alpine Path* in 1917 that this was a conclusion which she "regretted," she also indicated at the same time that, "when [she] wrote it [she] thought he must die, that there might be a necessity for self-sacrifice on Anne's part" (1917a, 75). On the one hand, this "necessity" is rooted in Montgomery's telling of the same kind of story which E. Pauline Johnson produced in "The Barnardo Boy" (included in the 1913 collection, *The Shagganappi*), which has an orphan (the kind of "street-Arab" which Marilla Cuthbert tells Rachel Lynde she does not want) saving his adoptive family from fire. On the other hand, however, Anne's "self-sacrifice" is a specifically "feminine" one: she chooses home and domestic duty over education and independence.

Although, as Kornfield and Jackson note, this conclusion is described in the novel as a much more limited one than Anne had anticipated while at school (Kornfield and Jackson 1992, 151), the point is also made that, "if the path set before her feet was to be narrow she knew that flowers of quiet happiness would bloom along it. The joys of sincere work and worthy aspiration and congenial friendship were to be hers" (Montgomery 1908, 308). In fact, we are to see that her decision was the *right* one: "[B]efore she went to bed," we are told, "there was a smile on her lips and peace in her heart. She had looked her duty courageously in the face and found it a friend—as duty ever is when we meet it frankly" (302). Anne's first story ends happily—if "quiet[ly]"—precisely *because*, when she is confronted by a choice between "new womanhood"—education and independence—and domestic duty, she chooses the latter. Thus, if Anne's story *had* ended here, instead of running for another seven instalments, what Temma Berg has described as the "independent, creative, and strong-willed heroine" (Berg 1992, 155) would have been left forever, not at the brink of a career, but finding "happiness" in domesticity and in "sincere work and worthy aspiration." Anne is shown, even this early in the series, to have "progressed" this far: she has come to believe that her primary vocation is domestic, and that "happiness" is to be found at home, within what are represented as the already determined boundaries of "womanly" duty.

Despite there being little explicit indication in the conclusion of *Anne of Green Gables* that the "domestic" path which Anne has chosen leads to motherhood—as the subsequent seven novels demonstrate it does—we are nonetheless already alerted to this trajectory for Anne's "progress" by the extent to which the narrative is shaped by a discourse of maternalism. *Anne of Green Gables* begins with the bringing together of an older woman characterized by childlessness and a girl who immediately draws our attention to her own motherlessness: telling Marilla the few details she knows of the mother who had died of typhoid when she was three months old, Anne says, "I do wish she'd lived long enough for me to remember calling her mother. I think it would be so sweet to say 'mother,' don't you?" (39). While Marilla resists any relational reconfiguration, and insists that Anne address her by her first name, she nonetheless does enter into a relationship with her adopted child that becomes progressively motherly.

It is Anne's desire to find her mother—the counterpart of her desire for children in the later novels, and the crucial element in Anne's "quest" throughout the first three novels—that sets in motion Marilla's "progress," or the story in which she discovers what is significantly represented as her own innate maternalism. When Anne "slip[s] her hand into the older woman's hard palm . . . [s]omething warm and pleasant well[s] up in Marilla's heart . . . a throb of the maternity she had missed, perhaps" (76). This "sudden sensation of startling sweetness thrill[s] her" again a little later when "Anne cast[s] herself into Marilla's arms and rapturously kisse[s] her sallow cheek" (9l): "It was the first time in [Marilla's] whole life," we are told, "that childish lips had voluntarily touched [her] face" (91). Rachel Lynde observes that Marilla is "a better and a happier woman" for having adopted Anne Shirley (236). Indeed, Anne's sacrifice at the end of the story indicates that Marilla is rewarded for taking in a child whom she initially regarded as "a sort of duty" (47) and came to see as "if [she] were [her] own flesh and blood" (297), "dearer to her than anything on earth" (186).

Kornfield and Jackson have suggested that Marilla is a model of "feminine duty" for Anne (1992, 150). In fact, however, Marilla's conversion is Anne's work, and it is she who awakens in the older woman what we see the novel implying is an essential female instinct, a "natural" desire to have children, and to care for them. Anne can "teach" the older woman to tap into this "instinct" because, as we see from her first appearance, she has it in abundance. From the beginning, Anne is configured as a child whose salient characteristic is not only her motherlessness, but her motherliness. At the age of eleven, she has been caring for children younger than herself for several years: she is, we are told, "handy with children" (Montgomery 1908, 40). This "natural" ability with children is dramatically foregrounded in the narrative when she saves Minnie May Barrie from an attack of croup (138–147). Anne, who first appears to Matthew Cuthbert as a "stray woman-child" (11), is represented as simultaneously maternal and in need of the kind of mothering which Marilla can offer once what is represented as her "natural" desire for a child is awakened.

If, on the one hand, Anne's work has been to awaken "mother-love" in Marilla Cuthbert, we might see Marilla's work, on the other, as the protection and cultivation of Anne's instinctive maternalism. Her "duty," that is, is to preserve Anne's best instincts for her own future domestic and, it is implicit, reproductive work: she is, after all, watching over a child who is described in this novel as a "Madonna" (267). Noted by Marilla as "a nice, teachable little thing" (41), Anne, we see, is already being primed for the motherhood which will so insistently be foregrounded throughout the series. There are, thus, two mutually reinforcing narratives of maternal identification in *Anne of Green Gables*: this first novel is not only about the conversion of an older woman from spinsterhood to a kind of spiritual motherhood, it is also about a young girl who is establishing, as the

teacher Miss Stacy puts it to all the girls in their "teens," "the foundation
. . . for [her] whole future life" (240) in what the remaining novels confirm is a maternal ideal.

It is, of course, the representation of motherhood as the "highest"
aspiration for a woman that has problematized feminist readings of the
"Anne" series. Gillian Thomas has not been alone in seeing Anne's rejection of a literary career in favour of domesticity as an indication of the
heroine's "decline," and her seeming failure to overcome what are seen to
be conventional notions of late nineteenth-century femininity a sign of
what T. D. MacLulich has suggested is Montgomery's "never dar[ing] to
let her protagonists put themselves deeply and permanently at odds with
their society" (1985, 471) and "[i]n her life and her art . . . always adher-
ing to the conventional pattern" (472).[1] But the series' foregrounding of
maternalism and its construction of a narrative which deliberately leads its
heroine to a conclusion in motherhood indicates that, in fact, Anne's
whole story is rooted in an early twentieth-century imperial notion of
progress, achieved through the advancement of women—or, at least,
white Anglo-Saxon and, in English Canada, Anglo-Celtic women—as
mothers. It is this notion that suggests that the Anne books—and even
Anne of Green Gables—ought to be positioned in relation to early twentieth-century feminist discourse.

If Anne is not generally regarded as a "feminist" heroine because
she chooses a path of domestic "duty" and not of "new womanhood," this
can only be because the series' politics of representation have usually been
discussed when they are treated historically—in relation to Montgomery's
own well-known lack of interest in the cause of woman suffrage, rather
than to the discursive basis of so-called "first-wave" feminism itself.[2]
Indeed, the Anne books serve to remind us that what is still rather inaccu-
rately called "first-wave" feminism is characterized in English Canada not
necessarily by suffragism, and, after the 1890s, not by the "new woman,"
but by the idea of woman as imperial "mother of the race," something
Anne Shirley arguably realizes more fully than any of her fictional contemporaries.

When Hazel Marr alludes to "those dreadful new women," she
conjures up an image which had first been given shape in the 1880s and
had first been named, according to Ellen Jordan and Ann Ardis, in 1894,
when novelist "Ouida" irritably "responded to Sarah Grand's essay, 'The

New Aspects of the Woman Question,' which had been published . . . in the March 1894 issue of *North American Review*" (Ardis 1990, 10). The primary characteristic of the new woman of the '90s—and the basis for "the tremendous amount of polemic which," as Ardis points out, "was wielded against her"—was her "choosing not to pursue the conventional bourgeois woman's career of marriage and motherhood" (1). "Indeed," Ardis suggests, "for her transgressions against the sex, gender, and class distinctions of Victorian England, she was accused of instigating the second fall of man" (1). But anxiety about the new woman's resistance to her reproductive "duty" focused on the possibility of another "fall": it was the British Empire itself that was threatened by her "transgressions."

Concerns about the continued dominance of what had come to be called the imperial Anglo-Saxon "race" were rampant by the turn of the century, as the British Empire undertook what John Strachey has noted was an unprecedentedly large and rapid territorial expansion (Strachey 1959, 79–81). Every census after 1881 had shown, Anna Davin points out, a decline in the British birth rate (Davin 1978, 10). The Boer War had been disastrous, not only in terms of the loss of South Africa, but in its revelation of the poor physical condition of so many young male recruits (Davin 1978, 11). Anxieties were increasing about the spread of what came to be called "racial diseases," infectious and incurable diseases such as tuberculosis, which acted through the individual upon the race by affecting reproduction and depleting the population. Venereal disease and alcohol, which eugenist Caleb Saleeby had argued in early twentieth century were affecting the quality of the imperial race, continued to be seen as a threat to future generations of Britons (See Saleeby 1909, 205–253). Since so many of these "problems" had to do with reproduction and with the perceived effect of a woman's influence upon the home, "those dreadful new women"—and, by extension, all feminists—were easy targets for blame. If the race was in decline, as it seemed to be, then one explanation was to be found, as Anna Davin has shown, in the argument that women were not doing their duty.

It is no doubt because of the burden of responsibility for imperial social decline laid upon the new woman that, early in the new century, Anglo-imperial feminist discourse struggled to distance itself from most of the ideas associated with what middle-class British women had appeared to want in the 1890s. In the years between the Boer War and World War

One, the new woman as the standard-bearer in the pursuit of women's rights was displaced by a figure who was profoundly maternal. Lucy Bland has noted that

> [t]he idea of "Woman as Mother" was mobilized by many feminists. It both empowered women, giving them a vantage point of superiority from which to speak, while simultaneously locating that vantage point within a discourse of racial superiority. For women were superior not as mothers in general, but as mothers of "the nation" and of "the race." Such constructions were inevitably placed within an Imperialist framework of which the vast majority of feminists were blithely uncritical. (Bland 1995, 70)

The promotion of motherhood for the purposes of populating the Empire had not always been concerned with the advancement of women, and eugenists such as Francis Galton, writing in the 1880s, did not necessarily endorse the notion that women had any duty beyond reproduction and the raising of children. Feminism, when it "appropriated" as Bland puts it, the idea of woman as "mother of the race" effectively undermined the position taken by such opponents as Galton, by affirming that the "advancement" of women and the race—and, of course, the Empire—were necessarily linked. Suffrage was to be one "advance," but it was arguably less important to most women than the empowerment, social validation, and professionalization of maternal work that is the hallmark of "first-wave" feminism in imperial English Canada.

If the new woman of the 1890s was represented as a sign and an index of imperial decline, the newer woman popularized as the "mother of the race" was positioned in feminist rhetoric as the Empire's last hope. Anglo-imperial feminists increasingly capitalized on the appeal of the idea of woman as mother, arguing, for instance, like Nellie McClung in 1915, that women were the last hope to "serve and save the race" (1915, 100): "The world needs the work and help of the women," wrote McClung in her 1915 suffrage manifesto, *In Times Like These*, "and the women must work, if the race will survive" (1915, 101). It is possible to see this idea powerfully resonating in English-Canadian feminist rhetoric during the expansionist years at the end of the nineteenth century and the beginning of the twentieth, primarily because English Canada—and especially the "new" prairie lands—had come to be configured in imperial immigrationist propaganda as the last place into which the Empire could hope to expand. In the context of the "last best west," it was not difficult to see Anglo-Saxon and Anglo-Celtic women as the Empire's last best reproductive "reserves" and its great "white hope," as McClung put it.

Anne Shirley epitomizes this imperial "hope": the first novel in her series is, after all, the story of the adoption of a girl ("native born" [Montgomery 1908, 61], and of Anglo-Celtic stock) who was supposed to be a boy. Indeed, her gender, far from being represented as a handicap or an explanation of what Kornfield and Jackson have described as her "limited" destiny, is foregrounded and insistently valorized, not only in this novel, with Matthew's parting comment that "[he'd] rather have [her] than a dozen boys" (293), but throughout the series, culminating in the last of the original six: we are reminded as Susan Baker salutes the Union Jack at the end of *Rilla of Ingleside* of "the women—courageous, unquailing, patient, heroic—who had made victory possible" (Montgomery 1920, 247). It is here, in the series' idea of progress—imperial progress, as Susan's gesture reminds us—staged in what is, through the whole eight parts, a maternal narrative, that we can locate the "feminism" of the Anne books. Montgomery, in other words, when she aims her heroine towards maternity, is not capitulating to "limited" late nineteenth-century ideas of womanhood, but, rather, is effectively engaging with first-wave feminism's discourse of imperial motherhood.

Carole Gerson has noted a comment which Montgomery made in her journal in November, 1933:

> In an old book today I came across the phrase "the new woman"—and smiled. It is so dead now—nobody would know what you meant if you used it. Yet it was a world-wide slogan in the '90s—and meant a woman who wanted "equal rights" and dared to think she ought to vote. To some it was a dreadful epithet; to others a boast. And now the new woman and the old woman are gone and the eternal woman remains—not much changed in reality and not, I am afraid, any happier. (Gerson 1995, 24)

In light of this comment, Montgomery's deliberate use of the term three years later in *Anne of Windy Poplars* to identify what her heroine is not is a compelling reminder of the extent to which we ought to be revising our understanding not only—as Gerson has done—of Montgomery's fiction as it reproduces early twentieth-century feminist ideology, but also of that ideology itself. The Anne books and the narrative of Anne's progress, that is, as they exemplify what we might see as the rise of the imperial mother in English Canada, enable us to have a better sense of "first-wave" feminism as it countered the new woman with the idea of woman as "mother of the race."

NOTES

1.   See Laura M. Robinson's discussion of what she sees as Montgomery's feminist "negotiations" in *Anne of Green Gables.*
2.   See, for instance, Mollie Gillen 85–6 and Montgomery's *Journal,* II:234.

WORKS CITED

Ardis, Anne L. *New Women, New Novels: Feminism and Early Modernism.* New Brunswick, NJ and London: Rutgers University Press, 1990.

Berg, Temma F. "Anne of Green Gables: A Girl's Reading." In *Such a Simple Little Tale: Critical Responses to L. M. Montgomery's* Anne of Green Gables. Ed. Mavis Reimer. Metuchen, NJ and London: The Children's Literature Association and the Scarecrow Press, 1992.

Bland, Lucy. *Banishing the Beast: Sexuality and the Early Feminists.* New York: New Press, 1995.

Davin, Anna. "Imperialism and Motherhood." *History Workshop Journal* 5 (1978): 9–65.

Gerson, Carole. "'Fitted to Earn Her Own Living': Figures of the New Woman in the Writing of L. M. Montgomery." In *Children's Voices in Atlantic Literature and Culture: Essays in Childhood.* Ed. Hilary Thompson. Guelph: Canadian Children's Press, 1995.

Gillen, Mollie. *The Wheel of Things.* Don Mills, Ontario: Fitzhenry and Whiteside, 1978.

Huse, Nancy. "Journeys of the Mother in the World of Green Gables." In *Such a Simple Little Tale: Critical Responses to L. M. Montgomery's* Anne of Green Gables. Ed. Mavis Reimer. Metuchen, NJ and London: The Children's Literature Association and the Scarecrow Press, 1992.

Johnson, E. Pauline. "The Barnardo Boy." In *The Shagganappi.* Toronto: Ryerson, 1913.

Kornfield, Eve and Susan Jackson. "The Female *Bildungsroman* in Nineteenth-Century America: Parameters of a Vision." In *Such a Simple Little Tale: Critical Responses to L. M. Montgomery's* Anne of Green Gables. Ed. Mavis Reimer. Metuchen, NJ and London: The Children's Literature Association and the Scarecrow Press, 1992.

MacLulich, T. D. "L. M. Montgomery's Portraits of the Artist: Realism, Idealism, and the Domestic Imagination." *English Studies in Canada* 11.4 (1985): 459–473.

McClung, Nellie L. *In Times Like These.* Toronto: McLeod and Allen, 1915.

Montgomery, Lucy Maud. *The Alpine Path: The Story of My Career.* 1917a. Don Mills, Ontario: Fitzhenry and Whiteside, 1974.

———. *Anne of Green Gables.* 1908. Toronto: McClelland-Bantam, n.d.

———. *Anne of the Island.* 1915. Toronto, New York, London: Bantam, 1976.

———. *Anne of Windy Poplars.* 1936. Toronto: McClelland-Bantam, 1981.

———. *Anne's House of Dreams.* 1917b. Toronto: McClelland and Stewart, 1972.

———. *Rilla of Ingleside.* 1920. Toronto: McClelland-Bantam, 1987.

Reimer, Mavis, ed. *Such a Simple Little Tale: Critical Responses to L. M. Montgomery's* Anne of Green Gables. Metuchen, NJ and London: The Children's Literature Association and the Scarecrow Press, 1992.

Robinson, Laura M. "'Pruned down and branched out': Embracing Contradiction in *Anne of Green Gables.*" In *Children's Voices in Atlantic Literature and Culture: Essays in Childhood.* Ed. Hilary Thompson. Guelph: Canadian Children's Press, 1995.

Saleeby, Caleb Williams. *Parenthood and Race Culture: An Outline of Eugenics.* London: Cassell, 1909.

Strachey, John. *The End of Empire.* 1959. New York: Frederick A. Praeger, 1960.

Thomas, Gillian. "The Decline of Anne: Matron vs. Child." In *Such a Simple Little Tale: Critical Responses to L. M. Montgomery's* Anne of Green Gables. Ed. Mavis Reimer. Metuchen, NJ and London: The Children's Literature Association and the Scarecrow Press, 1992.

Thompson, Hilary, ed. *Children's Voices in Atlantic Literature and Culture: Essays in Childhood.* Guelph: Canadian Children's Press, 1995.

L. M. Montgomery:
Canon or Cultural Capital?

HELEN SIOURBAS

In *Cultural Capital: The Problem of Literary Canon Formation*, John Guillory presents his theory on the relationship between the literary canon and cultural capital. Literary works have a cultural capital that is fixed by the university institution. If a work is part of the canon, a canon determined by the university, it has high cultural capital. By extension, noncanonical works are those not prized by the university, so they have little value as cultural capital. Works that have a high cultural capital are exclusive and canonical, and form the backbone of a country's national identity. Guillory's ideas about the canon, cultural capital, and their relationship to the university and the public are problematic in Canada because, firstly, the question of whether or not Canada has what he defines as a canon is ambiguous, and, secondly, works may have a high value as cultural capital yet not be part of the institutional curriculum of the university.

Lucy Maud Montgomery and her works are a perfect case in point. Though they are not generally taught in university settings, one would be hard-pressed to say that they have no value as cultural capital. In fact, Montgomery's value as cultural capital is very high, and has been so for decades, though her value as institutional capital has, until recently, been quite low. Examining these discrepancies will illuminate part of the canonical situation in Canada, and the fluid position of L. M. Montgomery within the canons of Canadian literature and Canadian children's literature.

Before Montgomery's place in the Canadian canon can be identified, the nature of the canon must be determined. Guillory's ideas on the canon are no longer valid when viewed from a contemporary Canadian perspective. In Canada, many works and authors are clearly both canonical—that is, they are part of a university-based curriculum—and, unlike many canonical works, popular within society at large. Authors such as Margaret Atwood and Mordecai Richler are among those who come to mind. Thus, it is ridiculous to state, as Guillory does, that "school culture does not unify the nation culturally" (1993, 38), for, in Canada, it does. A further distinction that needs to be made when studying the canon in Canada is the difference between Canon and canon. As Robert Lecker states in *Making It Real: The Canonization of English-Canadian Literature*, Canadian literary history has been too short to have developed into a stable canon (1995, 55). Canada has no Canon that can compare to that of the Unites States or Great Britain. There is no set of core courses in Canadian literature that university students must take to receive their degrees in English Literature; a single survey course is often all that is required. However, there are authors and texts, chosen as representative of Canadian literature, that do tend to reappear on the university syllabus, from *Wacousta* to *The Stone Angel*. "There may be no canon," Lecker writes, "but there may be an *imagined* canon" (52); in other words, there may be no Canon, but there may be a canon. Only a flexible canon is truly reflective of the Canadian literary situation.

The ambiguous nature of the Canadian canon also makes problematic Guillory's notion of cultural capital, since the "written works studied [which are part of the canon (1993, 86)] constitute a certain kind of cultural capital" (52). Since the dominant classes want to keep intellectual power to themselves, it is in their interest to restrict access to these canonical materials: the "*limit* of their dissemination, their relative exclusivity" (133) ensures their continued value. Guillory's model of canon as cultural capital is problematic when applied to Canada's literary landscape because Canada's canon has not been entirely determined by the university elite. As Lecker explains, "government, academia, and the publishing industry joined hands to create a national canon" (1995, 26). This cooperation created the New Canadian Library, which, according to Lecker, "*formed* this imagined tradition. [The NCL selections] influenced a generation of students, and helped to define which texts would become the subject of serious canonical inquiry during the 1960s and 1970s" (155). Because of Canada's small population, the canon had to be accessible to be profitable for the publishing industry. Furthermore, the canon was created to teach Canadians what it meant to be Canadian and to foster a sense of identity and nationalistic pride, goals that could not be achieved if the canon were a Canon—stoic, removed, and inflexible. The cultural capital of the Canadian canon, therefore, lies not in its exclusivity, but in its ability to touch the ordinary Canadian. An understanding of this relationship between canon and cultural capital clarifies the ambiguous value of L. M. Montgomery.

There are several issues to consider in a discussion of Montgomery's canonicity and her value as cultural capital. To begin with, Montgomery is and always has been the darling of Prince Edward Island. Her writing is revered for its portrayal of Island life, and her staunch nationalism make her a singularly Canadian hero. The early publishing history of Montgomery's books highlights the author's importance. Her first novel, *Anne of Green Gables*, was published by L. C. Page in Boston in 1908, as were her next seven novels. However, in 1916, McClelland and Stewart agreed to do what Page would not risk: publish her poetry collection, *The Watchman and Other Poems*. The ensuing legal battle for control over her works shows that, in the early 1920s, Montgomery's value as cultural capital was already very high. In contrast, because she was viewed as a writer of children's fiction, Montgomery fell out of favour with literary critics for almost thirty years after her death, a falling out that even the emergence of Canadian studies in the 1950s could not alleviate; she only re-entered the academic world around the centenary of her birth, thanks in large part to the emergence of studies in Canadian children's literature. After a decade of mild but renewed interest, her popularity exploded with the publication of her journals and with the release of a made-for-television adaptation of *Anne of Green Gables*.

Montgomery's value as cultural capital and her status as non/canonical is reflected in the literary and cultural criticism written about Montgomery and her works since her death. There are four main eras of Montgomery criticism: from her death to the centenary of her birth, from the centenary to the publication of her journals and the *Anne of Green Gables* film, the initial fallout from the journals and film, and the current prevailing attitudes.

Very little was written about Montgomery or her works from her death in 1942 until 1973. Soon after her death, Ephraim Weber, with whom she shared a correspondence, published two "nostalgic" (Waterston 1976, 24) articles in the *Dalhousie Review*, both claiming an important place for Montgomery in the history of Canadian literature. In the first article, "L. M. Montgomery as a Letter-Writer," Weber calls Montgomery's letters and her fiction "classics" (1942, 301) and compares her to canonical authors such as Carlyle and Wordsworth (306–307). In the second article, "L. M. Montgomery's 'Anne,'" Weber begins by paraphrasing the unnamed author of *Highways of Canadian Literature*, who "calls 1908 the real beginning of the Second Renaissance in Canadian fiction, for in that year were published three 'community novels' of note: L. M. Montgomery's *Anne of Green Gables*, Marian Keith's *Duncan Polite*, and Nellie McClung's *Sowing Seeds in Danny*" (1944, 64). Thus, a very clear picture of Canadian literature is presented: it is championed by female authors and glorifies the domestic ideal. Finally, Weber defends Montgomery against those critics who call her novels the "nadir of Canadian fiction" by asking, "Can so many people of so many kinds in so many lands be charmed by *cheap* fiction?" (68). Ironically, Weber used Montgomery's popularity to vindicate rather than to denigrate her writing.

Though literary critics may not have deigned to notice her during those years, Montgomery was still very much a Canadian, as well as an international, cultural icon. *The Atlantic Advocate* included two references to Montgomery in its society pages: in 1961, Prince of Wales College in Charlottetown opened a women's residence named "Montgomery Hall," the cornerstone of which was laid by Governor General Georges P. Vanier; and, in 1970, after five years of effort, the Confederation Centre Library finally obtained a "First Edition" of *Anne of Green Gables*. Montgomery's appeal was not limited to Canada, however: in 1969, a *Maclean's* editorial reports, with pride, that Anne of Green Gables would greet visitors to Canada's national pavilion at Expo '70 in Osaka, Japan, because of her immense popularity in that country, where "[the book] is a school classic" ("Good-by, Green Gables"). Thus, for the three decades after her death, Montgomery's status was ambiguous: though she held a special place in the popular heart, literary critics refused to write about, and thus to recognize, her achievements.

The decade that followed presents a heightened and self-conscious sense of that ambiguity. Nineteen-seventy-four marked the centenary of

L. M. Montgomery's birth, and both popular and literary culture wished to commemorate the occasion. Canada Post issued an eight-cent stamp in her honour (Cowan 1976, 48), and the P.E.I. Heritage Foundation published *The Years Before "Anne"* by Francis W. P. Bolger. Its preface recognizes Montgomery's importance to Canadian nationalism, if not to Canadian literature. In addition, Montgomery's autobiography, *The Alpine Path*, was published for the first time in book form in 1974. A biography and a CBC documentary were also made available to the public, creating and feeding the public's growing appetite for all things Montgomery.

The 1970s also marks the emergence of academic literary criticism on L. M. Montgomery, and on Canadian children's literature as a whole. The history of the *Canadian Children's Literature* journal is crucial to an examination of the literary value of L. M. Montgomery. The journal was co-founded by Mary Rubio in 1975 to fill a curricular void: at the time, Rubio noticed that all the books her young daughter was reading in school were by Americans, and, though an expatriate American herself, she worked to overcome that bias (McVittle 1985). *CCL* received so many essays on Montgomery that the editorial board decided to devote an entire issue to her. In 1976, seven of the *CCL* essays on Montgomery were reprinted in *L. M. Montgomery: An Assessment*, edited by John Robert Sorfleet; it was the first book devoted to literary criticism on Montgomery. In these essays, two perspectives on Montgomery and her work are emphasized: her national importance and the limitations of the genre in which she writes. While both Mary Rubio and Elizabeth Waterston declare Montgomery an important national literary icon because she "brought her country's literature a popular international recognition" (Waterston 1976, 9), other literary critics examine Montgomery's works through the lens of genre, and, since the recovery of the domestic novel had not yet begun, they find Montgomery's works lacking. Gillian Thomas, for example, explains that "in part the shortcomings of the sequels to *Anne of Green Gables* develop naturally from the genre of the sentimental novel to which they belong" (1975, 28). Jean Little praises Montgomery's efforts at capturing childhood, but emphatically states that Montgomery's "writing is flawed [because] she is overly sentimental and whimsical" (71). In the seventies, L. M. Montgomery's importance is contested: to the chagrin of many critic-fans, she is seen as having a cultural, but not a literary, importance because she writes sentimental children's fiction.

It is as a result of this interest in Montgomery as a writer of children's literature, however, that the author comes to the attention of other Canadian literary critics. In 1984, Montgomery's literary value was emphasized when Judith Miller published an essay in *Studies in Canadian Literature* entitled "Montgomery's Emily: Voices and Silences." This essay is the precursor to a new mode of thought in Montgomery criticism that began in earnest with the publication of Montgomery's journals in 1985. The significance of Montgomery's work outside the field of children's literature was at that time being examined. In her essay, Miller qualifies Emily's quest as a search for a personal and artistic voice, and categorizes her "struggle [as] curiously contemporary" (158). In addition to stating that the theme of this trilogy is, in essence, the search for self, Miller also proclaims that the trilogy creates a female world where orality and other "womanly arts . . . are protected" (161). In the *Emily* books, Miller concludes, Montgomery examines the societal "warning that it is best [for a woman] not to attempt serious 'Literature'" (163).

Are L. M. Montgomery's works serious literature? Is she canon? Is she valuable as more than a nationalistic commodity that can be packaged and sold to the Japanese? The turning point in the history of Montgomery's value as cultural and canonical capital occurred in 1985, when the first volume of *The Selected Journals of L. M. Montgomery*, edited by Rubio and Waterston, was published by Toronto's Oxford University Press. It is not, however, as literary entities that the journals are most important, although, as the preface states, they do "reveal the same literary qualities, in a relatively artless form, that have endeared Montgomery's fiction to generations of readers" (Rubio and Waterston 1985, xxi); according to the editors of the book, the journals are most valuable for their "autobiographical content" and "social history" (xxiv). Regardless, Montgomery is a "gifted storyteller" (1987, xviii) and "her words still have power" (xix). Rubio and Waterston's introductory statements and editorial work are encouraging the canonization of their subject.

The same year the journals were published, the release of the film version of *Anne of Green Gables* by Kevin Sullivan Productions made another major contribution to Montgomery's rising popularity. The film, aired over two nights on CBC prime time and as a four-part mini-series on PBS, won immediate critical acclaim as well a few Gemini awards. Aside from propelling Megan Follows to stardom and providing Sullivan with a cash cow that he would continue to milk for another decade—through

Anne of Green Gables: The Sequel, Jane of Lantern Hill, and the weekly television series *Road to Avonlea*—the movie brought Montgomery into the popular limelight, and publishers took notice. In the 1980s, McClelland and Stewart republished all of Montgomery's novels as popular Seal editions, using movie stills or paintings reminiscent of the movies as covers to target the mass market. Montgomery and her works were discussed in *Maclean's*, the *Toronto Star*, *Quill & Quire*, the *Globe and Mail*, the *Halifax Chronicle Herald*, and *Atlantic Insight*. As Harvey Sawler, marketing director of the Prince Edward Island tourism department, remarked, "Economically, [this renewed interest] is doing [for P.E.I.] what Mickey Mouse has done for Disneyland" (Johnson 1987, 50).

This interest in Montgomery was not limited to the popular sphere: the literary journals also took notice, though, once again, it was the journals of children's literature that took the initiative. *Canadian Children's Literature* published a theme issue on little women, in which half the articles included dealt with Montgomery's works and their presentation of progressive chronicles of adolescent life. Similarly, the *Children's Literature Association Quarterly* devoted much of its winter 1984-85 issue to Montgomery, examining the subtle feminism in her novels. However, Montgomery was not taken as seriously by non-children's literature journals. T. D. MacLulich, who praised Montgomery in an essay for *CCL*, also published an essay on Montgomery in *English Studies in Canada* where his kind words are attenuated when he writes that he "do[es] not want to make an absurdly inflated claim for Montgomery as an instance of neglected greatness" (1985b, 84). Significantly, the *Emily* trilogy appeared in the New Canadian Library series in 1989, suggesting its acceptance as canon, or, at least, as literarily important. Afterwords by Alice Munro and Jane Urquhart emphasize the great influence the struggling writer Emily had on their childhood lives, while P. K. Page, who admits that she only read the novels "as an adult" (1989, 237), finds that "as the [trilogy] progresses, and we ask more of it, it becomes thinner, offers us less" (240). This negative attitude is reflected in Heather Avery's review of the second volume of Montgomery's journals for *Resources for Feminist Research*. She writes, "one suspects that Montgomery viewed these journals, which she clearly intended to be read, as providing the explanation for her failure to make that more extensive contribution to Canadian literature" (1989, 61). At the end of the 1980s, though Montgomery's value as cultural capital was secure, her value as literary capital was still contested: she had great importance in the minds of theorists of Canadian children's literature, but had no place yet in the broader canon of Canadian literature.

Finally, in the 1990s, Montgomery's literary value has reached an all-time high, placing Montgomery and her works closer to elusive canonical status. Five books of criticism on Montgomery, as well as Rubio and Waterston's authorized biography, were published between 1990 and 1995. In *Such a Simple Tale*, previous articles on Montgomery from the seventies and eighties are collected because, as editor Mavis Reimer writes, there is a need for this criticism to be recognized—it has been ignored, just as the texts about which these critics write have been ignored, because it was considered children's literature. Reimer argues that, not only is there a separate canon of children's literature, but Montgomery is definitely part of it. In their biography of Montgomery, *Writing a Life*, Rubio and Waterston also condemn the "rather condescending treatment [of Montgomery] by academic reviewers" (1995, 65), and focus on the important literary contributions made by novels such as *Rilla of Ingleside* and the *Emily* trilogy. As Rubio explains in *CCL:*

> [only] now that foreign academics have started writing doctoral and M.A. dissertations on Montgomery, and a flood of articles have started appearing in American journals, [do] Canadians recognize that in Montgomery they have a truly unique figure who has embedded her imprint on generations of readers world-wide. (1992, 10)

Rubio also states that Montgomery's mass popularity makes her a greater writer than a canonized one because her works have endured without the help of "artificially" (12) inflated textbook sales. Montgomery's literary importance has never been more confidently proclaimed.

With the recognition that Canadian children's literature constitutes a separate literary canon and that Montgomery occupies a place of honour within this canon, literary critics have been forced to reevaluate their views on both children's literature and Montgomery as fields of study. As a result of this transition, Montgomery and her works are now considered subjects of serious literary study. Three developments in the 1990s best illustrate Montgomery's new-found value. Firstly, in 1993, the L. M. Montgomery Institute, a "research centre focused on Montgomery's work, career, and culture" was inaugurated at the University of Prince Edward Island, and Mary Rubio applauded the "author's long-deserved acceptance into the academic community" (quoted in "Author"). Secondly, in 1997, New York's Oxford University Press published a scholarly edition of Montgomery's first and most famous novel as *The Annotated Anne of Green Gables*. Thirdly, in 1994, the New Canadian Library, the reprint series that many critics suggest is the benchmark of canonicity in Canada, reprinted Montgomery's most famous novel, *Anne of Green Gables*, with a foreword by a member of the Canadian canon, Margaret Atwood.

Is L. M. Montgomery part of this broader Canadian canon? Since the author's death in 1942, literary criticism on Montgomery's work has gone from being absent to being apologetic to boldly proclaiming that Montgomery is canon. Her value as cultural capital has always been high, though it increased with the release of the films, and her value as literary capital skyrocketed with the inception of the *Canadian Children's Literature* literary journal and with the publication of Montgomery's personal journals. If acceptance into the canon means national and foreign academic respectability, then Montgomery has become part of the Canadian canon; however, if acceptance into the canon means high value as cultural capital, Montgomery has always been part of it.

WORKS CITED

"Author Finally Gaining Academic Recognition." *Globe and Mail.* 4 May 1993. C2.

Avery, Heather. Review of *The Selected Journals of Lucy Maud Montgomery, Volume II. 1910–1921*. Ed. Mary Rubio and Elizabeth Waterston. *Resources for Feminist Research* 18:2 (1989): 60–61.

Bolger, Francis W. L. *The Years Before "Anne."* Charlottetown: P.E.I. Heritage Foundation, 1974.

Cowan, Ann S. "Canadian Writers: Lucy Maud and Emily Byrd." In *L. M. Montgomery: An Assessment.* Ed. John Sorfleet. Guelph: Canadian Children's Press. 1976.

"First Edition." *Atlantic Advocate* 60 (Mar. 1970): 57.

"Good-by, Green Gables. Hello, Expo 70!" *Maclean's* 82:7 (1969): 11.

Guillory, John. *Cultural Capital: The Problem of Literary Canon Formation.* Chicago: Chicago University Press, 1993.

Johnson, Brian D. "Anne of Green Gables Grows Up." *Maclean's* 100:49 (1987): 46–50.

Lecker, Robert. *Making it Real: The Canonization of English-Canadian Literature.* Concord, Ontario: Anansi, 1995.

Little, Jean. "But what about Jane?" In *L. M. Montgomery: An Assessment.* Ed. John Sorfleet. Guelph: Canadian Children's Press, 1976.

MacLulich, T. D. "L. M. Montgomery and the Literary Heroine: Jo, Rebecca, Anne, and Emily." *Canadian Children's Literature* 37 (1985a): 5–17.

———. "L. M. Montgomery's Portraits of the Artist: Realism, Idealism, and the Domestic Imagination." 1985b. In *Such a Simple Little Tale: Critical Responses to L. M. Montgomery's* Anne of Green Gables. Ed. Mavis Reimer. Metuchen, NJ: Children's Literature Association, 1992. 83–100.

McVittle, Judy. "Anne's Creator Finds a Biographer." *Toronto Star* 6 Jan. 1985. D5.

Miller, Judith. "Montgomery's Emily: Voices and Silences." *Studies in Canadian Literature* (Fredericton) 9:2 (1984): 158–168.

"Montgomery Hall." *Atlantic Advocate* 51 (June 1961): 89.

Montgomery, L. M. *The Alpine Path: The Story of my Career.* 1917. Don Mills, Ontario: Fitzhenry & Whiteside, 1974.

Munro, Alice. Afterword. *Emily of New Moon.* Lucy Maud Montgomery. NCL. Toronto: McClelland and Stewart, 1989.

Page, P. K. Afterword. *Emily of New Moon.* Lucy Maud Montgomery. NCL. Toronto: McClelland and Stewart, 1989.

Reimer, Mavis, ed. *Such a Simple Little Tale: Critical Responses to L. M. Montgomery's* Anne of Green Gables. Metuchen, NJ: Children's Literature Association, 1992.

Rubio, Mary. "Subverting the Trite: L. M. Montgomery's 'Room of her Own.'" *Canadian Children's Literature* 65 (1992): 6–39.

Rubio, Mary, and Elizabeth Waterston. Introductions. *The Selected Journals of L. M. Montgomery.* 3 vols. Toronto: Oxford University Press, 1985, 1987, 1992.

———. *Writing a Life: L. M. Montgomery.* Toronto: ECW Press, 1995.

Sorfleet, John Robert, ed. *L. M. Montgomery: An Assessment.* Guelph: Canadian Children's Press, 1976.

Thomas, Gillian. "The Decline of Anne: Matron vs. Child." 1975. In *Such a Simple Little Tale: Critical Responses to L. M. Montgomery's* Anne of Green Gables. Ed. Mavis Reimer. Metuchen, NJ: Children's Literature Association, 1992.

Urquhart, Jane. Afterword. *Emily of New Moon.* Lucy Maud Montgomery. NCL. Toronto: McClelland and Stewart, 1989.

Waterston, Elizabeth. "Lucy Maud Montgomery: 1874–1942." In *L. M. Montgomery: An Assessment.* Ed. John Sorfleet. Guelph: Canadian Children's Press, 1976.

Weber, E. "L. M. Montgomery as a Letter Writer." *Dalhousie Review* 22 (Oct. 1942)" 300–310.

———. "L. M. Montgomery's 'Anne.'" *Dalhousie Review* 24 (Apr. 1944): 64–73.

L. M. Montgomery and Everybody Else: A Look at the Books

VIRGINIA A. S. CARELESS

SCHOLARS HAVE COMPARED L. M. Montgomery's books, and in particular *Anne of Green Gables*, to many others, including *The House of the Seven Gables* (Selkowitz 1993, 12), *Uncle Tom's Cabin* (E. Smith 1996, 20), *The Five Little Peppers and How They Grew* (Kornfeld and Jackson 1987, 141ff), *Little Women* (Berg 1994, 38ff; Kornfeld and Jackson 1987, 141ff; Litster 1997, 66; MacLulich 1985a, 5), *The Adventures of Tom Sawyer* (MacLulich 1985a, 5; Rubio 1976, 29ff), *Alice's Adventures in Wonderland* (Litster 1997, 61), *The Adventures of Huckleberry Finn* (Rubio 1985, 66), *The Little Princess* (McCabe 1995–96, 11), *The Country of the Pointed Firs* (Gay 1986, 103; Santelmann 1994, 68), *Heidi* (McCabe 1995–96, 11; Nodelman 1980, 29), *Treasure Island* (Weiss-Townsend 1986, 113ff), *Pride and Prejudice* (Santelmann 1994, 71), *Elizabeth and her German Garden* (Epperly 1992, 252 note 3; Waterston 1993, 67), *The Story of an African Farm* (Epperly 1992, 252 note 3; Waterston 1993, 67), and *Rebecca of Sunnybrook Farm* (Cadogan and Craig 1976, 94; Classen 1989, 42ff; Epperly 1992, 251 note 2; Kornfeld and Jackson 1987, 141ff; MacLulich 1985a, 10ff; McCabe 1995–96, 11; Nodelman 1980, 29; Townsend 1996, 59). L. M. Montgomery was compared (and still continues to be compared) to a number of different authors in her own time: in 1930, she herself listed twenty-two others to whom she had been likened (Montgomery 1998, 40).

Using comparisons to understand a topic is valid, in general as well as in scholarly life. By looking at two or more things together, we can see each more clearly. We see similarities and differences, and we can get a better understanding of each thing individually. We can understand something new in terms of what we know already. We can determine what is idiosyncratic in something, and what may be typical of a larger underlying principle. We can see general principles that emerge from the comparisons; and we can place what we are studying in context.

In the reading I have done, I have found that the comparisons of Montgomery's work to others' have gone into a great many topics. Some deal with aspects related to literary structure and style, such as genre (Classen 1989, 42; Gay 1986, 103; Kornfeld and Jackson 1987, 141ff; Litster 1997, 64; MacLulich 1985a, 5; MacLulich 1985b, 87; Rubio 1975, 29; Waterston 1993, 51), settings (Classen 1989, 42; Epperly 1992, 157ff; McGrath 1992, 65; Rubio 1994, 7; Townsend 1996, 59), characters (separate discussion of this will follow), plot twists (Waterston 1993, 75), use of particular expressions (Classen 1989, 46ff; Litster 1997, 70–71 note 3; MacLulich 1985a, 10; McGrath 1992, 65), use of allusions (Litster 1997, 71–72 note 7; MacLulich 1985a, 10–11; McGrath 1992, 62; Waterston 1993, 53), type of title (Litster 1997, 71 note 4; Townsend 1996, 59), and writing style (Townsend 1996, 59).

Other comparisons in the literature on Montgomery's writing discuss aspects of the society and culture being depicted, such as social rules (Epperly 1992, 155; McCabe 1995–96, 12; McGrath 1992, 64; E. Smith 1996, 20), child-rearing practices (Epperly 1992, 156–60; MacLulich 1985a, 10; McGrath 1992, 63), education (Classen 1989, 45–46; Gates 1989, 165ff; E. Smith 1996, 21), material culture (Classen 1989, 42–44; Litster 1997, 70–71 note 3; McGrath 1992, 63ff; E. Smith 1996, 20), travel and transportation (Drew 1995, 20; McCabe 1995–96, 11; Nodelman 1980, 29), transgenerational interaction (Drew 1995, 21; Epperly 1992, 155; MacLulich 1985a, 10; McCabe 1995–96, 11; McGrath 1992, 64–65; Nodelman 1980, 29, 31ff; Selkowitz 1993, 12; E. Smith 1996, 21; Townsend 1996, 59), family ties or lack of same, for instance if one were orphaned (Cadogan and Craig 1976, 88ff; Classen 1989, 42; Mills 1987, 227ff), religion (Rubio 1985, 77; Rubio 1985, 28ff; E. Smith 1996, 20), humour (Rubio 1975, 31; Townsend 1996, 59), and concern with nature (Drew 1995, 21; McCabe 1995–96, 11; Nodelman 1980, 35; Waterston 1993, 53).

Still other comparisons look at features of the individual, such as gender (McCabe 1995–96, 11; Nodelman 1980, 29; Selkowitz 1993, 12) and age (MacLulich 1985a, 5ff; McCabe 1995–96, 11; Selkowitz 1993, 12-13; Townsend 1996, 59), physical appearance (Classen 1989, 43ff; Nodelman 1980, 29; Santelmann 1994, 68; E. Smith 1996, 20), aspiring to be an artist/writer (Drew 1995, 21; Epperly 1992, 192ff; McGrath 1992, 63; Pike 1994, 50ff), and personality (Cadogan and Craig 1976, 94-6; Classen 1989, 44ff; Litster 1997, 70-71 note 3; McGrath 1992, 64; Townsend 1996, 59).

One very soon gets the sense, as I did with continued reading, of the large—and apparently growing—number of comparisons to which L. M. Montgomery's work has been subjected. For instance, in the case of book characters, we find that Anne has been compared to: Alice in Wonderland (Eggleston 1960, 80; Litster 1997, 61ff; MacLulich 1985a, 5; Mott 1947, 217; Whitaker 1975, 18), Heidi (McCabe 1995–96, 11; Nodelman 1980, 29), Rebecca of Sunnybrook Farm (Cadogan and Craig 1976, 94ff; Classen 1989, 42ff; Epperly 1992, 251 note 2; MacLulich 1985a, 10; McCabe 1995–96, 11; Townsend 1996, 59), Phoebe Pyncheon (Selkowitz 1993, 12), Jo March (Berg 1994, 38ff; MacLulich 1985a, 10), Topsy (E. Smith 1996, 20), and Dorothy Gale (Waterston 1993, 38).

Not to leave out the males in literature, she has also been compared to Huck Finn (Rubio 1985, 76–77; Rubio 1975, 29ff; Waterston 1993, 38; Whitaker 1975, 18), Tom Sawyer (MacLulich 1985a, 5; Rubio 1975, 29ff), Jim Hawkins (Weiss-Townsend 1986, 115–17), Kim (Waterston 1993, 38), and Freckles (Waterston 1993, 38).

It gets confusing, and Wonderland-ish, in itself, to find that Anne, Emily, and Marilla have been compared to Alice (Anne: {by Mark Twain} Eggleston 1960, 80; MacLulich 1985a, 5. Emily: McGrath 1992, 65. Marilla: Litster 1997, 71 note 3). Marilla has also been compared to Alice's Duchess (Litster 1997, 70 note 3; McGrath 1992, 64), and both Anne and Emily have been compared to Jo (Anne: Berg 1994, 38ff; MacLulich 1985a, 5, 10. Emily: MacLulich 1985a, 13; Pike 1994, 50ff). Validity of the comparative approach aside, it seems to be a growth industry!

Then too, many of these comparisons do more than just compare, that is, note similarities and differences. They go on to explain the similarities by positing a historical link between those works compared: that the first in date had a causal effect upon the second one. This link may only be hinted at, by suggesting that apparently coincidental similarities may not be so; or it may be actually stated, and the claim made that the later one was somehow the result of the earlier. The terms used in such studies show the different degrees of definiteness with which such a claim is made, and the different degrees of intentional derivation attributed to Montgomery.

Ordering some of these claims from the mildest to the strongest, we find, for example: "may have been influenced by" (Whitaker 1975, 18); "inherited a tradition of juvenile fiction" (MacLulich 1985a, 5); "belongs to a tradition that descends from" (MacLulich 1985a, 5); "recalls" (Waterston 1993, 51); "Montgomery's parallels and echoes" (Epperly 1992, 155); "likely . . . provided the stimulus" (MacLulich 1985a, 10); "drew associative force" (Waterston 1993, 51); "having offered inspiration" (E. Smith 1996, 20); "there is a connection with" (Waterston 1993, 54); "tipping her hat to" (Selkowitz 1993, 12); "had a few classic models" (Waterston 1993, 41); "modeled [sic]" (MacLulich 1985b, 87); "admired and was influenced by" (Litster 1997, 66); "a formative text" (Epperly 1992, 10); "very probably patterned after" (Classen 1989, 42); "borrowed liberally from" (McGrath 1992, 62); "resemblance . . . too close to be merely circumstantial" (Classen 1989, 42); "leaves very little doubt that the former was strongly influenced by" (Classen 1989, 49); "draws heavily on" (Litster 1997, 66); and "has openly appropriated, or modified only slightly" (Cadogan and Craig 1976, 94).

These latter kinds of comparisons are more charged, for their implications are serious. Some acceptance of literary borrowing has been discussed in the *Canadian Children's Literature* journal's editorial of 1989. This editorial makes reference to a historical literary tradition of derivation, conscious or unconscious, which has resulted in a rich web of interrelated books. Further, this practice has been recognized and sanctioned in the world of literature by the concept of "intertextuality" (2–3).

However, there are implications in a claim of derivation that can quickly go beyond the limits of acceptance. Even claiming that an author "echoes" another somewhat reduces the first's creativity and value. To go to the furthest extreme and claim actual copying is to accuse an author of plagiarism, the ultimate literary crime and degradation. To take the issue into the unconscious or subconscious realm in effect condemns accused—however lightly—authors to no defence, for the action is now beyond their conscious awareness and control.

Indeed, this crime—whether conscious, subconscious, or unconscious—may be hard to prove conclusively, as has been seen in the modern example of Colleen McCullough's *Ladies of Missalonghi* and its apparent close similarity to L. M. Montgomery's *The Blue Castle.* (Reimer 1992, 2–3; Rubio 1992, 10–11, 35–36 note 6; Wood 1988, 59). At least, however, McCullough can answer back; with a deceased author, the issue must be taken up by those who will speak for her.

In fact, in this case, Montgomery already has done some speaking for herself. It is obvious that she was well aware of the threat to an author's reputation from any charge of plagiarism, and was ready to make clear that this was a practice and a crime of which she was innocent. For instance, she wrote to Ephraim Weber on January 10, 1932 concerning someone's opinion that Aunt Becky of *A Tangled Web* and the grandmother in *Magic for Marigold* strongly resembled the grandmother in Mazo de la Roche's *Jalna* books. In answer, she said, after joking speculation as to whether de la Roche had "taken out a sort of copyright on the idea of sharp-tongued and autocratic old women": "I cannot see the least resemblance between any two of them beyond the fact that they are all old and like their own way." (Weber, Correspondence, Jan. 10, 1932).

Then too, on June 18, 1937, she expressed to Ephraim Weber her concern that the title of *Jane of Lantern Hill*, due out in August or September of that year, was so similar to Nellie McClung's *Leaves from Lantern Lane*, that being the name of McClung's actual house (McClung 3), published in 1936. As Montgomery explained, her title had been chosen, and approved by the publishers, two years previous. There had been discussion about changing this title, but as McClung's book was not published in the United States or England, and Montgomery felt that her choice was the most suitable for her book, they decided to retain it. However, she wrote, "no doubt many people will think I deliberately 'lifted' my title from McClung's book!!!" (Weber, Correspondence, June 18, 1937).

Again, and again associated with McClung, Montgomery expressed concern in her journal entry in December 1935 that her choice of a name, nationality, and personality for the Irish servant Judy, in *Pat of Silver Bush*, closely resembled a real Irish servant, also named Judy, that McClung described in her autobiographical *Clearing in the West.* Although *Pat* predated *Clearing*, Montgomery was aware that people could forget that, and instead think that her book must have plagiarized McClung's (Rubio Personal Communication 1990). Thus, Montgomery fully understood the implications of such an error, and was anxious to avoid being accused of it.

Besides the particular issue of L. M. Montgomery's works possibly being derivative from other authors, there is also the larger question to consider of why a claim like this is made: why are similarities noted in literary works explained in terms of some historical link between them? Is this the only answer possible, or are there other sorts of explanations that can be offered, which may be as, or more, valid than a causal one?

Drawing upon my own background, I would say that there are other explanations, and some may indeed be more valid. Much of my training has been in the discipline of anthropology, which deals with the study of culture in its various aspects, including literary expression. In the course of examining different societies, anthropologists regularly deal with cultural similarities and differences—so much so that the "comparative method" is regarded as a fundamental anthropological approach (Radcliffe-Brown 1952, 108–129; Barrett 1996, 76). Anthropologists, therefore, are no strangers to the types of exploration and findings that I have been discussing here as regards the field of literature. There have been different theories in anthropology put forth specifically to explain similarities in cultural phenomena. We can consider some of these to see how they may offer different ways of looking at similarities in literary works.

The theory which most closely resembles the literary historicist explanation which I have been dealing with above is Diffusionism, that is that cultural features are spread from one place and/or group to another (Barrett 1996, 53–55). Thus, according to this theory, for example, pottery and metallurgy in the New World could only have been brought by people from the Old (Gladwin 1947, xi, xiv–v, 12, 128–136). Thor Heyerdahl's Kon-tiki expedition was an attempt to prove a diffusionist theory about how settlement came about in Oceania (Heyerdahl 1950, 18–21). Von Daniken's explanation that pyramid-building in Egypt and in Middle America were both assisted by spacemen brings an extra-terrestrial element to diffusionism (Von Daniken 1970, 74–89, 97–107).

But many anthropologists long ago rejected this theory, arguing instead that Independent Invention—similar solutions to similar problems produced by similarly effective minds—is a better explanation (Barrett 1996, 53; Hudson 1973, 115). One notable instance that has been explained in this way is the invention of the sewing machine by Elias

Howe, as well as by a number of other people, in the mid-nineteenth century (Brandon 1977, chaps. 3–5). Another example is the simultaneous discovery of the laws of the evolution of species by both Charles Darwin and Alfred Russel Wallace (Desmond and Moore 1991, 467–472). Could this theory apply here, thus explaining similarities in literary output in terms of parallel but unconnected processes of perception and thought in different authors? Montgomery seems to have applied it herself, in fact, to herself: she labelled the similarity between her title for *Jane of Lantern Hill* and McClung's *Leaves from Lantern Lane*, "a devilish coincidence" (Weber, Correspondence, June 18, 1937).

There is also Cultural Ecology, which is somewhat similar to the last theory, but based more on a biological model. This framework of explanation states that similar environments, broadly defined beyond the merely physical, call forth similar responses (Barrett 1996, 83–84ff; Kuper 1996, 190). For example, two cultures each possessing the right kind of clay could produce pottery. Similarly, L. M. Montgomery, living in the Maritimes in a farming and fishing economy, had many of the same experiences as Kate Douglas Wiggin, living in Maine, which is also a farming and fishing economy, and would accordingly describe similar fictional life.

Then too, there is Structuralism, which defines similarities in culture as but surface manifestations of some deeper unity or underlying principles (Barrett 1996, 142–145ff; Hudson 1973, 121; Kuper 1996, 181–183). Here, one could point out that L. M. Montgomery and the many other authors to whom she has been compared, shared the same culture, in the anthropological sense of culture being the "entire way of life of a people, including belief system, social organization, technology, and environment" (Barrett 1996, 8). Although many of these authors and their readers were not English, or even English-speaking, still the lifestyle, values, norms, belief systems, economic bases, social stratification systems, socialization practices, and so forth, were very similar, across a large part of the literate world. Notwithstanding specific local traditions, the similarity in fashions and food across the world of those with a European or European immigrant background made it possible for works written in many different countries to be enjoyed and understood elsewhere.[1]

Thus, authors and their readers in Montgomery's time had a commonality of assumptions and experience, and their literature would reflect that. We today do not live in their time or their cultural context, and we have only the writings as its remains or legacy. Accordingly, we may regard these works as isolated, yet oddly similar phenomena, rather as if they were solo voices, when in fact they were all members of a choir, singing the same music. However, this situation does not negate the individual's ability and contribution—as in every choir, each voice has its own unique quality. They are still individually creative, but it must be remembered that they do exist within a cultural framework. Understanding that framework can help in understanding an author's work. When we know the context in which she and others wrote, we can in many cases attribute similarities in writing to similarities in context. In the discussion below, I will go into some examples of aspects of Montgomery's work in which an explanation in terms of context will make clearer the similarities between her and other authors.

Thus, it can be seen that just as there are different explanations for similar cultural features, so there can be different explanations for similarities found in literature. Just as similarities in aspects of culture do not necessarily come from some lineal connection, so too similarities in literary works are not necessarily the result of some kind of derivation. Perhaps an awareness of what other theories can explain similarities may lead to a broader treatment of the question in literary research.

In what follows, I take, in terms of the alternate explanations I have just discussed, a fundamentally structuralist approach, with something of a cultural ecological tinge. In other words, I want to show that knowing the context, that is, the cultural "environment" which is the underlying structure that is manifested in works of literature, will help immensely in explaining similarities between Montgomery and other authors.

In discussing the context of Montgomery's writing, we are moving from the general, or macro, level of the anthropological theories to the specific, or micro, level of a particular culture at a particular time. This culture, as I have discussed above, was widespread and can be, for ease of identity, labelled "Victorian"—allowing, of course, for the fact that it was not only also found in places where Victoria was not queen, but also continued into the early twentieth century, when she no longer reigned. But the term is apt in applying to the period Montgomery, and many of those to whom she was compared, lived in, worked in, and wrote about.

In discussing aspects of this Victorian culture, I bring my work experience in the field of history to my training in anthropology. The two fields meet where history can supply the details of the culture of this particular period. I will draw upon my knowledge of Victorian history in addressing various topics, as I listed earlier, in which Montgomery's writing has been found similar to others.

As a historian approaching some of these topics, I do not find many of the apparent similarities in the comparisons between books as significant as do some of the literary scholars. Take, for instance, the question of physical appearance. Constance Classen discusses and compares the descriptions of both Rebecca and Anne, first quoting Kate Douglas Wiggin's description of Rebecca:

> The buff calico was faded, but scrupulously clean and starched within an inch of its life . . . the head looked small to bear the weight of dark hair that hung in a thick braid to her waist. She wore an odd little vizored cap . . . Her face was without color and sharp in outline. (Classen 1989, 43)

Classen next quotes some of L. M. Montgomery's description of Anne:

> . . . garbed in a very short, very tight, very ugly dress of yellowish gray wincey . . . She wore a faded brown sailor hat and beneath the hat, extending down her back, were two braids of very thick, decidedly red hair. Her face was small, white and thin . . . . (43)

According to Classen, the similarity between these two examples is among the proofs that Anne "had as its model an American import" (49). However, to a historian, there are other and more obvious, cultural reasons for the similarity.

What is being described in both cases is more telling about the fabrics, dyes, and laundry techniques of the books' periods. Many dyes were fugitive, even the synthetic aniline dyes that came into being in the mid-nineteenth century. Fabrics made completely or partially of cotton, as were calico and wincey (Caulfield 1887, 521; Farnfield 1975, 219), did not hold aniline dyes well (*Cassell's* 1878, vol. I: 360–361; vol. II: 22). Buff, a dye made from iron, was not a bright colour to begin with (Adrosko 1968, 49). Washable clothes, including ones made of cotton, were generally boiled with harsh soaps to clean them, and this treatment faded dyes, wore fibres, and shrunk clothing (*Cassell's* 1878, vol. I: 299; vol. II: 51).

What the historian further sees in these passages is that the two girls had clothes that had been washed a great deal, with the common detrimental results for both garment and wearer. But the important question is why the girls were wearing such clothes. And the answer is that the girls were poor. The 1887 *Dictionary of Needlework* described wincey as being "used by the poorer class of people" (Caulfield 521). Barrie's *Sentimental Tommy* illustrates this point well: his working class characters in Thrums wear wincey, in contrast to Tommy's mother's aspiration to silk as a sign of socio-economic success in London (Barrie 1896, 35). The issue in the descriptions of Rebecca's and Anne's clothing, therefore, is not about whether or not Montgomery copied Wiggin. Both authors depicted the physical evidence of poverty.

The fact that each girl is wearing a hat is also of little significance to the historian. In fact, apart from some curiosity about the different hat styles the two girls are wearing, the historian would find much more of note if both of them were not wearing hats. As Gwen Raverat pointed out in her reminiscences of Victorian Cambridge, wearing hats then was as normal as wearing shoes today (Raverat 1952, 259–60). In future, when perhaps human beings are born with some space-age surface on their feet that obviates the need for any added footwear, literary scholars may find two books from our period that have characters wearing shoes, and perhaps they will postulate that the later book was a copy of the first.

The similarity of the girls' hairstyles is also not of much significance for one who knows the period being described. There was not much choice of style available: long hair was common, unless a girl had a mother or guardian who went against the prevailing style perhaps for medical reasons. As she has recorded, Montgomery's own hair in childhood was very long (Montgomery 1987, 42; photograph in Bolger 1974, 45).

Furthermore, with long hair, there were not many style options: loose, in one braid, or in two. The first of these tended to be found if it was in style in a particular period—apart from being a popular style for portrait photographs. Rebecca's one braid and Anne's two would not alert a historian to some possible causal link between the two books. They both depict styles that existed in the periods in which the books are set. Similarly, two writers setting books in the 1960s could have girls in "Sassoon" haircuts, with the later writer having no fear of being accused of "borrowing."

Classen also sees evidence of Montgomery's taking from Wiggin in their shared emphasis on their heroines' "large, expressive eyes" (Classen 1989, 43). Other scholars who see a causal link between Rebecca and Anne have noted this feature also (Cadogan and Craig 1976, 91; Nodelman 1980, 29). Again, this is not that significant a comparison, when one sees how many of their fellow authors similarly described characters with eyes that were arresting of attention through colour, size, or quality of expression (Barrie 1900, 44; Burnett 1887–88, 98; Ewing 1885, 7; Finley 1889, 9, 71; Jewett 1886, 84, 86; Molesworth 1876, 93; Schreiner 1883, 3; Thackeray 1847–48, 23). Indeed, such attention to this feature is not limited to those authors or their times. In the culture of our own day, eyes are still referred to as the "mirrors of the soul," and there are huge-eyed children in popular, if not high, art. The Disney corporation has used the appeal that a child's large eyes have for most human beings in the designing of its cartoon characters, many of which have child-like facial proportions (*Nova*, Roller Coaster).

On the other hand, literary scholars often miss some very fine nuances that would be obvious to dwellers in the times described in the books, and to historians of those times. Nodelman has reduced the story of many books written around the time of *Anne*, including *Anne*, by listing what he sees as basic and sweeping similarities (Nodelman 1980, 29–30ff). For instance, he talks of all of these books having a solitary young girl travelling and he groups together the types of conveyance that she might be found in, as if the vehicle itself is not of particular importance (29).

However, the type of conveyance had a lot of meaning and would not have been arbitrarily chosen, by either the characters or by the author. That a girl was in a stage coach, or in a buggy, or on a train spoke volumes to people of the time as to her family's economic status, the stage of development of her locale, the age, taste, ethnic group, and even religion of those who sent her in this way, and so on. A modern illustration of this would be whether one travels in a sports car or an eighteen-wheeled truck.

Therefore, those doing the comparisons need to have a good understanding of the cultural context in which they are doing their comparing, and the meaning, to the people then, of the features that they have chosen. Besides choosing a theory for explaining a comparison's findings, they must also consider the elements being compared. Is the comparison in fact valid? What is the nature of the "population sampled"? How representative, or atypical, is it of its times? Are actually comparable units being studied? Without perhaps subjecting the comparisons to the demands of statistical standards, those doing such work in literature also have to take care that the approach used ensures that the results are as reliable as possible.

Next, I want to look more closely at some other examples of how Montgomery's work has been compared to others'. It should become more evident from these that when one does know something about the culture of Montgomery's times, the comparisons may not be that easy to make or, in fact, really that significant.

One obvious topic to consider from the list at the beginning of this paper is orphans. It has been noted that Anne, Rebecca (Cadogan and Craig 1976, 88–110; Classen 1989, 42; Mills 1987, 228; Waterston 1993, 39), Heidi, Sara Crewe (the Little Princess) (McCabe 1995–96, 11; Nodelman 1980, 30); Emily St. Aubert (Drew 1995, 20), Huck (Waterston 1993, 38), Kim (Waterston 1993, 38), Freckles (Waterston 1993, 38), and Dorothy Gale (Waterston 1993, 38) all were orphans, and that the orphan tale was obviously a very popular genre (Mills 1987, 227–239).

Explanations for this popularity take into consideration the freedom and power that, in some ways, an orphan has, divorced from family ties and restrictions (Auerbach 1985, 58; Mills 1987, 228). Florence Nightingale talked about the advantages for the Victorian female who was free of family expectations and controls, saying that "the family uses people, not for what they are . . . but for what it wants them for . . . ." (quoted in Showalter 1978, 105–106). Then too, explanations for the pervasiveness of orphan stories consider the difficulties that orphans face, having been neglected, abandoned, and deserted through their parents' death: these very difficulties elicit the interest that readers have in such lives (Auerbach 1985, 57–58; Mills 1987, 227).

Yet, it is also a fact that there were a great many orphans in Victorian times; and this fact documents both the good and the bad sides of that period's health conditions. Many more children were surviving infancy in this than in previous centuries. Life expectancy was rising (Banks and Banks 1964, 28) as was the size of families. Where the typically large family between 1800 and 1850 had 4.5 children (Roberts 1978, 60), couples married in the mid-Victorian period would have an average family of 5.5 to 6 live children (Banks 1954, 3). G. Kitson Clark has attributed this reduction in mortality to improvements in sanitation and hygiene, as well as a good supply of food and the lack of a killing agent, such as any serious epidemic (Clark 1962, 71–72).

However, many adults were still dying, whether mothers in child-birth—even in 1882, women were cautioned that preparing for birth might also mean preparing for death (Miller 1978, 25–26)—or mothers and fathers as a result of other disease or injury (Barry et al. 1997, 424; Roberts 1978, 59). Because more children were surviving, potentially more might become orphans. Then too, larger families meant additional stress on often very limited family finances. As a result, many children, even with living parents, were sent to orphanages, or to relatives, for foster care. This happened in the fictional Rebecca's case—she was not in fact an orphan (Wiggin 1903, 12)—and, under slightly different circumstances, in the real Montgomery's case also (Rubio 1985, 71–72).

Another theme discussed by those who have compared Montgomery to other authors is Nature. A strong response to the natural world in L. M. Montgomery's books, and in others to which they are compared, has also been seen as indicative of links between Montgomery and those books' authors. In some of the examples that have been discussed in scholarly literature, the explanation is given that Montgomery and these authors were all influenced by Romanticism, in which Nature figures so strongly (Cadogan and Craig 1976, 90; Drew 1995, 21; McCabe 1995–96, 12; Nodelman 1980, 34–35; Waterston 1993, 40; Weiss-Townsend 1986, 114). But, again, there were other and more recent cultural influences in these authors' lives that could make them, and their fictional characters, so attuned to Nature.

Popular literature from the mid-nineteenth to late-nineteenth century in Canada and abroad reflects a concern with the natural world. A survey of the topics in the magazines of the time quickly makes this apparent (e.g. "Some New Nature Books"; *Canadian Magazine*, Toronto; *The Outlook*, New York). This concern came about partly as a reaction to the damage created by the Industrial Revolution, and it is against this background, Houghton has argued, that the English Victorian nature poetry and the popularity of Wordsworth in particular is to be understood (Houghton 1957, 79–80).

The geological and archaeological discoveries of the time, as well as the development of evolutionary theory, carried with them the implication that Man had now to be seen as a part of Nature, and not as something distinct from it (Raven 1949, 173–179). The view of an immanent God in Nature, as expressed by Wordsworth, Kingsley, and others, was one way of accepting this new view of the whole natural world without abandoning religious belief (Raven 1949, 178–179). Also, on a more practical level, there was concern about the loss of the connection with the earth through the continuing rural depopulation in many countries at the turn of the century. Sir Andrew Macphail, in L. M. Montgomery's own home province, was one of those trying to halt this process (Robertson 1976, 16–17).

There were many other instances of a broad and active interest in Nature in its varied aspects. For example, there was a Conservation movement, as exemplified by the establishment of the National Trust in England in late-Victorian England (Lane 1968, 46; Taylor 1986, 39), the concern with the preservation of wilderness in the United States from the 1870s on (Baker 1903, 365ff; Hummel 1995, 19), and the efforts to establish national parks systems in North America (R. Careless 1997, 23; Hummel 1995, 21). There was the growth of vegetarianism (Freeman 1989, 94–95, 250–270), the establishment of societies for the protection of animals (Barry et al. 1997, 423; French 1975, 27–35), anti-vivisection campaigns (Desmond 1994, 457–459; Rupke 1987, 2–3; Society for the Abolition . . . ad, May 30, 1903), a widespread interest in gardening (Highstone 1982, 1–10; Hume 1989, 30–31), with a related expression in the genre of flower garden paintings (Clayton-Payne and Elliott 1988, 7–11), and so forth. Readers in Canada today may know only the examples of Anne, Rebecca, and Heidi, among others in literature, and their response to Nature, but these characters, and their authors, all existed within a context in which such concerns were not at all unusual.

At the outset of this paper, I discussed comparisons made between L. M. Montgomery's and other's books, among which figured similarities noted between her *Anne of Green Gables* and Kate Douglas Wiggin's earlier published *Rebecca of Sunnybrook Farm*. These similarities have been taken by some modern scholars as proof of a causal link between the two works. Thus far, I have discussed some of the variables that these scholars have found significant, in order to show that an understanding of the books' and authors' historical context yields other explanations for many of these similarities. Now, I want to address the question of the similarities between the two books in a more general sense.

This topic is of interest for more than the chance to look more closely at particular comparisons that have been made in Montgomery's case. It is still a current issue, as is evident in articles on the matter published in the *National Post* in 1999 (Lamey 1999, A1, B12). At some point in this discussion, no matter how gently any claim may be worded, the serious charge of plagiarism is always close at hand, even if it is only implied and is not directly stated.

It is interesting, and important, given the implications, to explore this particular comparison at greater length. It does seem that if such a charge is only implied, some attempt at proof, apart from apparent similarities in texts, should be undertaken. For instance, is there in fact proof that Montgomery read *Rebecca of Sunnybrook Farm?* Elizabeth Epperly thinks that there is, in that both Montgomery and Wiggin similarly misquote Emerson in their books (Epperly 1992, 5, 251–252 note 2). One might wonder, however, whether they both might have had a common source of the version of Emerson they used.

Montgomery read widely, and likely did keep up to date with the popular books of her period (Rubio Personal Communication, 1999). Thus, in fact, she may have read *Rebecca.* However, there is no mention of *Rebecca* in her published letters or journals (own survey: Bolger 1974; Bolger and Epperly 1980; Eggleston 1960; Gillen 1975; Gillen 1978; Montgomery 1985, 1987, 1992, 1998; Ridley 1956; Epperly 1992, 251 note 2); nor is there in the list of what survives of her library at the University of Guelph (Doody Jones 1994). Montgomery, however, did have a much larger library than the 175 or so books listed in the Guelph collection: in 1926, she talked of packing forty-two boxes of books (Montgomery 1992, 272), and even if many of those books belonged to her husband and sons, she surely had more than a couple of hundred. Rubio has also noted that Montgomery recorded five hundred titles in her journals between 1889 and 1942, talked of having several thousand books at one time, and, according to her son, often read one book a day (Rubio 1992, 17; 36, note 15). Maybe *Rebecca* was among them.

The scholars who have claimed derivation of *Anne of Green Gables* from *Rebecca of Sunnybrook Farm* do not refer to any of Montgomery's letters other than the selected ones which have been published. Yet in one of her unpublished manuscript letters to George Boyd Macmillan, I found mention of a work by Wiggin, *Penelope's Progress*, the plot of which Montgomery discussed at some length. However, she did not mention the author, or indicate that she had ever previously discussed that author or her works with Macmillan. Nor did she say anything at all about *Rebecca of Sunnybrook Farm* (Macmillan Correspondence, April 7, 1904).

Further, although various scholars have noted similarities between Anne and Rebecca, it is also important and necessary to note the differences between these two novels. For instance, in the discussion above on orphans, I have pointed out that Anne was one, but that Rebecca was not. She knew her parents and her siblings, her extended family, and her origins. Also, Rebecca was invited to her new home, albeit with some reservations (Wiggin 1903, 32), was welcomed with a kiss (34), and had a room specifically prepared and waiting for her (37). Similarly, although a parallel has been found in Anne and Rebecca's both caring for ailing older persons, in fact, Rebecca was absent—home with her family—when Aunt Miranda was dying (Wiggin 1903, 316ff).

The historian W. L. Burn has cautioned students of the nineteenth century against "the game of selective Victorianism" in which "there is only one important rule: to determine beforehand the 'pattern' you wish to discover or the 'trend' you wish to follow and then go on to find the evidence for its existence" (Burn 1964, 36). Similarly, he has pointed out to those who would study this period that "[w]hat is not permissible . . . is to select from the past only those factors which we happen to like and to separate them from their contemporary context" (48). There is a parallel process at work, with similar attendant drawbacks, if literary scholars only look only at apparent similarities, while omitting the differences, between two works, without reference to the culture that produced them.

With these cautions in mind, we should look the more closely when selecting relevant features for comparison, not only at the context of a book, but also at the context of its author's life. Mary Rubio has pointed out that Montgomery was describing many of her own experiences in *Anne of Green Gables* (Rubio 1985, 71–72). She, motherless with an absent father, thus in essence an orphan, was raised by an elderly couple, aspects of whose personalities could be found in Montgomery's characters. Many details of Montgomery's own life can be found to parallel ones in Anne's (Montgomery 1987, 38–44). Although, as will be discussed presently, Montgomery saw similarities between P.E.I. and New England, there were other places too that resemble the one that she knew and drew upon for her writing. In 1932, writing of two books by Ian Maclaren, she noted the similarity between rural Scotland and the Cavendish of her childhood (Montgomery 1998, 162; 397 note). Then again, although MacLulich uses as evidence for influence of *Rebecca of Sunnybrook Farm* on *Anne of Green Gables* the experience of both girls having an unsympathetic teacher in a one-room local school (MacLulich 1985a, 10), the source of both of these circumstances is more likely the authors' own lives. Montgomery, reading Wiggin's autobiography in 1932, pointed out how they had each had an unpleasant teacher, and how each had dealt with her (Montgomery 1998, 161).

Some of the scholars who have deduced a causal link between these two novels have quoted a contemporary review that made the same comparison (Classen 1989, 47; MacLulich 1985a, 11 note 18). However, they did not go on to quote the remainder of that review which states definitely that *Anne of Green Gables* was indeed not a mere imitation (*The Outlook*, New York, in Barry et al. 1997, 487). Classen also refers to a review that Montgomery quoted to Ephraim Weber, in which the reviewer notes the similarity of P.E.I., as she had described it in *Anne*, to that of New England (Classen 1989, 50 note 6). Classen presents this as part of her evidence that *Anne* was copying *Rebecca*. But there is more that needs to be told. Montgomery mentioned the review to Weber because she was amused and surprised by the fact that the reviewer had expected the two places to be very different. She went on to wonder about another American reviewer who commented, in a similar vein, on how much "the people of Canada *resemble ourselves* [her emphasis]," and she added "*what* did that poor man suppose we were like here???" (Eggleston 1960, 72). The similarities in descriptions of place found in the two books is because of similarity in reality, not because of any form of borrowing.

I have been able to locate a total of sixteen reviews of *Anne of Green Gables*, which includes two review-like ads by Montgomery's publisher (Barry et al. 1997, 483–89; Garner and Harker 1989: *St. John Globe*, 38–40; *Girl's Own Annual* 1909–10, 297-298; Reimer 1992, 170–175). I found that two of the contemporary reviewers mentioned a likeness to Alcott's works, but not copying (Garner and Harker 1989: *St. John Globe*, 39; *The Spectator*, 40). In their review of *Anne of Green Gables*, Montgomery's publishers likened it to Alice Hegan Rice's *Mrs. Wiggs of the Cabbage Patch* (Barry et al. 1997, 483). Three other reviewers of *Anne of Green*

Gables mentioned *Rebecca* (Barry et al. 1997: *Boston Budget and Beacon*, 485; *The Outlook*, New York, 487; *The Spectator*, London, 489). Of these the two that might give any impression to the prospective reader that Montgomery's novel was derived from Wiggin's hasten to assure the prospective reader that there is no question of imitation (Barry et al. 1997: *The Outlook* 487; *The Spectator* 489).

It is interesting, informative, and important to put these reviews in some context themselves. I was able to locate seven contemporary reviews of *Rebecca of Sunnybrook Farm*, as well as four of the sequel, *New Chronicles of Rebecca*, the latter which I included as it predated *Anne*, and was also about Rebecca. Four of the reviews of *Rebecca of Sunnybrook Farm* and three of the sequel's reviews made comparisons. Wiggin was compared as an author to Alcott (*The Spectator* June 29, 1907), and to Dickens (*The Atlantic Monthly* Dec. 1903). Her works were compared to Smollett's *Peregrine Pickle* (*The Atlantic Monthly* Dec. 1903), J. M. Barrie's *Sentimental Tommy* (Ford, *The Bookman*, Feb. 1904), and Mrs. Ewing's *Six to Sixteen* (*The Spectator*, Nov. 21, 1903). Wiggin's style was compared in three different instances to that of Marjorie Fleming's, a short-lived precocious young Scottish diarist and poet of the early nineteenth century (Stephen and Lee 1917, 281; *The Nation*, Jan. 21, 1904; *The Nation*, Apr. 18, 1907; Ford, *The Bookman*, May 1907).

Therefore, finding similarities to previous writing was not a phenomenon limited to Montgomery's work in her own time. Moreover, we see that the two authors' contemporaries found more similarities to note between Wiggin's works and others' than between Montgomery's and her literary antecedents. It seems most significant that the original reviewers of *Anne of Green Gables*, who were Montgomery's contemporaries, and lived in the same culture, did not see her work as so similar to or derivative from her literary forebears—and in particular so similar to or derived from *Rebecca of Sunnybrook Farm*—as our contemporaries do. It is significant too that although another of her contemporaries, Mark Twain, knew the works of both women, and wrote to congratulate first Wiggin on *Rebecca of Sunnybrook Farm* (N. Smith 1925, 314) and then Montgomery on *Anne of Green Gables* (Eggleston 1960, 80), he did not link the two together. It was Alice in *Alice's Adventures in Wonderland* to whom he compared Anne, and not to Rebecca.

Positing and not proving causal links between L. M. Montgomery, or any author, and another, is detrimental to an author's reputation, and so this should not be lightly done. Given the serious implications of such a procedure, scholars engaging in it should be prepared to make a clear and well-supported case for such interpretation. Can they prove that the author did in fact read the identified antecedent work and also left definite evidence that she did in fact echo, borrow, or copy? Otherwise the author, and certainly a dead author, is unable to defend herself against the negative consequences of such a claim.

For one thing, claiming that an author's work is derived from another, whether to a greater or lesser degree, minimizes that author's creativity and originality for, of course, she got her ideas from somebody else. Thus her work at best is but a patchwork of snippets from the works of other writers. Such a claim also denies the legitimacy of an author's own experiences, observations, and perceptions, even if these bear some similarity to those of other people. It suggests that all she did was read and absorb other authors' writing. Further, it diminishes not only an appreciation of her wide reading, but also of her artistic acumen in making literary allusions.

Furthermore, consider how absurd it can be as the years pass and more and more scholars find more and more similarities between L. M. Montgomery and more and more authors. These findings may of course only be significant in telling us what other works these scholars have read, not what else Montgomery read. Still, we are faced with the image of Montgomery ever busy reading others' works, and squirrelling their ideas away to cut and paste them into her own. When would she have the time to do any writing?

Also, we get into the awkward and never-ending problem of establishing who was the very first in the chain of causal links. With two authors, it may seem relatively easy to sort them historically: obviously, the later one copied the earlier. But whom did the earlier author copy or, at least, derive her ideas or words from? And whom did that one copy, and the one before that? And so on. We get ourselves into a march of infinite regression, a kind of literary version of (almost) perpetual motion.

An example of this kind of exercise can be seen if we take Montgomery's well-known phrase, "kindred spirits." Many readers of the *Anne* books today believe that it originated with Montgomery and subsequent use of it is likely regarded as being traceable back to her. While this may be the case, it is also a fact that she was not the first one to use the phrase. Epperly has connected it to Biblical examples, to Thomas Gray's 1751 *Elegy in a Country Churchyard* (Gray 1751, 16–21), Olive Schreiner's 1883 *Story of an African Farm* (Schreiner), and Elizabeth Russell's 1901 *Elizabeth and her German Garden*, (Epperly 1992, 5, 252 note 3; Russell). In her opinion, it is the last of these works, which Montgomery read in 1905, which was probably the most immediate influence on its use in *Anne of Green Gables* (Epperly 1992, citing Montgomery, 252 note 3). However, Montgomery's published journals show that she had used the phrase at least as early as Dec. 10, 1890 (Montgomery 1985, 36).

In *The Annotated Anne of Green Gables,* Gray's *Elegy in a Country Churchyard* is listed as the source for Montgomery's use of "kindred spirits" (Barry et al. 458). Another possible source that has been identified is the painting *Kindred Spirits* by the American artist, Asher B. Durand, of the painter Thomas Cole and the poet William Cullen Bryant in New York, dated 1849 (Uthoff 1994, 6). Of course, both Gray's poem and Durand's painting do predate Montgomery's journal use of the term.

In my research on this issue, I found that the Biblical references in the Concordance I consulted only had examples in which "kindred" was used as a noun (*Baker's* 1974, 309); Gray and Montgomery use it as an adjective. Gray used it in this way in at least three other poems, with three other nouns (Cook 1908, 70). I also found "kindred" used as an adjective by various authors who preceded Montgomery: Mary Russell Mitford used it at least once in her sketches between 1824 and 1832 (Mitford, 183); Susanna Moodie used it at least nine times from 1827 to 1854 (Moodie, "To Mary, Leaving England" cited in Thurston [1996], 1827, 229; "Sailor's Return" 1841, 59; "The Well in the Wilderness" 1847, 91; "Trifles" 1851, 196; *Life in the Clearings* 1853, 139, 260; *Flora Lyndsay* 1854, 18, 88, 168); Hawthorne used it at least twice in 1851 (Hawthorne 165, 245); the friends of Harriet Scott, a girl from Ontario, used it in her autograph album twice in 1873 (Scott 35, 95); and Sarah Orne Jewett also used it at least twice, in 1884 (119) and in 1886 (*The Story of the Normans* cited in Howard 1994, 42). Thus the use of "kindred" in this grammatical form was probably known quite widely, when one adds to the individual authors all the readers who read their works.

I also found other instances of "kindred spirits" itself, apart from the examples already cited above. Mary Russell Mitford, in England, used it in *Our Village*, 1824–32 (Mitford 308). Susan Sibbald, who came from Scotland and England to settle on the shore of Lake Simcoe in Ontario in the 1830s used it in her memoirs of 1853-58 (Hett 1926, xi; 22). Another of Harriet Scott's friends in Ontario used it c. 1873, in Harriet's autograph album (Scott 83). I found various other examples of the phrase but, because they postdate Montgomery's 1890 use, they are not included in this sample.

Given these various examples of phrases so similar, or even identical, to Montgomery's, and given how such instances in literature are frequently interpreted as being historically connected, an obvious question arises. If the similarities are evidence of causal links from one user to another, can we reconstruct the lineage of this phrase to trace it through time to Montgomery? In the interests of exemplifying an exercise in this diffusionist approach, I will attempt a reconstruction.

Thomas Gray is our first recorded user of "kindred spirits" in 1751. Many years separated him from the next one, Mary Russell Mitford, but as they both lived in England, his words could have reached her through some as yet undisclosed route, or through her reading his work. It is highly likely that Mitford knew Gray's *Elegy*, as do many people today who are much further removed from it in time. The Canadian pioneer and author, Susanna Moodie, also a native of England, in 1829 sent Mitford a poem which contained the very similar phrase about kindred souls (L'Estrange 1882, 141–142). Perhaps Moodie used this in recognition of, or in response to, Mitford's use of the phrase that we are tracking here.

In 1836, L. M. Montgomery's grandmother emigrated to Prince Edward Island from the same region that Moodie's family of origin, the Stricklands, came from (Montgomery 1987, 56; L'Estrange 1882, 150). Maybe the phrase was one that she learned in England, or from correspondence with those left at home. In fact, L. M. Montgomery also used the phrase "kindred souls" (Bolger and Epperly 1980, 16), and so this [souls] may be evidence of a link to this line of literary influence. Or there may have been a less direct Canadian path which led to Montgomery's "kindred spirits": via Moodie to her friend Susan Sibbald (Sibbald Brown, June 22, 1999), and through various links to Harriet Scott's friends in Penetang, Kingston, and Cobourg, Ontario (Scott, various).

However, a more direct route may have been through the United States. In 1829, Thomas Cole, one of the subjects in Asher Durand's painting, went to Europe for three years in 1829 (Richardson 1956, 167). Perhaps there he came into contact with Mitford, and brought the phrase back to his country, eventually to be used by Durand for the painting that he set in upper New York State. Maria Beebe, the daughter of an upper New York State physician (Kos-Rabcewicz-Zubkowski 1959, 23) may have been exposed to the phrase through some historically traceable connection with Cole. In 1839, Maria married Casimir Gzowski, an exiled Polish nobleman, with whom she moved to Canada in 1842 (Nelles 1990, 389–391). Casimir's increasingly successful career was capped in 1890 by a knighthood recommended by his business associate and friend, the Canadian Prime Minister, Sir John A. Macdonald (Nelles 1990, 395). As a Canadian Senator, Donald Montgomery was Macdonald's associate and friend, as well as being L. M. Montgomery's grandfather (Montgomery 1985, 25). In 1890, the Senator took L. M. Montgomery from Prince Edward Island to relocate with her father in Saskatchewan (19). On the trip West, Montgomery met Sir John A. (25) and it was following that date that she wrote the phrase "kindred spirits" in her journal (36).

Therefore there could have been a line of diffusion of the phrase "kindred spirits" from Gray to Mitford to Cole to Maria Beebe Gzowski and other New Yorkers like Durand to Sir Casimir to John A. via—or not—the Senator to L. M. Montgomery. If, as is often claimed, similarities found in literature come from somewhere else, all this is highly likely. But, as this exercise also shows, this approach can often be of dubious validity.

As I have discussed and illustrated with certain examples above, my approach in explaining the similarities found in Montgomery's and her antecedent authors' works is what in anthropological terms could be called a structuralist-cultural ecological one. Essential to understanding the literary similarities is a good understanding of the similar cultural environment in which the authors lived. This environment in its geographical, economic, temporal, ethnic, religious, educational, and political aspects formed the cultural structure underlying the authors' life experiences. In turn, these experiences led to the works that the authors produced.

One cannot, of course, go so far as to argue for cultural determinism in the creation of literature. Still, to the extent that an author draws upon her own culture, and to the extent that that culture is similar to another author's, it is not so surprising to find similarities in their works. Certainly, as we know from the examples of literary comparisons given at the beginning of this paper, a great many similarities have been found between the work of L. M. Montgomery and other authors. As the detailed examination of some of those similarities has shown here, reference to the authors' shared cultural context does yield useful explanations. Satisfactory explanations do result from this approach, without our needing any diffusionist interpretation in terms of possible causal links between works of literature. It helps to return the text to its context.

NOTES

1.   My research on the O'Reilly family, of Victoria, B.C., gives some illustration of the fact of a culture shared by many across the world. Like many others in the nineteenth and early twentieth centuries, the O'Reillys shopped in Canada, America, and England, had clothing made in keeping with fashions available in the United States, Britain, and the Continent, and ate food prepared in English and other European styles. See *Responding to Fashion* and *Clue to a Culture*. See also my *Bibliography for the Study of British Columbia's Domestic Material History* that documents the various origins of sources for home life and furnishing at the turn of the century.

WORKS CITED

Adrosko, Rita J. *Natural Dyes and Home Dyeing*. 1968. New York: Dover, 1971.

Auerbach, Nina. *Romantic Imprisonment: Women and Other Glorified Outcasts*. New York: Columbia University Press, 1985.

Baker, Ray Stannard. "John Muir." *The Outlook* vol. 74, New York, 1903: 365–377.

Baker's Pocket Bible Concordance. Grand Rapids, MI: Baker Book House, 1974.

Banks, J. A. *Prosperity and Parenthood: a Study of Family Planning among the Victorian Middle Classes*. 1954. London: Routledge and Kegan Paul Ltd. 1965.

Banks, J. A. and Olive. *Feminism and Family Planning in Victorian England*. New York: Schocken Books, 1964.

Barrett, Stanley R. *Anthropology: a Student's Guide to Theory and Method*. Toronto: University of Toronto Press, 1996.

Barrie, James M. *Sentimental Tommy: The Story of his Boyhood*. London: Cassell and Co. Ltd., 1896.

166

————. *Tommy and Grizel.* London: Cassell and Co. Ltd., 1900.

Barry, Wendy E., Margaret Anne Doody, and Mary E. Doody Jones, eds. *The Annotated Anne of Green Gables.* New York: Oxford University Press, 1997.

Berg, Temma F. "Sisterhood is Fearful: Female Friendship in L. M. Montgomery." In *Harvesting Thistles: The Textual Garden of L. M. Montgomery: Essays on her Novels and Journals.* Ed. Mary Rubio. Guelph: Canadian Children's Press, 1994.

Bolger, Francis W. P. *The Years Before "Anne."* Charlottetown: P.E.I. Heritage Foundation, 1974.

Bolger, Francis W. P. and Elizabeth R. Epperly, eds. *My Dear Mr. M: Letters to G. B. MacMillan from L. M. Montgomery, Author of* Anne of Green Gables. Toronto: McGraw-Hill Ryerson, 1980.

Brandon, Ruth. *A Capitalist Romance: Singer and the Sewing Machine.* Philadelphia and New York: J. B. Lippincott Co., 1977.

Burn, W. L. *The Age of Equipoise: a Study of the Mid-Victorian Generation.* London: George Allen and Unwin Ltd., (1964) 1968.

Burnett, Frances Hodgson. "Sara Crewe or What Happened at Miss Minchin's." *St. Nicholas,* vol. XV, part 1, Nov. 1887–Apr. 1888. New York: The Century Co.

Cadogan, Mary and Patricia Craig. *You're a Brick, Angela!: a New Look at Girls' Fiction from 1839–1975.* London: Victor Gollancz Ltd., 1976.

Careless, Ric. *To Save the Wild Earth: Field Notes from the Environmental Frontline.* Vancouver: Raincoast Books, 1997.

Careless, Virginia A. S. *Bibliography for the Study of British Columbia's Domestic Material History.* National Museum of Man, History Division Mercury Series, #20. Ottawa: National Museums of Canada, 1976.

————. *Clue to a Culture: Food Preparation of the O'Reilly Family.* Victoria, B.C.: Royal B. C. Museum, 1993.

————. *Responding to Fashion: the Clothing of the O'Reilly Family.* Victoria, B.C.: Royal B. C. Museum, 1993.

Cassell's Household Guide, being a Complete Encyclopaedia of Domestic and Social Economy, and Forming a Guide to Every Department of Practical Life. 4 vols. London: Cassell, Petter, and Galpin, c. 1878.

Caulfield, S. F. A. *The Dictionary of Needlework.* London 1887. New York: Dover, 1972.

Clark, G. Kitson. *The Making of Victorian England.* London: Methuen, (1962) 1965.

Classen, Constance. "Is *Anne of Green Gables* an American Import?" *Canadian Children's Literature* 55 (1989): 42–50.

Clayton-Payne, Andrew and Brent Elliott. *Victorian Flower Gardens*. London: Weidenfeld and Nicolson, 1988.

Cook, Albert S., ed. *A Concordance to the English Poems of Thomas Gray.* 1908. Folcroft, PA: The Folcroft Press Inc., 1969.

Daniken, Erich Von. *Chariots of the Gods? Unsolved Mysteries of the Past.* Trans. Michael Heron. New York: Bantam Books, (1970) 1971.

Desmond, Adrian. *Huxley: from Devil's Disciple to Evolution's High Priest.* Reading, MA: Addison-Wesley, (1994) 1997.

Desmond, Adrian and James Moore. *Darwin: the Life of a Tormented Evolutionist.* New York: Warner Books (1991) 1992.

Doody Jones, Mary E. *Summary List of Books in L. M. Montgomery's Personal Library.* Based upon the catalogue of the L. M. Montgomery Collection, Special Collections, University of Guelph Library, unpublished, 1994.

Drew, Lorna. "The Emily Connection: Ann Radcliffe, L. M. Montgomery and 'The Female Gothic'." *Canadian Children's Literature* 77 (1995): 19–32.

"Editorial: On Literary Debts." *Canadian Children's Literature* 55 (1989): 2–3.

Eggleston, Wilfrid, ed. *The Green Gables Letters from L. M. Montgomery to Ephraim Weber, 1905-1909.* Toronto: Ryerson Press, 1960.

Epperly, Elizabeth R. *The Fragrance of Sweet Grass: L. M. Montgomery's Heroines and the Pursuit of Romance.* Toronto: University of Toronto Press, 1992.

Ewing, Juliana. *The Story of a Short Life*. London: Society for Promoting Christian Knowledge, 1885.

Farnfield, Carolyn A. and P. J. Alvey. *Textile Terms and Definitions*. Compiled by the Textile Terms and Definitions Committee, 7th ed. Manchester: The Textile Institute, 1975.

Finley, Martha. *Elsie Dinsmore*. London: George Routledge and Sons, Ltd., 1889.

Ford, Mary K. Review of *Rebecca of Sunnybrook Farm* by Kate Douglas Wiggin. *The Bookman*, New York, Feb. 1904, vol. 18: 652–653.

Ford, Mary K. Review of *New Chronicles of Rebecca* by Kate Douglas Wiggin. *The Bookman*, New York, May, 1907, vol. 25: 304–305.

Freeman, Sarah. *Mutton and Oysters: the Victorians and their Food.* London: Victor Gollancz Ltd., 1989.

French, Richard D. *Antivivisection and Medical Science in Victorian Society.* Princeton: Princeton University Press, 1975.

Garner, Barbara Carman and Mary Harker. "*Anne of Green Gables*: An Annotated Bibliography." *Canadian Children's Literature* 55 (1989): 18–41.

Gates, Charlene. "Image, Imagination and Initiation: Teaching as a Rite of Passage in the Novels of L. M. Montgomery and Laura Ingalls Wilder." *Children's Literature in Education* 20.3 (1989): 165–173.

Gay, Carol. "Kindred Spirits All: Green Gables Revisited." 1986. In *Such a Sim-*

168

ple Little Tale: Critical Responses to L. M. Montgomery's Anne of Green Gables. Ed. Mavis Reimer. Metchuen, NJ and London: The Children's Literature Association and The Scarecrow Press, 1992.

Gillen, Mollie. *Lucy Maud Montgomery.* "The Canadians" series. Don Mills, Ont.: Fitzhenry & Whiteside Ltd., 1978.

————. *The Wheel of Things: a Biography of Lucy Maud Montgomery, Author of* Anne of Green Gables. Don Mills, Ont.: Fitzhenry & Whiteside Ltd., 1975.

Girl's Own Annual. "The International Reading Club." Includes a review of *Anne of Green Gables.* Vol. 31, London, England, 1909–10.

Gladwin, Harold Stanley. *Men out of Asia.* New York: McGraw Hill Book Co. Ltd., 1947.

Gray, Thomas. "Elegy Written in a Country Churchyard." 1751. In *Selections from the Poetry and Prose of Thomas Gray.* Ed. William Lyon Phelps. Boston: Ginn & Co., 1894.

Halpenny, Francess G., ed. *Dictionary of Canadian Biography, 1891–1900.* Vol. XII, Toronto: University of Toronto Press, 1990.

Hawthorne, Nathaniel. *The House of the Seven Gables.* 1851. Ed. Seymour L. Gross. A Norton Critical Edition. New York: W. W. Norton & Co. Inc., 1967.

Hett, Francis Paget, ed. *The Memoirs of Susan Sibbald.* London: John Lane Bodley Head, 1926.

Heyerdahl, Thor. *The Kon-Tiki Expedition by Raft across the South Seas.* 1950. Trans. F. H. Lyon. London: George Allen & Unwin Ltd., 1966.

Highstone, John. *Victorian Gardens.* San Francisco: Harper & Row, 1982.

Honigmann, John J., ed. *Handbook of Social and Cultural Anthropology.* Chicago: Rand McNally Publishing Co., 1973.

Houghton, Walter E. *The Victorian Frame of Mind 1830–1870.* 1957. New Haven & London: Yale University Press, 1971.

Howard, June, ed. *New Essays on "The Country of the Pointed Firs."* Cambridge: Cambridge University Press, 1994.

Hudson, Charles. "The Historical Approach in Anthropology." In *Handbook of Social and Cultural Anthropology.* Ed. John J. Honigmann. Chicago: Rand McNally Publishing Co., 1973.

Hume, Cyril. "The Point Ellice House Garden: Recovery and Restoration." *APT Bulletin: the Journal of Preservation Technology* 29.2 (1989): 28–42.

Hummel, Monte, ed. *Protecting Canada's Endangered Species: an Owner's Manual.* Toronto: Key Porter Books, 1995.

Ideas and Beliefs of the Victorians: an Historic Revaluation of the Victorian Age. 1949. New York: E. P. Dutton & Co., Inc., 1966.

Jewett, Sarah Orne. "The White Heron". 1886. In *Best Stories of Sarah Orne Jewett*. Ed. Charles G. Waugh et al. Augusta, ME: Lance Tepley, 1988.

———. *A Country Doctor*. Boston: Houghton, Mifflin & Co.; Cambridge: The Riverside Press, 1884.

Kornfeld, Eve and Susan Jackson. "The Female *Bildungsroman* in Nineteenth-Century America: Parameters of Vision." 1987. In *Such a Simple Little Tale: Critical Responses to L. M. Montgomery's* Anne of Green Gables. Ed. Mavis Reimer. Metchuen, NJ and London: The Children's Literature Association and The Scarecrow Press, 1992.

Kos-Rabcewicz-Zubkowski, Ludwik and William Edward Greening. *Sir Casimir Stanislaus Gzowski: a Biography.* Toronto: Burns & MacEachern, 1959.

Kuper, Adam. *Anthropology and Anthropologists: the Modern British School.* 1973. Third revised and enlarged edition. London: Routledge, 1996.

L'Estrange, the Rev. A. G., ed. *The Friendships of Mary Mitford as Recorded in Letters from her Literary Correspondents.* New York: Harper & Bros., 1882.

Lamey, Andy. "Is Anne of Green Gables really from Sunnybrook Farm?" *National Post*, Apr. 10, 1999, A 1.

———. "Was our Anne born in Maine?" *National Post*, Apr. 10, 1999, B 12.

Lane, Margaret. *The Tale of Beatrix Potter.* 1968. London: Collins, 1972.

Litster, Jennifer H. "An Annotated 'Anne': the History and the Dream." Review of *The Annotated Anne of Green Gables*, Wendy E. Barry, Margaret Anne Doody and Mary E. Doody Jones, eds. *Canadian Children's Literature* 88 vol. 23:4 (Winter, 1997): 61–73.

MacLulich, T. D. "L. M. Montgomery and the Literary Heroine: Jo, Rebecca, Anne and Emily." *Canadian Children's Literature* 37 (1985): 5–17.

———. "L. M. Montgomery's Portraits of the Artist: Realism, Idealism and the Domestic Imagination." 1985b. In *Such a Simple Little Tale: Critical Responses to L. M. Montgomery's* Anne of Green Gables. Ed. Mavis Reimer. Metchuen, NJ and London: The Children's Literature Association and The Scarecrow Press, 1992.

MacMillan, George Boyd. Papers, MG 30 D 185. Correspondence to Feb. 12, 1915, microfilm #C-10689, National Archives of Canada, Ottawa, Ont.

McCabe, Kevin. "Orphans Sunny Side Up: Anne and her Kinfolk." *Kindred Spirits*, Winter 1995-96: 11–12.

McClung, Nellie. *Leaves from Lantern Lane.* Toronto: Thomas Allen, 1936.

McGrath, Robin. "Alice of New Moon: the Influence of Lewis Carroll on L. M. Montgomery's Emily Bird [sic] Starr." *Canadian Children's Literature* 65 (1992): 62–67.

Miller, John Hawkins. "'Temple and Sewer': Childbirth, Prudery, and Victoria

Regina." In *The Victorian Family: Structure and Stresses*. Ed. Anthony S. Wohl. London: Croom Helm, 1978.

Mills, Claudia. "Children in Search of a Family: Orphan Novels through the Century." *Children's Literature in Education* 18.4 (1987): 227–239.

Mitford, Mary Russell. *Our Village*. 1824–1832. Ed. Sir John Squire. London: Dent, Everyman's Library, (1936) 1970.

Molesworth, Mrs. Mary Louisa. *Carrots—Just a Little Boy*. 1876. London: Macmillan & Co., 1957.

Montgomery, L. M. *Jane of Lantern Hill*. 1937. Toronto: McClelland-Bantam Inc., Seal Books, 1988.

———. *The Selected Journals of L. M. Montgomery. Volume I: 1889–1910*. Ed. Mary Rubio and Elizabeth Waterston. Toronto: Oxford University Press, 1985.

———. *The Selected Journals of L. M. Montgomery. Volume II: 1910–1921*. Ed. Mary Rubio and Elizabeth Waterston. Toronto: Oxford University Press, 1987.

———. *The Selected Journals of L. M. Montgomery. Volume III: 1921–1929*. Ed. Mary Rubio and Elizabeth Waterston. Toronto: Oxford University Press, 1992.

———. *The Selected Journals of L. M. Montgomery. Volume IV: 1929–1935*. Ed. Mary Rubio and Elizabeth Waterston. Toronto, Oxford University Press, 1998.

Moodie, Susanna. *Flora Lyndsay, or, Passages in an Eventful Life*. 1854. New York: Robert M. Dewitt, 1880.

———. *Life in the Clearings versus the Bush*. 1853. Toronto: McClelland and Stewart, New Canadian Library complete edition, 1989.

———. "The Sailor's Return, or Reminiscences of our Parish." 1841. In *Voyages: Short Narratives of Susanna Moodie*. Ed. John Thurston. Ottawa and Paris: University of Ottawa Press, 1991.

———. "Trifles from the Burthen of a Life." 1851. In *Voyages: Short Narratives of Susanna Moodie*. Ed. John Thurston. Ottawa and Paris: University of Ottawa Press, 1991.

———. *Voyages: Short Narratives of Susanna Moodie*. Ed. John Thurston. Ottawa and Paris: University of Ottawa Press, Canadian Short Story Library, #15, 1991.

———. "The Well in the Wilderness: a Tale of the Prairie—Founded upon Facts." 1847. In *Voyages: Short Narratives of Susanna Moodie*. Ed. John Thurston. Ottawa and Paris: University of Ottawa Press, 1991.

Mott, Frank Luther. *Golden Multitudes: the Story of Best Sellers in the United States*. 1947. New York: R. R. Bowker & Co., 1960.

Nelles, H. V. "Sir Casimir Stanislaus Gzowski." In *Dictionary of Canadian Biography*, vol. XII, 1990. Toronto: University of Toronto Press, 1990.

Nodelman, Perry. "Progressive Utopia, or, How to Grow Up Without Growing Up." 1980. In *Such A Simple Little Tale: Critical Responses to L. M. Montgomery's* Anne of Green Gables. Ed. Mavis Reimer. Metuchen, NJ and London: The Children's Literature Association and The Scarecrow Press, 1992.

Nova. "Roller Coaster." PBS. KCTS, Seattle, WA, June 15, 1999.

Phelps, William Lyon, ed. *Selections from the Poetry and Prose of Thomas Gray.* Boston: Ginn & Co., 1894.

Pike, E. Holly. "The Heroine who Writes and her Creator." In *Harvesting Thistles: the Textual Garden of L. M. Montgomery: Essays on her Novels and Journals.* Ed. Mary Rubio. Guelph: Canadian Children's Press, 1994.

Radcliffe-Brown, A. R. "The Comparative Method in Social Anthropology." *Journal of the Royal Anthropological Institute*, LXXXI (1952) in *Method in Social Anthropology: Collected Essays by P. R. Radcliffe-Brown.* Ed. M. N. Srivnas. Chicago and London: University of Chicago Press, 1966.

Raven, Canon C. E. "Men and Nature." In *Ideas and Beliefs of the Victorians: an Historic Revaluation of the Victorian Age.* 1949. New York: E.P. Dutton and Co., Inc., 1966.

Raverat, Gwen. *Period Piece: a Cambridge Childhood.* 1952. London: Faber & Faber, 1974.

Reimer, Mavis, ed. *Such a Simple Little Tale: Critical Responses to L. M. Montgomery's* Anne of Green Gables. Metuchen, NJ and London: The Children's Literature Association and The Scarecrow Press, 1992.

Review of *New Chronicles of Rebecca* by Kate Douglas Wiggin. *The Outlook,* New York, May 18, 1907, vol. 86: 115.

Review of *New Chronicles of Rebecca* by Kate Douglas Wiggin. *The Nation,* New York, New York Evening Post Co., April 18, 1907, vol. 84, #2181: 362.

Review of *New Chronicles of Rebecca* by Kate Douglas Wiggin. *The Spectator,* London, June 29, 1907, vol. 98: 1037–1038.

Review of *Rebecca of Sunnybrook Farm* by Kate Douglas Wiggin. *The Dial,* New York, Oct. 16, 1903, vol. 35: 264.

Review of *Rebecca of Sunnybrook Farm* by Kate Douglas Wiggin. *The Canadian Magazine*, Toronto, March 1904, vol. 22, #5: 496–497.

Review of *Rebecca of Sunnybrook Farm* by Kate Douglas Wiggin. *The Atlantic Monthly,* Boston and New York: Houghton, Mifflin & Co.[who later became Wiggin's publisher], Dec. 1903, vol. 92: 858–860.

Review of *Rebecca of Sunnybrook Farm* by Kate Douglas Wiggin. *The Outlook,* New York, Dec. 5, 1903, vol. 75: 850.

Review of *Rebecca of Sunnybrook Farm* by Kate Douglas Wiggin. *The Nation*, New York, New York Evening Post Co., Jan. 21, 1904, vol. 78, #2012, "Recent Novels": 54–55.

Review of *Rebecca of Sunnybrook Farm* by Kate Douglas Wiggin. *The Spectator*, London, Nov. 21, 1903, vol. 91: 873.

Richardson, Edgar P. *Painting in America: the Story of 450 Years*. New York: Thomas Y. Crowell Co., 1956.

Ridley, Hilda M. *The Story of L. M. Montgomery*. Toronto: The Ryerson Press, 1956.

Roberts, David. "The Paterfamilias of the Victorian Governing Classes." In *The Victorian Family: Structure and Stresses*. Ed. Anthony S. Wohl. London: Croom Helm, 1978.

Robertson, Ian Ross. "Sir Andrew Macphail and Orwell." 1976. *Kindred Spirits* (Winter 1997–98): 16–17.

Rubio, Mary. "Anne of Green Gables: the Architect of Adolescence." 1985. In *Such a Simple Little Tale: Critical Responses to L. M. Montgomery's Anne of Green Gables*. Ed. Mavis Reimer. Metuchen, NJ and London: The Children's Literature Association and The Scarecrow Press, 1992.

———. Personal Communication, December 16, 1990.

———. Personal Communication re: L. M. Montgomery's reading. May 16, 1999.

———. "Satire, Realism and Imagination in *Anne of Green Gables*." 1975. In *L. M. Montgomery: an Assessment*. Ed. John R. Sorfleet. Guelph: Canadian Children's Press, 1976.

———. "Subverting the Trite: L. M. Montgomery's 'room of her own'." *Canadian Children's Literature* 65 (1992): 6–39.

———, ed. *Harvesting Thistles: the Textual Garden of L. M. Montgomery: Essays on her Novels and Journals*. Guelph: Canadian Children's Press, 1994.

Rupke, Nicolas A. *Vivisection in Historical Perspective*. London: Croom Helm, 1987.

Russell, Elizabeth. *Elizabeth and her German Garden*. New York: George Munro's Sons, 1901.

Santelmann, Patricia Kelly. "Written as Women Write: *Anne of Green Gables* within the Female Literary Tradition." In *Harvesting Thistles: the Textual Garden of L. M. Montgomery: Essays on her Novels and Journals*. Ed. Mary Rubio. Guelph: Canadian Children's Press, 1994.

Schreiner, Olive. *The Story of an African Farm*. 1883. Chicago: Cassandra Editions, Academy Press Ltd. (1924), 1977.

Scott, Harriet B. *Autograph Album*. unpublished, c. 1864–73.

Selkowitz, Robert. "*Anne of Green Gables* Meets *The House of the Seven Gables*." *Kindred Spirits* (Summer) 1993: 12–13.

Showalter, Elaine. "Family Secrets and Domestic Subversion: Rebellion in the Novels of the 1860s." In *The Victorian Family: Structure and Stresses*. Ed. Anthony S. Wohl. London: Croom Helm, 1978.

Sibbald Brown, Peter. Personal Communication re: Susan Sibbald and Susanna Moodie. June 22, 1999.

Smith, Edith K. "Adoption in Shades of Black and Red: the Taming of Topsy and Adoption of Anne." *Kindred Spirits* (Autumn) 1996: 20–21.

Smith, Nora Archibald. *Kate Douglas Wiggin as her Sister Knew her*. Boston and New York: Houghton Mifflin Co.; Cambridge: The Riverside Press, 1925.

Society for the Abolition of Vivisection, London, England. Advertisement, *The Spectator*, London, May 30, 1903, vol. 90: 873.

"Some New Nature Books." In "The New Books: Notes on Recent American Publications." *The American Monthly Review of Reviews*. New York, vol. 29, January-June, 1904; Feb., 1904: 256.

Sorfleet, John Robert, ed. *L. M. Montgomery: An Assessment*. Guelph: Canadian Children's Press, 1976.

Srinivas, M. N. *Method in Social Anthropology: Collected Essays by P. R. Radcliffe-Brown*. 1958. Chicago and London: University of Chicago Press, 1966.

Stephen, Sir Leslie and Sir Sidney Lee, eds. *The Dictionary of National Biography*. 1917. Vol. 7: 281, entry on Margaret (Marjorie) Fleming. London: Oxford University Press, 1937–8.

Taylor, Judy. *Beatrix Potter: Artist, Storyteller, and Countrywoman*. Harmondworth, MX: Frederick Warne, 1986.

Thackeray, William Makepeace. *Vanity Fair*. 1847–48. Signet Classic. Afterword by V. S. Pritchett. New York: The New American Library, 1962.

Thurston, John. *The Work of Words: the Writing of Susanna Strickland Moodie*. Montreal and Kingston: McGill-Queen's University Press, 1996.

Townsend, John Rowe. *Written for Children: an Outline of English-language Children's Literature*. Lanham, MD, and London: The Scarecrow Press, 1996.

Uthoff, Sarah S. "Our Kindred Spirits Share." *Kindred Spirits* (Spring) 1994: 6.

Waterston, Elizabeth. *Kindling Spirit: L. M. Montgomery's Anne of Green Gables*. Toronto: E.C.W. Press, 1993.

Waugh, Charles G., Martin H. Greenberg and Josephine Donovan, eds. *Best Stories of Sarah Orne Jewett*. Introduction by Josephine Donovan. Augusta, ME: Lance Tapley, 1988.

Weber, Ephraim. Correspondence, 1905–1909, 1916–1941. MG 30 D 36. National Archives of Canada.

Weiss-Townsend, Janet. "Sexism Down on the Farm? *Anne of Green Gables*." 1986. In *Such a Simple Little Tale: Critical Responses to L. M. Montgomery's*

Anne of Green Gables. Ed. Mavis Reimer. Metuchen, NJ and London: The Children's Literature Association and The Scarecrow Press, 1992.

Whitaker, Muriel A. "'Queer Children': L. M. Montgomery's Heroines." 1975. In *Such A Simple Little Tale: Critical Responses to L. M. Montgomery's* Anne of Green Gables. Ed. Mavis Reimer. Metuchen, NJ and London: The Children's Literature Association and The Scarecrow Press, 1992.

Wiggin, Kate Douglas. *Rebecca of Sunnybrook Farm*. 1903. Boston and New York: Houghton Mifflin & Co.; Cambridge: The Riverside Press, 1931.

Wohl, Anthony S., ed. *The Victorian Family: Structure and Stresses*. London: Croom Helm, 1978.

Wood, Chris. "A Tale of Twin Spinsters." *Maclean's Magazine* 15 Feb. 1988: 59.

From Pagan to Christian: The Symbolic Journey of Anne of Green Gables

JOHN R. SORFLEET

On July 5, 1911, Lucy Maud Montgomery married a Presbyterian minister named Ewan MacDonald to whom she had been secretly engaged for five years, since October 12, 1906. In subsequent years Maud's ideas about Christian doctrine went through some significant changes, but at the time *Anne of Green Gables* was written they were comparatively orthodox. Indeed, she afterwards noted that the very evening she started to write the novel was the first day that Ewan came up to get his mail (Montgomery 1987, 147), and they made a regular practice of talking "for an hour or so" on various matters: "I began to enjoy our chats on theology and philosophy—the only subjects he had a real grasp of—and moreover, I began to be attracted by the man himself" (Montgomery 1985, 321). Further, in a May 1907 letter to Ephraim Weber, her long-time pen-pal, when she first mentions writing most of *Anne of Green Gables* "last fall and winter" (Eggleston 1981, 51), she also says she had spent the last year reading the Bible—"really, *reading it*" (53)—a logical activity for a woman who had become interested in (and later engaged to) a minister while writing the novel. It is only natural to consider how her relationship with Ewan and her careful Bible study might be reflected in *Anne of Green Gables*.

What we have in the novel is Anne's life-journey from childhood (age eleven) to young adulthood (age sixteen and a half). Anne's growing-up has various dimensions: physical, educational, social, moral, and spiritual. I'm going to focus most on the moral and spiritual journey, as conveyed through the fairy tale elements, imagery, symbolism, and religious allusions.

Montgomery adds force to the details of her depiction by drawing on the power of archetype, especially fairy tale archetype. Anne is the orphaned heroine, the outsider coming to an unknown land, where she is involved in a case of mistaken identity, is strongly associated with nature and natural forces, gains protectors who are themselves atypical—indeed, she can even be said to wake them from a kind of sleep—demonstrates her competence and worthiness, defeats her enemies, helps transform Avonlea society, and is finally reconciled with her Prince Charming, Gilbert Blythe. She is, then, a powerful personality in terms of fairy tale archetype.

Anne's unusual qualities are apparent in the novel's first description of her: "no commonplace soul inhabited the body of this stray woman-child" (Montgomery 1908, 12–13). She soon shows remarkable powers, including the ability to pick the Cuthbert homestead out of many in a panoramic landscape before she first arrives there. On her initial trip to Green Gables in Chapter Two, she is also described in fairy tale terms, as "this freckled witch" (16). Similar uses of imagery and symbolism occur later in the novel. In Chapter Three, Marilla says: "Matthew Cuthbert, I believe that child has bewitched you!" (31). In Chapter Four, we are told that Marilla "had an uncomfortable feeling that while this odd child's body might be there at the table her spirit was far away in some remote airy cloudland, borne aloft on the wings of imagination" (36). Later she says to herself, "She'll be casting a spell over me, too. She's cast it over Matthew" (38). In Chapter Seven, Anne is again described as "this freckled witch of a girl who knew and cared nothing about God's love, since she had never had it translated to her through the medium of human love" (55). In Chapter Fourteen, Marilla says, "I declare I believe Green Gables is bewitched" (108), while in Chapter Thirty Rachel Lynde declares, "an odder, unexpecteder witch of a child there never was in this world" (265).

Anne also imagines she is "a frost fairy" (133), tells "beautiful fairy stor[ies]" (128), believes in fairies (263) and dryads (183), is compared to "[s]ome wild divinity of the shadowy plain" (121) and a "sprite" (189), plays "a red-haired fairy" at the school concert (205), imagines she is "an enchanted princess" (173), and proves to be a female ugly duckling who becomes a beautiful swan.

Fairies and witches and dryads, of course, are intrinsically linked

with nature and with nature-based or pagan religious perspectives—
hence, the novel's narrator refers to "the witcheries of the spring world"
(272)—and they are non-Christian in origin.[1] The colours most strongly
associated with such nature religions are red and green—colours also associated with Anne (especially her hair—a strong symbol of female identity). Anne too, at the beginning of the novel, is not a Christian. Chapter
Seven, "Anne Says Her Prayers," makes this very clear.

> "I never say any prayers," announced Anne . . . .
> Marilla . . . had intended to teach Anne the childish classic, "Now
> I lay me down to sleep." But . . . it suddenly occurred to her that that sim-
> ple prayer, sacred to white-robed childhood lisping at motherly knees, was
> entirely unsuited to this freckled witch of a girl who knew and cared noth-
> ing about God's love, since she had never had it translated to her through
> the medium of human love.
> "You're old enough to pray for yourself, Anne," she said finally.
> "Just thank God for your blessings and ask Him humbly for the things
> you want . . . ."
> "Matthew Cuthbert, it's about time somebody adopted that child
> and taught her something. She's next door to a perfect heathen. Will you
> believe that she never said a prayer in her life till to-night? . . . I foresee
> that I shall have my hands full." (53–56)

The most important points to note in this chapter, besides Anne's initial
non-Christian status, are the insistence on human love as the medium
through which we come to understand something about God's love,
Marilla's assumption of her responsibility as a Christian to adopt this "hea-
then" (56) and teach her something about Christianity, and Anne's first
prayer, which contains thanks and then two petitions—to stay at Green
Gables and to be good-looking when she grows up—both of which are subsequently fulfilled.

Anne's religious education begins the next day. Marilla intends for
Anne to learn the Lord's Prayer from a printed card, but Anne is detained
on her way to get it by a picture (alluding to Mark 10: 13–16) titled "Christ
Blessing Little Children"—in which she identifies with one of them:

> I was just imagining that I was one of them—that I was the little girl in
> the blue dress, standing off by herself in the corner as if she didn't belong

to anybody, like me. She looks lonely and sad, don't you think? I guess she hadn't any father or mother of her own. But she wanted to be blessed, too, so she just crept shyly up on the outside of the crowd, hoping nobody would notice her—except Him. I'm sure I know just how she felt. Her heart must have beat and her hands must have got cold, like mine did when I asked you if I could stay. She was afraid He mightn't notice her. But it's likely He did, don't you think? I've been trying to imagine it all out—her edging a little nearer all the time until she was quite close to Him; and then He would look at her and put His hand on her hair and oh, such a thrill of joy as would run over her! (60)

It is only after this that she reads, learns, and admires the Lord's Prayer: in doctrinal terms, she comes to the Father through the Son. As the novel progresses she eventually becomes a regular church and Sunday school goer, regularly gives thanks to God, and says prayers. As she puts it to Marilla after meeting Diana, "I'll say my prayers with a right good will tonight" (92). Further, she identifies herself as a Protestant (132); "repent[s]" of sins of omission as well as commission (245); and models herself on the new minister's wife, Mrs. Allan, a kindred spirit. "Mrs. Allan said we ought always to try to influence people for good. She talked so nice about every-thing. I never knew before that religion was such a cheerful thing. I always thought it was kind of melancholy, but Mrs. Allan's isn't, and I'd like to be a Christian if I could be one like her" (181). She also prays for help when in danger of drowning during the Lily Maid episode and says "a grateful prayer" after her earlier prayer is answered (238); further, she decides she'd "like to be a minister's wife when she grows up" (192), and later states that "[I]f I were a man I think I'd be a minister. They can have such an influence for good if their theology is sound" (267).

In addition, she is compared by Mrs. Allan to "a Madonna" (283), is described as having a "spiritual face" (288), and shows Christian love and selflessness when she decides to give up her Avery scholarship to stay with Marilla after Matthew's death and Marilla's eye-trouble. The human love that Marilla realized Anne needed to experience in order to understand God's sacrificial love comes back to benefit the elderly couple themselves; as Anne declares to Marilla and Matthew, "at heart I shall always be your lit-tle Anne, who will love you and Matthew and dear Green Gables more and more every day of her life" (293). And, in the last lines of the novel's last page, the extent of Anne's Christian journey is made clear: as she says, "'God's in his heaven, all's right with the world'" (329). In spite of troubles, in spite of change, she trusts in God's providence. Further, in this passage Montgomery is quoting Browning's poetic drama "Pippa Passes"—and the lines suggest that, like Browning's Pippa, Anne too has become an influence for spiritual good in a world where evil is all too common.

This last point, of course, indicates that the religious influences in the novel are not all one-sided. Though Anne gains a religious, moral, and social education, as well as an academic one, she also educates or influences Avonlea. Anne is childhood spontaneity and imagination confronting adult conventionalism and social dogmatism. Her words and actions effectively undermine the hypocrisies of the adult world and deflate its pretensions, while at the same time asserting the value of imaginative reality—attuned to nature—in a society which tends to deny it. When Anne first comes to Avonlea, she comes to a town that is socially, educationally, and religiously stagnant. The community is bound by convention, by concern about what the neighbours might say, by boring, unimaginative, everyday practicality. It needs revivifying; it needs to be brought back to an awareness of the importance of the spirit behind the letter of its social, educational, and religious institutions and customs; it needs transformation by the powers of the imagination and by the energy of undomesticated nature. This dialectic in the novel is represented by the symbolic geography of Avonlea, indicating in Chapter One an opposition between Green Gables and the rest of Avonlea. This dialectic is summarized in the description of the brook in the novel's first paragraph:

> [the] brook had its source away back in the woods of the old Cuthbert place; it was reputed to be an intricate, headlong brook in its earlier course through these woods, with dark secrets of pool and cascade; but by the time it reached Lynde's Hollow it was a quiet, well-conducted little stream, for not even a brook could run past Mrs. Lynde's door without a due regard for decency and decorum. (1)

Similarly, when the avidly curious Rachel Lynde goes to Green Gables to unravel the mystery of Matthew's buggy trip, the narrator observes that

> where the Cuthberts lived was a scant quarter of a mile up the road from

Lynde's Hollow. To be sure, the long lane made it a good deal further. Matthew Cuthbert's father, as shy and silent as his son after him, had got as far away as he possibly could from his fellow men without actually retreating into the woods when he founded his homestead. Green Gables was built at the furthest edge of his cleared land and there it was to this day, barely visible from the main road along which all the other Avonlea houses were so sociably situated. Mrs. Rachel Lynde did not call living in such a place *living* at all.

"It's just *staying*, that's what," she said as she stepped along the deep-rutted, grassy lane bordered with wild rose bushes. (3–4)

Green Gables is a place where nature has not yet been totally tamed by Avonlea's stultifying values, where brook and wild rose bushes can thrive and be true to themselves, where Anne will be able to find an empathetic natural environment.

Into this world comes Anne, attuned to nature and the powers of the imagination—an outstanding example of the child as conceived of by the Romantic poets (also suggested by the allusions to Wordsworth, etc., in the novel). She begins by appreciating the beauties of Nature she sees around her and renaming the geographical features—e.g. the White Way of Delight and the Lake of Shining Waters—that she encounters on her initial trip to Green Gables. Once there, she continues the naming process, extending it to individual trees and flowers and even to her own identity: she later says to herself that "it's a million times nicer to be Anne of Green Gables than Anne of nowhere in particular, isn't it?" (65) In the act of naming she is claiming the landscape, putting her mark on it, and internalizing and representing its values—values that she links with herself and the brook (17, 35, 38). And she brings those values of Nature—life and beauty—into the closed-up Cuthbert house. On her first morning she opens the resistant window (33) of her sterile, rigid room (29–30) and lets in the beautiful sights and aromatic scents and joyous sounds of the outside world (34). Later, when told to learn the Lord's Prayer, she props the printed prayer-card "against the jugful of apple blossoms she had brought in to decorate the dinner-table—Marilla had eyed that decoration askance, but had said nothing" (61). This combination symbolizes the idea that a healthy Christianity has room for the values associated with nature—beauty and vitality and life—as well as the printed word. This message is reinforced when Anne first attends church in a hat decorated with flowers: she is bringing her values into the church and is helping revivify Avonlea religious services which have become stultified, as Marilla herself admits at the end of Chapter Eleven (87). It is no accident that the text for that sermon is, ironically, Jesus's words to the Church in Revelations 3: 2–3: "Wake up, and strengthen the things that remain, which were about to die; for I have not found your deeds completed in the sight of My God. Remember therefore what you have received and heard; and keep it, and repent." The message to the congregation and minister—to apply their faith and not to let it stagnate—is one that Anne with her hat is visibly representing: she is the little child that shall lead them—all, of course, in accordance with the earlier message of the "Christ Blessing Little Children" picture.

As time goes on, both Matthew and Marilla are awakened and transformed by the values associated with Anne. In Mrs. Lynde's words about Matthew and Anne, "That man is waking up after being asleep for over sixty years" (212); St. Cuthbert, incidentally, was a hermit, with some parallels in Matthew and the comparatively isolated Cuthbert house. As for Marilla, whose name and role can be linked with that of the Virgin Mary, mother of the Child Jesus who brings salvation to the world, she learns the joys of life under Anne's influence: first she is moved to release reluctant, rusty smiles, then laughter, and, eventually, by the novel's final chapters, she is able to voice her deep love for Anne. "It's never been easy for me to say things out of my heart, but . . . I love you as dear as if you were my own flesh and blood and you've been my joy and comfort ever since you came to Green Gables" (316). Indeed, Anne's budding romance with Gilbert is a symbolic surrogate—a younger generation's resurrection—of Marilla's blighted romance with Gilbert's father (she had let a minor quarrel escalate so that life passed her by for many decades). In this regard the parallel between Anne's name (meaning "grace") and that of Anne the mother of the Virgin Mary may indicate an oblique cyclic reference to the prefatory passage of Wordsworth's "Intimations Ode" ("The child is father [mother] of the man [woman] . . ."), a poem also used as the source of Montgomery's title for Chapter Thirty-Six.

Important too is that Avonlea as well as Anne experiences transformation. The dialectical opposition between Green Gables and Avonlea is resolved into a new synthesis, as Anne, the Cuthberts, and Green Gables are integrated into an Avonlea society that is itself significantly altered by the values associated with Anne. The former minister and the former teacher leave and are replaced by kindred spirits, hence church and school are changed; the lives of Anne's school chums are transformed by her imaginative play with them; and even such authority figures as Mrs. Rachel Lynde and Aunt Josephine Barry are positively influenced by Anne. Thus, by the novel's end, Anne, the outsider representing the world of the imagination, and the beauty and life associated with nature, has become an integral part of the changed Avonlea world—and it is to her that the School Board entrusts the responsibility of guiding the future of Avonlea youth as their teacher. As well, her presence by the window at the novel's end symbolically supplants the presence of Mrs. Lynde at the window at the novel's beginning: Anne's wider vision has replaced Rachel's narrow one. Anne's original values, based in nature and the imagination, have subsequently been enriched by Christian love and ethics, and Anne's concomitant mental, moral, social, and spiritual growth, have accordingly both merged with, and transformed, the community of Avonlea.

NOTES

1.   Compare Montgomery's comment, in her *Journals*, in November 1907: "when I left the lane I . . . felt as if I had escaped from some fascinating but not altogether hallowed locality—a place still given over to paganism and the revels of fauns and satyrs. None of the wild places are ever wholly Christianized in the darkness . . ." (1:332).

WORKS CITED

The Bible (NASB translation).
Eggleston, Wilfrid, ed. *The Green Gables Letters from L. M. Montgomery to Ephraim Weber,* 1905–1909. Second Edition. Ottawa: Borealis Press, 1981.
Montgomery, L. M. *Anne of Green Gables.* 1908. First Canadian Edition. Toronto: Ryerson Press, 1942.
———. *The Selected Journals of L. M. Montgomery, Volume I: 1889–1910.* Eds. Mary Rubio and Elizabeth Waterston. Toronto: Oxford University Press, 1985.

———. *The Selected Journals of L. M. Montgomery, Volume II: 1910–1921*. Eds. Mary Rubio and Elizabeth Waterston. Toronto: Oxford University Press, 1985 and 1987.

Wordsworth, William. *Poetical Works*. Ed. Thomas Hutchinson, rev. Ernest De Selincourt. London: Oxford University Press, 1950.

The Picture Book: A Commentary

JANET LUNN

I HAVE PUBLISHED FOUR PICTURE BOOKS and two illustrated stories in picture book format. Generally I write for older children and, when I consider the work of Michael Solomon, the art director of so many fine picture books or the picture books written and illustrated by Marie-Louise Gay, I know myself to be an apprentice. But then I have known this for some time. Years ago I was a reviewer of children's books—I still am, once in a while—and I know how a picture book should work, but knowing how it should work and getting it to work are very different.

The first problem is brevity. Think of great picture books like *Goodnight Moon, Harry the Dirty Dog* or *Red is Best*. There's not an extra word in any of them. Brevity. For one thing young children can't —or won't—listen to a long, wordy story so every word, every single one, has to matter. What's more, the rhythm of those words must be as strong as it is in a poem. Only think of Maurice Sendak's *Where the Wild Things Are*. I defy you to take a single word out of that book without losing something important.

The man who sent his friend a letter, apologizing at the end by saying, "I'm sorry this letter is so long, I hadn't time for a brief one," might have been speaking for me in my efforts at picture book writing. I haven't yet brought off brevity. When I read my picture book stories to children, I can see, at once, that there are too many words and I always pull some out as I read. I may never achieve the kind of distilled language the genre demands—not the way Maurice Sendak or Margaret Wise Brown have done—but I know what I'm striving for. My job is to write my story—over and over and over—until I have some degree of confidence that it's the best sketch I can make for what's going to be the written half of a picture book.

Then comes the second problem. This is one Marie-Louise Gay and other writers like her who are also visual artists don't have. I can't draw, or paint, or create pictures in collage, plasticine or any other medium. I have to trust an artist to create the other half of the book. The problem is that, in the course of writing the story, I've conjured up a vision of its characters and setting. I've thought of scenes I'd let my pencil dream over if I could draw. I've all but polished off the whole book in my imagination.

The artist is bound to have a different vision. This can be painful for the writer. Of the four picture books I've had published, two have been with Kim La Fave, *Amos's Sweater* and *Duck Cakes for Sale*, one, *The Umbrella Party* with Kady MacDonald Denton, and one, *Come to the Fair*, with Gilles Pelletier. This last one was constructed differently, so I'll talk about it separately, but the others are good illustrations of what I mean—especially *Amos's Sweater*.

This is how the procedure works. The writer takes a story to a publisher. If the picture book editor thinks it will make a saleable book, he/she will set about to find an artist. If the writer is an established writer, he/she will be in on the consultation. That doesn't always mean complete freedom of choice, it often means only the right to veto an unacceptable choice. The choice gets made, the artist makes his/her pictures then, when the writer and artist have completed their work—or, at least have neared completion of it—the designer is invited in to move the words and pictures around until they make an artistic whole. That's Michael's job.[1]

When I'd done all I could with the writing of my sheep story, *Amos's Sweater*, I took it to Patsy Aldana at Groundwood. She liked it and we discussed possible artists. I suggested Kim La Fave because I had liked the pictures in Judith Saltman's and his *Goldie and the Sea*. Patsy agreed and we shipped the story off to Kim. He liked it and, pronto, created a watercolour of a large, white, fluffy, self-satisfied-looking sheep.

Patsy liked the picture. I liked the picture. I did not like the picture for my story. I'd written about a sheep I really knew, a small, grey, grumpy old ram who belonged to my friend Peg Fraser on her farm in Vermont.

Peg had made me a shawl from Amos's undyed wool (it's grey and grumpy, too). I'd taken a lot of photographs of Amos and I'd sent them all to Kim. So why had he elected to send back an image of this big, white imposter?

I called Kim on the phone. "I like your sheep," I said politely. It was true, I did like it. It just wasn't my Amos (by this time, I was thinking about him as my Amos, you'll notice). And I told Kim that. Quite firmly.

"Well . . ." Kim sounded cautious, "I like your story, too, and it's brought a lot of picture ideas to mind and I think this sheep will work a lot better with what I'm planning on doing."

I began to argue with him. Then I remembered the argument I'd had with the artist friend who had done some tentative drawings for this story a couple of years back; he had died before anything could come of our partnership. This friend was not a man who'd ever drawn pictures for children's books and he'd objected strenuously when I'd asked him to draw Amos looking angry. "Sheep don't look angry; they're not people," he said. He should have known Amos.

"They do in picture books," I said and we'd had a long—quite heated—discussion about pictures in animal-study books and pictures in books for children. It suddenly occurred to me while I was talking to Kim La Fave that, if I didn't want him to tell me how to write my story, I'd better not tell him how to make his pictures. His Amos did not have to look exactly like my Amos; I gave up—not without pain, though—and waited anxiously for more sketches.

He made a whole series of sketches, doing exactly what Marie-Louise Gay described as the artist's process with a new story: he let ideas sift through his imagination, trying them all out on paper. His ideas were definitely not the same as the ones I'd had. They were better. I certainly hadn't imagined Amos naked and blue and covered with Band-Aids. That picture got across the misery and embarrassment the Amos of my story would feel with his wool shorn better than a whole page of words could possibly have done. At once I could see that Kim was right about the big, white sheep.

In *Duck Cakes for Sale*, the second book Kim and I made together, Kim put Amos in his sweater in a field in view of the little white house where he'd put the old woman in the new story. The words don't have to say that the old woman has moved to a house near the farm where Amos lives.

When Kady Denton and I made *The Umbrella Party* together we faxed rough drafts of story and pictures back and forth many times, discussing the characters, their relationships, and the story's setting. What happened was a sort of counterpoint between the artist's drawings and writer's words. It was lovely working this way and I must say that it was a great pleasure working that closely with Kady Denton.

It's not the only way to work, of course. There have been many brilliant collaborations between artists and writers who have never met one another. Most editors prefer that, I think because they feel that it gives them better control of the book. There have been collaborations when one of the partners has been dead for years. Two of Frank Stockton's stories were illustrated by Maurice Sendak in the 1960s when Stockton had been dead at least sixty years—and, of course, the age-old fairy tales are always being illustrated anew. As Marie-Louise said with Rumplestiltskin, "this is a very old story and the story you can't change but you can bring a whole new feel to the story by the kind of pictures you're making."

I've always been happy to be the one creating the idea for the picture book and I've often wondered how the artist feels getting a story to work with that can't, essentially, be changed. I know how it feels now because I was sent the completed pictures for *Come to the Fair* and asked to write a story for them. It was a challenge. Gilles Pelletier is a French-Canadian artist and his pictures for this fall-fair story have a very French-Canadian flavour. They're strong, bold, and colourful and I love them. But I live in Ontario and our fall fairs are not exactly the same as the ones in Quebec. The ingredients are all there— the jams, pickles, pies, pumpkins, the cattle judging, and the horse races—but the farms and villages are different. My job was to write the words for the story of a family's day at the fair that would work in both French and English. I chose to call the family Martin. I was very careful about the names of both neighbors and pets and I did not mention the farms or villages—but then, M. Pelletier's pictures were telling that story, so I didn't really need to. I laboured long and hard over the story, appreciating, more and more, with every passing moment, the difficulties artists face when given a story they cannot change but must mold and enlarge with their pictures. I think that *Come to the Fair* works, but it works because of Gilles Pelletier's pictures. All I really managed to do was write cut lines for them.

When I look at a picture book in which the artist has added characters and action that are not in the words, I feel satisfied with the story. Marie-Louise Gay always has characters in her books that have a pictorial story all their own. They complete the story the words have started. In fact, in good picture books, the words and pictures have to be true partners. The story may exist without its pictures, but it's thin, incomplete, unsatisfying. It's just as true for the pictures. Only imagine *Where the Wild Things Are* without either its pictures or its words or Jan Andrews's and Ian Wallace's *The Very Last First Time* or any of Maryann Kovalski's books. There are exceptions, of course. We all know *Good Dog Carl*, for instance, and there are a great many picture book stories that will stand alone, but the best picture books are a good marriage of pictures and story.

In other words, a picture book is not an illustrated story. The pictures in an illustrated story enhance the story, but they do not complete it and they, unlike the story, will not stand alone, not as stories. When I was a child, most of the books I read had illustrations in them. I loved those pictures. They were the artist's idea of what the characters and their settings looked like. Jessie Wilcox Smith's illustrations for *Little Women*, *Heidi*, and *A Child's Garden of Verses* helped to bring those books to life for me, but they did not, in any way, help to create the story.

There are still illustrated books for children. These are not the novels for the *Little Women*-aged children, unless they are novels in deluxe editions, but there are illustrations in stories for younger children. Ann Blades' pictures in both Betty Waterton's *Pettranella* and Sue Ann Alderson's *Ida and the Wool Smugglers*, for example, are illustrations for story books, not the visual portions of picture books. But, even in books like these, the illustrator sometimes does a bit of freelancing. In my own story, *One Hundred Shining Candles*, Lindsay Grater added a splendid cat who is not in the story I wrote. He has his own part in the finished book, though, and he's a great addition. Even so, the story still works on its own as it was meant to do and the pictures don't—as they weren't meant to do.

I love picture books and I think the true picture book is a high art form, aesthetically and emotionally satisfying. I also think that few picture books ever achieve this high art form, the standard their young audience demand of them. Only think about how many handsome but over-illustrated, over-written picture books lie discarded on the nursery floor while the children who left them there pore over *Goodnight Moon*, *Harry the Dirty Dog*, or *Red is Best*. There are so many lessons to be learned from these wonderful, simple, straightforward books both for you who choose them or write about them and for us who write and create pictures for them that I can only be grateful for them.

Thank you for giving me this chance to talk about one of my favourite subjects.

NOTE

1.   Janet Lunn's commentary is a transcription from a brief talk given at a panel discussion with Marie-Louise Gay and Michael Solomon held during the Canadian Children's Literature Symposium.

Publishing Children's Picture Books: The Role of Design and Art Direction

MICHAEL SOLOMON

A FREQUENTLY ENCOUNTERED RECURRING THEME in the self-perception of graphic designers seems to be that encapsulated in Rodney Dangerfield's famous formula. A recent column by Roy Behrens, a professor of art and teacher of design history, asks why it is that architects, playwrights, composers, actors, choreographers, even fashion designers are known to a general audience outside their fields, and are even widely celebrated, but graphic designers rarely are so recognized. Behrens's article makes a good attempt at answering this question, for his theme is the "transparency" which has always been held as the rigorous and chastening ideal of the typographer's art. We don't get no respect because at our best we do work that lives up to this ideal of transparency—the page design is to be a neutral, unobtrusive medium for the transmission of the author's thought. Nor are we, like an author, the primary producers of a work of art but rather the servant of the writer, illustrator, photographer, and, most important, the reader. The temptation designers feel to struggle against the constraints of transparency are indeed great. That way perhaps lies glory. And a great deal of the typography of the last twenty years has been characterized by a radical self-assertion, seemingly motivated expressly in reaction to transparency and sensitivity. Art, of course, may advance by means of such reactions. Conversely typography's tradition may stand as a constant rule and critique against what we may call "opacity" and design self-expression. This is a real critique based in a living tradition. Typography's conservatism is essential and organic. When we bring adverse judgement against an exemplar of the anti-transparent tendency we may use as our standard examples that are tried and true in an era now over five hundred years long. The history of typography is the history of fashions and innovations as well, but its conservative tradition is embodied in the type designs and techniques that have not fallen into disuse or curiosity or quaintness, but have managed to stay the course and weather trends and pressures even to the practice of today. It was apt and sharply descriptive of typographic practice that D. B. Updike subtitled his classic history of printing types "A Study of Survivals."

So the tradition, being a vital one, permits us to enjoy and work creatively within its limits. As I take my place beside Janet Lunn and Marie-Louise Gay, two of the great "primary producers"—to use a term for, I promise, the last time—I am reminded of how great is the reward of servitude to the reading public, of allowing the art of design silently to bring, a rich, literary, and illustrative art to life through the book.[1]

If the Dangerfield syndrome is thus rendered less painful, there remains another theme that haunts the designer's biography that was brought back to me anew, when I read, I think in *Adobe* magazine in a brief throwaway line by a designer now approaching a well-established phase of her career, of her sudden realization that it no longer concerned her to make the Herculean effort of explaining to her parents what it was exactly that she did for a living. She is referring—it came to me with some force— to a very real fact of life. I remember the looks I too would attract when I attempted an apologia of my nine-to-five (in those days more like nine-to-nine) job; in some few cases the eyes of the hearer would glaze over—this was clearly diagnostic and I would gratefully shut up. But more often the looks were of incredulity or suspicion that seemed to accuse me of pulling off some sort of rare scam. "Let me get this straight," would begin the comfortable listener possessed of a real job. "You don't make the pictures, you don't set the type, you don't edit texts, you don't print the books, you certainly don't write them—so what exactly is it . . .?" Then there was the danger to merely polite inquirers of being frightened off by my attempt at an answer. I remember once being asked by an uncle of mine the same heavy question, and I, being of course in my first innocent design youth, began the disquisition which always held so much charm for me, but which, I was too new to be anything like aware, caused so much doubt and misgivings in the layperson. Duly interrupting my patient lecture, he turned to my father and exclaimed, "Gee, ask a guy the time and he tells you how to make a watch!"

Time wounds all heels. And in time I've grown content with the obscurity in which I dwell. For it is the rich and abounding shade of any long-lived and arcane art—and arcane indeed are the further reaches and inlets of typography. The terms themselves are proof of both age and complexity. There are, for instance, the terms that, even though some may date back the nearly five-and-a-half centuries since Gutenberg set up shop, still survive in the lexicon of the personal computer and desk-top publishing software: words like "font," "roman," "italic," "small caps," "leading," "measure," "rule." Then there are the words that any educated person will have a grasp of, but yet whose typographic definitions will almost certainly be different from those automatically called to mind: I mean pitfalls such as "gothic," "folio," "colour," "modern," "antiqua," and "grotesque." Finally there are the great lost words—words with which only the bibliographer, paleographer, or typographic historian will be on friendly terms: "Aldine," "nonpareil," "Paragon," "lettre batarde," "lettre de forme," "Didot point."

I mention these intoxicating words only to suggest something of the charm that the book arts can exert on the susceptible. Many an unlikely one otherwise gainfully engaged has proven so. I will conclude my introductory remarks with the oft-quoted words of one of the great book-men who fell under the spell. John Baskerville was an eighteenth-century artisan and businessman of Birmingham who enjoyed a great success in the production of fine engraved metalwork and japanned (lacquer) ware. These words are preserved in a great many histories of the book. He wrote:

> Amongst the several mechanic arts that have engaged my attention, there is no one which I have pursued with so much steadiness and pleasure, as that of letter-founding. Having been an early admirer of the beauty of letters, I became insensibly desirous of contributing to the perfection of them.

Birmingham was for the eighteenth century what we should call today a high tech centre, and because he had already made his fortune,

Baskerville was able to satisfy his insatiable desire by establishing not only a type foundry and printing office but also a paper mill where he invented the technique of pressing the wet sheets between heated copper plates to produce an unheard of silky smooth finish, which contributed nearly as much as his letter designs to advancing the book arts to a new stage. The paper itself was the last word in suave luxury, and the *éditions de luxe* that came from his shop were the envy of the continent for several decades.

For me, of course, page design takes place not in the grimy industrial setting of a printing plant but in the overstuffed and creaking offices of a children's book publisher. I have been art director at Groundwood for six years, but for seventeen years before that I freelanced, becoming a children's book specialist for reasons a bit obscure to me now but which I cover with the expression "by default." Groundwood's publisher, Patricia Aldana, asked me to design some picture books in the inaugural season, and so my association with Groundwood really goes back to the beginning—twenty-one years ago. I took on a wider variety of projects over the years, adding fiction and non-fiction, poetry and music books, but picture books remain my most absorbing challenge.

Now I am part of the editorial department where two or three decades before much of what I do might have been (indeed was) conducted in an attic studio. The small computer and numerous other developments, most important perhaps the dissemination of Adobe's Postscript language and the software products developed from and dependent on it, mean that many of the tasks that once would have been performed in an industrial setting—including typesetting itself—have now moved under the publisher's or designer's roof (where they were performed in the days following Gutenberg when printer, publisher, and bookseller were one thing or very intimately allied).

Once I have received an edited picture book manuscript (usually now already captured on diskette in a word-processing program), I create a complete page layout on the computer with many determinations, such as the editor's (sometimes my) page breaks, fonts, sizes, measure, leading, and the grid (comprising text and picture column placement, margins, and bleeds) made but not "carved in stone." For this layout is then sent to the illustrator, with the overriding proviso that all of this, though professional and final-looking, should be treated only as a starting point. I am asking the artist to try it on for size and to determine how my format and arrangement suits his or her compositional, technical, and stylistic intentions. I will sometimes incorporate sketches to make clear how I envisaged the impending pictures' engagement with the dramatic and narrative episodes, and I will also note my sense of the degree of uniformity, variety, and rhythm among the pictures. I might judge, for example, as follows: "We have before us a long, noble tale with an apparent fairy tale lineage; I see the text running in full-page columns interrupted now and again by full-page, full-colour paintings which fix on and interpret the most dramatic or romantic moments. Look at a classic Anglo-American fairy tale from the turn of the century." Or I might advise: "This is a sprightly comic fable, the characters are madcap performers with personality to burn. Furthermore the illustrator's style is quirky, light, rapid, calligraphic, with a dynamic sense of rhythm and design. Let's make only one third of the pictures full-page quads with full palette and saturated coverage right to the edges; the rest of the pictures will be free, open-edged vignettes of characters and objects and bits of setting and atmosphere disposed against the white of the page and poised above, below, beside and even among the spidery lines of type." Of course the illustrator will often report back with an entirely different conception, often radically different, so that I will have to recast the entire layout, instructing the artist meanwhile to proceed with rough sketches and compositions but not to fall in love with any particular arrangement until I can catch up and supply a tightly corresponding layout. I insist on the parallel development of the type layout, because I've learned that many illustrators in their enthusiasm for their compositional and storytelling solutions will conveniently ignore or wish away text if it seems at all tentative or is not firmly part of the page design in uncompromising and uncompromisable black and white.

After I have reviewed and approved the thumbnails and storybreaks with author and editor, the illustrator next proceeds to draw full-size pencil roughs, and often a sample final to show intended medium and technique. This sample can be studied and tested by the prepress suppliers and printer in advance of the artist's undertaking the bulk of the work; the printer's timely advice has been known to assist in avoiding peril and preventing heartache. Some artists stick to a well-loved technique that yields reliably colour-separable and printable art for project after project. Others audaciously make the adoption of a new medium or technique a crucial part of their interpretive strategy when face to face with a fresh new story.

Of the illustrators I have worked with over many years I would name Harvey Chan and Ian Wallace as the most restless and questing in this regard. Such artists can especially benefit from trouble-shooting and proofing a fully executed sample at scanning film and press stages.

An artist will work from three months to more than a year on a typical thirty-two-page picture book. The entire process from receipt of manuscript to finding the right illustrator, to printed and bound book may in fact take two to three years, and sometimes even longer.

When the corrected, approved art work is finally received at our office, the pictures are prepared for scanning and colour separation, sized and coordinated with the digital layout file, and sent to the printer. Most of our full-colour picture books are manufactured, for reasons of optimum balance of quality and economy, in the Far East. (Illustrated first novels, junior and young adult fiction, and non-fiction with black and white or non-critical colour illustrations, whether paperbacks or hardcovers, are all produced in Canada.) Our Chinese printer will show us press proofs, that is, printed proofs on the specified stock, in reader's spreads, even bound—on special request—into dummy books. Author, artist, editor, publisher, sales manager, prospective domestic and foreign co-editors, major buyers, and, of course, I, all get a chance to examine the proofs for accuracy, colour and tonal fidelity, general attractiveness, etc. Adjustments and corrections are shown if necessary in second proofs. Once the proofs are approved and all co-editions integrated, the button is pushed, and printing, binding, and shipping of the finished books ensue.

These are the bare outlines of the designer's role. According to my business card, I wear an art director's hat as well, but because I design most of the children's list and nearly all of the picture books, it is not easy to distinguish between the two roles. The description above of my original conceptions of the look and pacing of an illustrated book is a large part of the quasi-editorial activity that belongs under the rubric of art direction. My art director self does have the wisdom to tell my designer self to kick back and give it a rest when working on a picture book by the likes of Marie-Louise Gay, whose spare, bright, and lively design sense informs her work right from its earliest manifestation, usually as a complete and detailed folded, gathered, and sewn thumbnail dummy. I'm more than content to contrive a type arrangement that agrees as closely as possible to her design, with usually slight tweaking or refinements for the purposes of legibility or conformity to the admittedly rather wide and open tracts of the house picture book style. For both her *Rumpelstiltskin* and *Stella, Star of the Sea,* I made the digital pages match her careful and unfussy layout, even to the point of adopting (for Stella) a light, sans-serif type of uniformly weighted stroke for the reading text. I chose, however, Futura rather than the Avant Garde shown in her sketches. Avant Garde's genesis was as a display font for magazines and advertising; it suffers from serious legibility problems that are admittedly not as grievous when it is deployed in one or two lines of 16-point but I'm averse to using any type or setting for young readers where word-recognition and word-group cohesion is compromised. But even my choice was scrapped after the strong objections of the picture book editor. Patricia Aldana harbours a strong distaste for any sans-serifs in juvenile text-settings. I, on the other hand, am fascinated by sans-serifs, and, intrigued by Marie-Louise Gay's layout, saw it as a rare opportunity for an appropriate deployment. Insofar as the strict requirements for legibility go, the editor is right. Although specially adapted sans-serifs are still used in earliest school readers where letter discrimination is crucial, as soon as reading fluency begins, children contend with serif types whereby word recognition and phrase and sentence cohesion are all assisted. (When I worked in educational publishing some ten years ago the rule seemed to be to commence the use of serif fonts—albeit sometimes with special characters—at the Grade Two level.) And so, for *Stella*, I switched to Old Style No. 7, a charming Modern with bracketed serifs and a family resemblance to a line of early reader and primer fonts. In the Futura I was looking for a certain contrast between type and illustration, though a gentle one. With the Old Style No. 7, with its thick-thin contrasts, the result is closer to a harmony with the lively lines and transparent tones of the pictures. But in either case something of the unfussy spareness and innocence of Marie-Louise Gay's mock-up was answered.

I have spoken about design's concern with being sensitive to the artist's creative expression. But I would be giving a falsely generous impression of freedom if I did not duly contract the horizons somewhat by acknowledging the constraining influences that the business of publishing and international publishing bring to the designer's activity.

If the designer's responsibility includes the overall appearance of the book and the care brought to the sensitive yoking together of story and picture and typographic treatment, the art director moreover looks at all of the publisher's books as a whole (the list), and imparts to it a look that embodies or reflects the publisher's philosophy and mission. This may mean the strict application of a strong "corporate" identity to be jealously guarded from raids by imitators. In Groundwood's case, the individuality of the books is apparent, but still they do manage to participate in a "Groundwood look" especially in the medium- and large-format picture books; our emphasis on literarily excellent stories and high-quality illustration are given a stable visual "home."

Book design is constantly tried and tested in numerous markets—the trade, libraries, wholesalers, book clubs—at home and in the United States. Covers and jackets especially, which are regarded more as advertising vehicles than as integral parts of the book, are very often subject to revision after they are seen in mock-up form by buyers. Reports come back to me from the sales and marketing managers on their return from trade fairs and distributors' offices. Our American distribution initiative, having reached a critical scale in the past few years, is particularly influential on design practice. The U.S. sales force was recently asked to consider my cover proposal for a rather unusual non-fiction picture book, a photo essay on the children in a small village in Guatemala who make great tissue paper kites and fly them each year on the Day of the Dead. In my design I showed not a kite entire, but a close-up of the gorgeous multi-coloured tissue paper collage that forms the webbing. Moreover the pattern was shown masked by the title lettering so that the title itself appeared made of the coloured paper, and allowed to glow through a black background in the style of a stained-glass window. It made for a clean and striking design but was too abstract, the American buyers thought, for the young audience. They felt that a book about kites must have an entire, readily-apprehendable kite on the cover. I went back to the drawing board, computer, and a binder full of photographs, and came up with a new design that answered their main requirement, but that also, because a different photographic treatment was entailed, forced changes to type, composition, mechanical colours, even background, so that now we had an essentially white cover where before it had been black. The result was less sophisticated perhaps than the first version, but it was undeniably more readable, accessible, and above all, "younger."

Similarly, and perhaps to a greater extent, since it is forming an increasing part of our business, the sale of foreign rights has an influence on design and execution decisions. We've learned, for example, to curb enthusiasm for colored title type or lettering, and to instruct illustrators to be sure to keep to a separate overlay any English-language lettering that forms a part of the pictures, so that it may be scanned separately and combined on the press with the black language plate, overprinting the four-colour image rather than being enmeshed in the picture's web of coloured ink dots. This permits foreign editors to buy the four-colour film or digital files untouched by English and easily to insert text in the territorial language.

Bologna, Italy is well-known and much loved by publishers as the venue for the most important fair at which children's book rights are traded. Held in late March or early April every year, it is attended by publishers, foreign rights professionals, editors, agents, and occasionally authors and illustrators, and produces for me an annual report on our offerings by a foreign jury that is often surprising, sometimes dismaying, but always interesting. Every year, we and many other Canadian publishers increasingly sell rights abroad. For us Scandinavia, France, and Germany have proved our steadiest buyers of fiction, non-fiction, and picture books. And we have recently expanded our initiatives to include commerce with Spanish- and Portuguese-language publishers in the Western Hemisphere.

I have hinted already at how cost restraints—our current commitment to four-colour printing in Asia being indicative—limit design exuberance. The exposure to markets around the world has intensified the cost squeeze that publishers have eternally faced: the demand to keep quality high and prices low. Opulent and expensive effects and processes are generally avoided. When we use foil stamping, fluorescent inks, or other extra colours, it is for carefully weighed editorial reasons, never merely for the sake of glamour. Sometimes, for example, the requirement to keep to black text only is felt to be too inhibiting of a desired effect of colour harmony, and so a fifth spot colour may be run to carry type and lettering, yet still leave the four-colour plates untainted by English. As producers of high-quality, low cost books, we are compelled to concentrate our resources in the areas of faithful reproduction, good but not extravagant paper, and bindings strong enough to meet the standards of institutional book buyers.

NOTE

1.   Michael Solomon's contribution was part of a panel discussion on the picture book with Marie-Louise Gay and Janet Lunn at the Canadian Children's Literature Symposium.

The Changing Faces of Canadian Children: Pictures, Power, and Pedagogy

ANDREA MCKENZIE

W E'RE ALL AWARE OF THE OLD CLICHÉ, "Don't judge a book by its cover." But the cover of an unknown work can attract us with its visual design, and the illustrations often draw us further into the work. Who hasn't read a page or so of the work and then flipped through the pictures to get an idea of the story or worth of the text? Although we know that the pictures sometimes don't reflect the text, they contain values and implications that we consciously or unconsciously agree or disagree with, and that can make us drop the book on the spot or take it home with us. Illustrations, however, continue to be downplayed in favour of the text. Arguing against this subordination of image to text, Gunther Kress and Theo van Leeuwen contend that "language and visual communication both realize the same . . . fundamental and far-reaching systems of meaning that constitute our culture, each by means of its own specific forms, and independently" (1990, 4). Illustrations are not merely adjuncts to the text, but can, as well-known illustrations of children's text demonstrate, influence the development of attitudes and values: text and illustrations dynamically interact, each shaping future narratives, both in pictures and in words. Children and stories targeted at children are of particular concern, especially because the images used usually replicate the popular social values and moral attitudes of the times and of the culture, often without the realization that the child is unconsciously absorbing these values and attitudes from the images presented. As Perry Nodelman argues, "Whether we are conscious of it or not, illustrations always convey information, not just about what things look like, but how we should understand and what we should feel about the things depicted" (1993, 6). Although we're much more conscious today of visual imagery and visual literacy, why, given that the images conveyed in movies, television, and on the World Wide Web are obvious targets of concern, do we still largely ignore book illustrations? Kress and van Leeuwen argue that societies where written language predominates suppress visual literacy, because it is seen as "a threat; a sign of the decline of culture" and is seen as a "non-literate," or more "oral and primitive" form of communication (1990, 3). The growing dominance of images means that unpacking not just the artistic composition of the image, but the power relations and meanings of pictures and their reverberations in the text, has become increasingly urgent. In fact, "visual literacy should be an equal partner along with verbal literacy or mathematical literacy in the education of children" (Schwartz and Sommerfeld 1990, 26).

Canada is a country still in transition, both in our literature and in our landscape. For children reading, the images of children as they interact with the landscape, according to Kress and van Leeuwen's theory, form a path separate from the literature in developing attitudes and images about the country and their place in its society. Authors such as L. M. Montgomery and Ernest Thompson Seton, growing up before the turn of the century, had few books that, in text or in illustration, depicted the land that they knew, or themselves as they acted and interacted with the land. Their books, when they in turn grew up, depicted Canada as it had not been seen before: Canada as perceived by Canadians. These authors and others transformed the land in their literature; as this paper shows, however, the illustrations that accompanied their books sometimes worked with, and sometimes against, the vision they upheld. Using Kress and van Leeuwen's "grammar" of visual rhetoric to examine the composition, planes, participant perspectives, presence, and exclusion, this paper demonstrates how images can communicate subtle and influential messages of power, place, and presence or absence to the child reader. In particular, I explore illustrations of representative Canadian children's literature before and shortly after the turn of the century, demonstrating the changing landscape of Canada and children's place in it.

Kress and van Leeuwen, influenced by Michael Halliday, summarize their theory that "pictures, like language, can realize not only representations, but also interactions, and . . . can cohere together into texts" (1990, 21), by examining three aspects of visual grammar: the ideational, the interpersonal, and the textual. Ideational metafunctions can be read by examining the "symmetrical arrangements" and vectors to discover "ways of relating represented participants" in the pictures. Interpersonal metafunctions, "a range of ways of relating interactive participants," can be explored by looking at the direction of the depicted person's gaze at the viewer and the perspective and angles at which the illustration is depicted. And finally, the "horizontal and vertical placement" and the characteristics of the represented elements determine the textual metafunctions (1990, 21). Each of these three areas contains its own more detailed methods of analysis, and the three work together to create a reading of the power relations of the illustration.

The cover and frontispiece of a children's book are attempts to immediately capture the potential reader's interest, and to engage him or her in the text. "Because pictures don't actually move," comments Perry Nodelman, "illustrators can choose one moment only of stopped action out of all the events the text accompanying it describes; and the ones they choose focus our attention on the events in a highly specific way" (1993, 21). Kress and van Leeuwen don't mention the part that choice plays in illustrations, but obviously the publisher, illustrator, and sometimes the author determine the images that define the genre of the text for the reader. For every picture included, a range of choices is omitted, much like our choice of words in theories of language. The cover and the frontispiece are representational, tools to engage our attention and draw us into the book, and so become crucial in how we envision the story without having read it.

The cover of *The Boy Tramps or Across Canada* by J. Macdonald Oxley, illustrated by Henry Sandham, provides an entry point to Kress and van Leeuwen's grammar of reading images. First, Kress and van Leeuwen stress the relation of the participants in and outside the picture: the people in the picture and the viewer's perspective. We discover where the viewer "stands" by looking at the perspective and the direction of the gaze in the actual picture. The boys in the picture are above the tiny picture of the city behind them, emphasized by the position of the clouds in the middle of the picture, as though they've conquered the city and left it

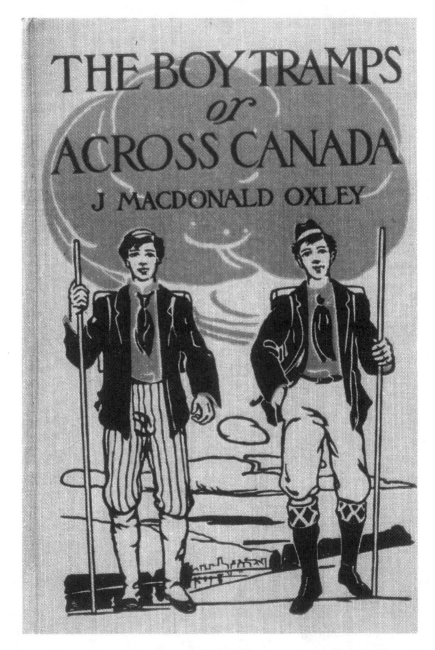

FIGURE 1.   Cover illustration: *The Boy Tramps or Across Canada*. Illustrator Henry Sandham. Edition copyright Musson Book, n.d.

behind, moving on to new, unknown country. Because of this downward perspective, the actual viewer is slightly above the boys, looking down on them. Next, the two boys in the picture are gazing out towards the viewer. The boy on the left gazes at an unknown object slightly to the right. If you look closely, the boy on the right is actually looking directly at the viewer, or potential reader. Both boys are smiling, looking pleasant, and both are stepping out of the solid line at the bottom that frames the picture towards the reader. These gestures—the direct engagement of the viewer by the boy on the right, the smiles, and the step out of the picture towards the reader—form what Kress and Leeuwen call a "demand," in which the reader is "asked imaginarily to enter a relation of social affinity with the represented participant(s)" (1990, 27). The lack of distinction between the two boys—they look the same, and are dressed alike, apart from the actual pattern of their clothes, and the hat that one wears—emphasizes their similarity as representational types: male, white, better class adolescents. Essentially, what this picture asks is that the reader—presumably a male, white, better class adolescent, or one who aspires to belong to that class—place himself in the picture and join the two boys in conquering this decontextualized, unknown country, literally "taking a step up" with them on their climb. There is no place in this picture for girls or for adolescents of other origins.

If the cover invites the reader inside by focusing on the boys, the frontispiece entices by focusing on the country. Here, if we look at perspective and the vectors formed by the relations of objects within the pictures, the railway line draws the viewer's gaze from the foreground and bottom to the top, where the mountains, clouded with mist, represent the unknown country and the site of adventure. The viewer is now placed, by the perspective, at the bottom of the picture gazing up, as the boys must, at the mountains. The telegraph line emphasizes the vanishing point of the railway; both serve as reminders that humankind's technology has conquered the wilderness, and that the boys follow this path. In this picture, neither boy gazes at the reader, and the mountains become the objects of contemplation. The viewer, of course, can always imagine himself as a third in the picture, about to enter it, behind the boys and just out of sight, but the demand for social engagement is not present. The boys' lack of action highlights the focus of the mountains, as does the play of sunshine and shadow: formidable, yet beckoning, a barrier to be climbed and a promise of adventure. This illustration shows a scene near the end of the book, when the

In the Gorge of Bear Creek. —P. 283.

Tramps.

FIGURE 2. Frontispiece illustration: *The Boy Tramps or Across Canada.* Illustrator Henry Sandham. Edition copyright Musson Book, n.d.

boys have travelled across most of Canada, and are at the last and hardest part of their journey—the tramp through the Rocky Mountains. The shift from the decontextualized city, which the boys have left behind on the cover, to sharply detailed mountains emphasizes the main structuring theme of the text. Oxley organizes the book by place: each new adventure, each new excitement, heralds another shift towards the west, away from the settled parts and on to the wilder sections of the country.

Oxley uses the ploy of a Scottish boy and an English boy, with distinctly developed characters, spending their summer in Canada. The imposition of boys from Britain allows Oxley to undercut the stereotype of Canada as uncultured and unrefined: in Montreal and Ottawa, the boys are impressed by the refinement and culture of the inhabitants, albeit the few they meet are extremely wealthy; they travel on trains that are far more comfortable than those back home; and they're constantly surprised by the quality of the people and the country. Unfortunately, few Canadians apparently inhabit the land Oxley describes so beautifully and accurately; even the ranchers the boys meet are younger sons of the British aristocracy. Farmers, townspeople, and native Canadians are not particularly well-treated; the Canadian girl or boy picking up this book would not find themselves or their parents in the text. Canada is a land to travel through, exclaim about, and leave. Canada is an adventure and a memory, but not a place to live.

Canada in illustrations is seen as a land of adventure in turn-of-the-century boys' books; Canada as pastoral is depicted in the works of the author whose name made the Canadian landscape known internationally: Lucy Maud Montgomery.

Montgomery's first books were published by L. C. Page and Company, a large American firm. Page seems to have already established visual conventions for his books: a beige cover, with the title and author's name in gold, and a portrait of the main character in a frame in the middle. Before the reader even picks up the book, the quality and type are already established. This pattern holds for *Anne of Green Gables*, although the portrait is unusual in that it's a side profile. This portrait has been described as a "typical Gibson Girl"; although she is "the epitome of American beauty" with "no suggestion of a vulnerable orphan waif" (Hutton and Jackson-Hutton 1999, 200), she is not a Gibson girl, for she lacks the typical pout and pose, though later Montgomery heroines were depicted as such.

FIGURE 3. Cover illustration: *Anne of Green Gables.* Illustrators M. A. and W. A. J. Claus. Edition copyright L. C. Page & Company, 1908. Twelfth impression, June 1909.

From Kress and van Leeuwen's perspective, the picture of Anne on the cover is a portrait, intended as a timeless, decontextualized image set in a frame to be studied; portraits "are about 'being,' and try to capture the timeless essence of a person," as opposed to showing us "particular moments in time" (1990, 74). Anne does not engage the viewer, but gazes away, presenting her profile to the viewer. No clothing gives away the time period; only the hair, richly waved and piled, indicates, as the painting of a portrait would in those times, wealth and status. This is no orphan or even country girl: this portrait is of a beautiful, classic, timeless adolescent, whose status is to be desired by the reader. However, part of the Gibson Girl pose was the frontal portrait, seen in illustrations as diverse as cold cream advertisements and First World War American recruitment posters. Part of the visual convention was the seductive pout and the pose; the hairstyle changed with the years, but the pose and the facial expression did not. Anne escapes these attributes, gazing perpetually into the distance and presenting that classic profile to the viewer. She presents no demand, for she does not look at us; instead, she offers herself to view.

If *Anne of Green Gables* is opened to the frontispiece, we discover that the world of the outdoors has disappeared: the image chosen by the publisher to represent the book is one of two girls obviously dressing for a party, which in turn makes it equally obvious that this book is one that is intended for girls. The outdoors is presented in the last three illustrations in the book. In the first, Anne is about to fall off the roof and break her ankle. In the second, Gilbert is rescuing Anne from the pond, which appears to be amazingly tranquil and unthreatening; despite its peacefulness, the female is threatened by the great outdoors. The sardonic comment that L. M. Montgomery made in her diary about the mistake the illustrator made in endowing Anne with "long hair" instead of "short curly ringlets" (Montgomery 1998, 195) fails to ask why the illustrator might have done so; it is, of course, traditional to depict a female in distress, especially one about to drown, with long, "streaming tresses" (Eggleston 1981, 73) to emphasize the romance of the rescue. Noticeably, Anne's rejection of the romance fails to show up. The third illustration again includes Gilbert, this time as the traditional suitor. Canada has become domesticated and gendered, confined to being seen out a kitchen window if a male is not present to mitigate its dangers. But worse is to follow.

The cover and frontispiece of the *Golden Road* depict Sara Stanley, the Story Girl, ready to travel to Europe. Here is the Gibson Girl in a typical pose, pouting seductively at the artist. This portrait, with its grown-up Sara, complete with rich hat, pompadour, and lace collar, epitomizes Kress and van Leeuwen's description of enticement, in which the represented figure "seductively pout[s] at the viewer, in which case the (supposedly male) viewer is asked imaginarily to 'possess' the represented participant" (1990, 27). In the case of women viewers, doubling takes place, as the viewer imagines herself as the object of the male gaze; she wants to enter the picture to become the represented image doing the seductive pouting and thus creating desire. The sexuality is subtle, but it is present; it also happens to be an American image of desire. We see a similar event in the frontispiece of *Anne of Avonlea*, which depicts a three-quarter portrait of Anne, arms raised to her hat, which only emphasizes her swan-like Gibson-girl figure, again gazing directly at the reader in a sexual demand stance.

How do these pictures affect the reader? The intended reader is obviously the adolescent girl, but we know that *Anne of Green Gables* and Montgomery's other works were read by men and women, girls and boys of many countries. The portraits on the covers would probably serve both as reassurance to middle and upperclass parents that values were not being undermined, and as an object of desire to younger readers. The sexuality is hidden: in *The Golden Road*, it is cut off at the neck and evident only in the expression. In *Anne of Avonlea*, the softened colours hint at romance, rather than sexuality, somewhat mitigating the demand. The directness of the gaze, however, engages the reader in social action. For the younger reader, especially of *Anne of Green Gables*, if the girl of the text can become this object and status symbol on the cover, so too can the girl in less affluent circumstances, whether she's from a small rural community or from a large city. The portraits reassure, yet demand.

Fortunately for Montgomery and Canada, Montgomery changed publishers in 1917, switching to the Canadian firm of McClelland, Goodchild, and Stewart. The new publisher presented an attractive cover, and repeated the same picture in full colour as the frontispiece, minus the flowery frame. No other illustrations were offered. *Anne's House of Dreams* is the first new depiction of Canada as pastoral and romanticized, but I've chosen to present *Emily of New Moon* because Emily is a child. M. L. Kirk, an American illustrator, did both covers, but managed to tone down the Americanization and status symbol aspect of the picture considerably. The established visual cues include the frame which forms part of the pic-

FIGURE 4.   Frontispiece illustration: *Anne of Avonlea*. Illustrator George Gibbs. Edition copyright L. C. Page & Company, 1909. First impression, September 1909.

ture, in this case a combination of flowers and filigree, which connect the title and author's name to the combined portrait/landscape. There is little perspective in this picture, except for the line of trees on the hill: Emily is the main focus, and the line of trees curves gently towards her. She does not engage our gaze, but gazes into the distance. She is herself placed to the right, in the world of the new, and if you look closely, you can see the faint image of a woman, probably the Wind Woman, immediately behind Emily, connecting Emily, nature, and the imagination as things of enchantment and beauty. The reader is not "invited" into this picture; no demand is made. The colours are muted and delicate, with the colours of the landscape reflected in Emily's clothing, again subtly connecting her with the beauty of the scene. Her clothing reflects the ordinary, neither affluent nor poverty-stricken, and her hair escapes the hood in wisps, suggesting escape from convention. As with the cover of *Anne's House of Dreams,* and unlike the boys' stories, Emily is reacting, seemingly, to the beauty of the landscape, though we could argue that the Wind Woman in the background transforms that landscape and is an action in itself. The power of the imagination, rather than of the body, is suggested. Canada has become a land of dreams and imagination, instead of a land to be overpowered with technology, and perhaps a land more welcoming to its readers, especially the female half, and especially the less affluent.

The illustration ignores Emily's alienation and the conflicts she encounters throughout the book. As Elizabeth Epperley notes, "Montgomery's novels suggest how radically life scripts must change if the female is to read herself as heroine," because her female relatives are "not supportive" of Emily's writing, and "the underlying and encoded messages about woman's place in the male literary establishment eventually make their quality of support suspect" (1992, 152–153). Emily's abilities are threatened continually with suppression, and it is this conflict that shapes her writing; she must "write against" the traditional script. Just as Anne of Green Gables' illustrations largely suppress Anne's orphan status, focusing on conventional girls' roles and traditions—dressing up, rescue, and romance—so the cover of Emily suppresses the conflict and alienation that she battles against, presenting only the romance and beauty of her imagined world. This pattern is repeated in all of M. L. Kirk's covers. *Anne's House of Dreams, Rainbow Valley, Emily of New Moon,* and *Rilla of Ingleside* depict portraits of women in pastoral, romanticized landscapes, always framed as a world of beauty. None of the darker traits or moods of

FIGURE 5. Cover illustration: *Emily of New Moon*. Illustrator M. L. Kirk. Edition copyright McClelland and Stewart Limited, Toronto, 1923.

the text are portrayed. Even the First World War escapes depiction in *Rilla of Ingleside*, since the moment chosen to be depicted is the one where she reads her first love letter. Romance is emphasized; conflict is hidden. None of the women, except perhaps Emily, act on the landscape, though they may react to an incident, as Rilla does. This lack of power and action in the illustrations may, in fact, have coloured later critical reactions to the books, diminishing them to juvenile works of pretty landscapes and playful, romantic heroines, and relegating Montgomery to being "aggressively unliterary . . . satisfied to truckle to mediocre taste" (Brown 1977, 4). Fortunately, Montgomery's complexities and those of her work have been recovered and re-envisioned by scholars such as Mary Rubio and Elizabeth Waterston, Elizabeth Epperley, and numerous others in recent years. Today's Canadian literature for children reflects their changing faces and landscapes in a proliferation of literature and illustrations created by Canadians. Noticeably, most of the early illustrations don't depict urban Canada at all, nor do they reflect the many landscapes contained within the country, even across the range of books available. Perhaps one of the best known Canadian illustrators of our times is Michael Martchenko, whose pairing with Robert Munsch demonstrates the interplay of text and picture, as well as the influence of illustrations when read by themselves. Perry Nodelman's analysis of illustrators of Munsch's work argues that Martchenko "makes an equally assured, equally masterful, and equally important contribution to the final effect" (1993, 23) of Munsch's text, comparing the success of his illustrations to those of Munsch's books done by other illustrators. The illustrations "release the energy that was inherent in the story's genesis all along" (Thorpe 1993, 10), making the illustrations a text in and of themselves that also shapes our reading of the story.

Munsch's figures of children are representational rather than realistic; they suggest openness, rather than the detailed closure of reality seen in the illustrations in Montgomery's work. In this way, the child reader can find him or herself more readily in the illustration, unbound by finely detailed reality. The cartoon-like figures are comic and lively, not status symbols of wealth and class. Perspective and viewpoint become less obvious and compelling as a result of the large shapes and bright colouring. In the illustration to *Pigs!*, perspective is certainly present, but it recedes into the background, formed by the proportions of the bus, the teacher, and the other children, placing the artist and viewer directly in front of Megan, on an equal level.

FIGURE 6.   Illustration: *Pigs!* by Robert Munsch. Illustrator Michael Martchenko. Edition copyright Annick Press, 1989.

Megan's single eye is shut, and the other people are gazing at the pig. We could say that the representation of their eyes by dots reduces the force of gaze, undercutting the idea of demand or offer that the represented figures would normally make on the viewer. The direction of the teacher and children's gaze, in fact, draws attention to the pig, whose expression, with closed eye and small grin, is a duplication of Megan's. The teacher and the line of children draw our eye from left to right, to the pig, the upright pole, and to Megan, whose detailed dress focuses our attention on this figure of comic anarchy, as does the brightly coloured tree against which her head is centred. The schoolbus, of course, approaching in its cloud of dust with one wheel raised and a blank pair of front windows, represents movement, not to mention deviation from normal safe driving standards. The teacher and children represent the established, into which Martchenko drops the pig, undercutting convention; Megan stands approximately in the centre, the focus of both established and new; and the schoolbus, emphasizing its movement and the windows into which we cannot see, is on the right, in the place of the unknown. Megan's act of holding the leash with the pig on it, poised to move towards the schoolbus, the unknown, is a presentational act, which captures a snapshot of the moment. The gaze of the others provides the reaction, the slightly troubled stare which transfixes the pig as an incongruity in the landscape. The pig is shining clean, contrary to convention; its "dirt" has been transferred to Megan in a reversal of animal-human characteristics. Even Megan's feet, one with shoe on, one with shoe off, places her, like her position, between the established and the adventurous. She is an open figure, able to be read and engaged by the viewer, thus placing power in the imagination of the viewer.

And what of the landscape itself? Megan's pig transforms the established into the new, but the background, though not explicitly set in Canada, suggests it. The flame of the tree behind Megan, again representational instead of a detailed type, allows the reader to again read into the picture what he or she is familiar with. (I instantly read it as my childhood maple.) The brick wall of the elementary school and the pole with the bus stop sign suggest an urban landscape, but the school bus, correct in every detail, and labelled to reinforce its purpose, suggests a departure to the rural. Much of the comedy, of course, lies in the incongruous placement of the pig in an urban setting. Finally, the variety of children depicted, again representationally, again suggests openness. This picture, in other words, contains both urban and rural elements that suggest familiar settings, peopled by a mixture of types, focused by the anarchic figure of Megan, who contradicts all the tenets of wealth, status, and establishment we have seen in previous illustrators' depictions of children. This child, with her pig, holds the power to transform the landscape and to undercut established conventions; the openness of the represented figures and the landscape to the viewer's imagination and experience makes this illustration a gesture of power for the viewer, reminiscent, but new.

Canada and its children, then, when read through Kress and van Leeuwen's theory of visual grammar, present the portrait of a country in transition, where children's place is determined by the values inherent, whether consciously or unconsciously, in the illustrations. In the early years, Canadian children were left out of the visual text and landscape, relegated to nothingness in their own country; Canada itself was not a place to live, but a country to travel across or to hunt in, and then leave. The illustrations of Montgomery's work show the range of transformations possible, from gendered, traditional, often sexual roles to romanticized figures of reaction set in a pastoral landscape. Across the years, many of today's illustrators, represented here by Martchenko, depict children with power and agency to transform an open landscape, where children can read themselves into the picture. The power of visual literacy lies in its ability to uncover the power relations and social values of the illustrations that sometimes work with, and sometimes against, the accompanying text. It is a literacy that lends itself to the classroom to enable children and adults to become critically aware of the values incorporated into images, either through bringing books into the classroom or by building electronic art galleries to reach a wider audience. Kress and van Leeuwen's vision of illustrations and pictures forming their own text, and one that can be read, allows the critical reader to follow the paths of openness and closure, of demand and its lack, that shape our children's view of their world and themselves in it.

WORKS CITED

Brown, E. K. "The Problem of a Canadian Literature." In *Responses and Evaluations: Essays on Canada by E. K. Brown.* Ed. David Staines. Toronto: McClelland and Stewart, 1977.

Eggleston, Wilfrid. *The Green Gables Letters*. Ottawa: Borealis Press, 1981.

Epperley, Elizabeth Rollins. *The Fragrance of Sweetgrass: L. M. Montgomery's Heroines and the Pursuit of Romance*. Toronto: University of Toronto Press, 1992.

Hutton, Jack, and Linda Jackson-Hutton. "Images of Anne throughout the Years." In *The Lucy Maud Montgomery Album*. Comp. Kevin McCabe. Ed. Alexandra Hutton. Toronto: Fitzhenry and Whiteside, 1999.

Kress, Gunther, and Theo van Leeuwen. *Reading Images*. Victoria, Australia: Deakin University Press, 1990.

Montgomery, L. M. *Anne of Avonlea*. Illus. George Gibbs. Boston: Page, 1909.

———. *Anne of Green Gables*. Illus. M. A. and W. A. J. Claus. Boston: Page, 1908.

———. *Anne's House of Dreams*. Illus. M. L. Kirk. Toronto: McClelland, Goodchild, and Stewart, 1917.

———. *Emily of New Moon*. Illus. M. L. Kirk. Toronto: McClelland and Stewart, 1923.

———. *The Golden Road*. Illus. George Gibbs. Boston: Page, 1913.

———. *Rainbow Valley*. Illus. M. L. Kirk. Toronto: McClelland and Stewart, 1919.

———. *Rilla of Ingleside*. Illus. M. L. Kirk. Toronto: McClelland and Stewart, 1921.

———. *The Selected Journals of L. M. Montgomery, Volume IV: 1929–1935*. Ed. Mary Rubio and Elizabeth Waterston. Toronto: Oxford University Press, 1998.

Munsch, Robert. *Pigs!* Art by Michael Martchenko. Toronto: Annick Press, 1989.

Nodelman, Perry. "The Illustrators of Munsch." *Canadian Children's Literature* 71 (1993): 5–25.

Oxley, J. Macdonald. *The Boy Tramps or Across Canada*. Illus. Henry Sandham. Toronto: Musson Book, n.d.

Rubio, Mary Henley. "Introduction: Harvesting Thistles in Montgomery's Textual Garden." *Harvesting Thistles: The Textual Garden of L. M. Montgomery*. Ed. Mary Rubio. Guelph: Canadian Children's Press, 1994.

Schwartz, Bernard, and JoAnn Sommerfeld. "Visual Images in Books, a Neglected Resource in Children's Aesthetic Education." *Canadian Children's Literature* 60 (1990): 25–33.

Thorpe, Douglas. "'Why Don't We See Him?': Questioning the Frame in Illustrated Children's Stories." *Canadian Children's Literature* 70 (1993): 5–21.

The Nature of Canadian Children's Literature: A Commentary

JOHN R. SORFLEET

PROFESSOR BECKETT HAS DISCUSSED some international aspects of Canadian children's literature, and Professor Waterston has examined some aspects of children's literature outside Canada. Accordingly, I'll begin by linking my comments to theirs with a look at the nature of Canadian children's literature in relation to international and national factors.[1]

Canadian children's literature: how can such a field be justified? Once we have American and British and French and German and other children's books, surely there is no need for Canadian ones! Is not international children's literature enough? Well, it depends on what "international" means to you. The word "international," used in culturally dominant nations—say England, the United States, or Russia—has a slightly condescending content: it means that the culturally dominant nation—secure in its belief as to the superior quality of its own literature—is also willing to recognize that there may be occasional good works produced by minor countries. But there is another side to the meaning of international—the connotations it has for smaller nations. To citizens of such countries, the emphasis of "international" is on both "inter" and "national"—but from a different perspective: it equals an assertion that their nation and their national literature have a significant place in the world, not merely as local colour, but as valuable in and of themselves. In both cases "international" is an extension of "national," but in the former case the importance of the home nation is supposedly self-evident; in the latter, it is a statement of independence. I draw this distinction not to promote argument or controversy, but simply to indicate that there are at least two modes of perception applicable to children's literature: the viewpoint of the culturally dominant nations—what one might term the imperial perspective—and the viewpoint of the culturally dominated nations—what one might term the independent or local perspective.

It is this independent local perspective—what one can term a sense of one's own place or home ground—which is most important to any understanding of the *raison d'être* of children's literature in Canada and other relatively young nations. Perhaps I can illustrate with a personal anecdote. By an accident of location I was born in England while my parents were visiting there—though they brought me back to Canada when I was still little more than an infant. However, my father's parents were English and regularly sent me Christmas or birthday copies of the *Boy's Own Annual*, the *Schoolboy's Annual*, and similar works. The stories, of course, were almost always set in England, but occasional mention of the colonies would occur. In these books, Canada was equated with Eskimos and Mounties; Australia was equated with gold-mining, deserts, and sheep-farming; New Zealand was equated with boating, Maoris, and hunting for birds' eggs. The image of Canada did cause me some doubtful moments because I'd never seen an Eskimo and saw only one Mountie before I was twelve, but I passed it off as being due to my somewhat unadventurous life—at least unadventurous in comparison with the exploits of the boy heroes in the books. But then one Christmas I received an Annual that had a *Real Canadian* in it. The protagonist was a Canadian boy attending an English boarding school. The school had an ice-hockey team which had continually lost in games with a rival school. (The prefix "ice," incidentally, surprised me; I'd never heard of any other kind of hockey at that time.) Our clean-cut Canadian, of course, was no mere puck-pusher: he was good, having played hockey at home in Canada. Needless to say, he proved to be the star of the big game, rescuing victory from the jaws of defeat. (I have to speak in clichés about the story because it *was* a series of clichés.) Hail the triumphant hero—fine and good! But then, as the winning players were returning to the dormitory, a teammate asked if our Canadian had enjoyed the game as much as those he'd played in Canada.

Nostalgically, he replied: "Yes, the game was good. But what I really miss is walking home under the beautiful Northern Lights, and listening to the twittering of the penguins."

There are no penguins in Canada—they're Antarctic birds. And they don't twitter.

Reading that, I was incredulous. All of a sudden, I realized that the world of the schoolboy's annuals, that the world in all the English and American children's books I was reading, *was not my world*. It was a foreign world, a false reality. The writers *didn't know my country*. It was an instant of shockingly clear insight, a flash of identity realization, a moment of mental awakening.

Their world was not my world; their Canada was not my Canada. My country was different. I needed books about life as I knew it, here and now, in this place. In this place. My own country. At that point I learned the importance of a national children's literature. And the conviction of its importance has stayed with me and grown—and is one reason why I'm talking to you today about the nature of Canadian children's literature, especially as it relates to the significance of home ground.

In fact, the history of children's literature in Canada is the developing story of how Canadians have come to terms with the place in which we live, Canada: its location, its climate, its peoples, its history, its politics, and its potential. I'm not going to chronicle Canadian children's literature—Egoff and Saltman's *The New Republic of Childhood* does a good job of that—but I will discuss some features of the field. First, it seems to me significant that some concerns of our nineteenth-century children's writers remain areas of interest to our contemporary ones. For example, the realistic animal stories of Charles G. D. Roberts and Ernest Thompson Seton, from the 1890s on, inaugurated a genre which was clearly Canadian and profoundly different from the over-sentimentalized and humanized animal stories of Anna Sewell, Rudyard Kipling, Kenneth Grahame, Felix Salten, and other foreign writers. Instead, the animals of Roberts and Seton exemplified the reality of the struggle for survival, of nature *as it is in Canada*. Our environment is not the peaceable British countryside or the conquered American landscape; it is still, in large part, a wilderness. Thus the animals face the problem of survival of the fittest by engaging in heroic struggle; indeed, the title of one of Seton's books is *Animal Heroes* (1905). Both authors gave to their animal biographies the kind of serious attention most writers give only to human biographies. Through such serious treatment, these two writers and their successors attempted to come to terms with Canada as a place distinct from all others, as a country which Canadians need to understand so that they can inhabit it psychologically as well as physically. These two Canadians were in tune with a Canadian respect for nature and ecology which is reflected in more recent twentieth-century animal stories by Roderick Haig-Brown, Cameron Langford, Fred Bodsworth, and Farley Mowat.

Similarly, Catherine Parr Traill's *Canadian Crusoes*, later retitled *Lost in the Backwoods* (1852), portrayed multi-ethnic cooperation in the context of an adventurous and exciting Canadian natural environment, concerns which are also central to Farley Mowat's *Lost in the Barrens* (1956) and *The Curse of the Viking Grave* (1966). Both authors, having experienced the challenge and rigours of the Canadian climate and wilderness, could not ignore the physical and psychological importance of Canada as a *place*. In particular, Mowat's work presents an intrinsically Canadian lesson about the environment: as Jamie comes to learn from his Cree Indian chum Awasin, the way to survive in the Canadian wilderness—and Canada is still two-thirds wilderness—is not to struggle against nature or attempt to conquer it, but rather to adjust to it, to live in tune with nature. The boys—like us—must recognize that this place, Canada, is *our* place, our home ground: it is where we must live, and it is what we must *accept*. In acceptance, allying ourselves with the reality of our land, so to speak, is the secret to Canada's strength and potential.

Further, given Tim Wynne-Jones's comments in his keynote address, his interest in mysteries, and his presence on this panel, it seems appropriate to examine briefly that genre for what it reveals about the nature of Canadian children's literature. The history of Canadian children's mystery stories begins with James De Mille's nineteenth-century schoolboy adventure and mystery series, the B.O.W.C. (Brethren of the White Cross) books. Among De Mille's successors was Leslie McFarlane who, under the name of Franklin W. Dixon, wrote twenty-one of the first twenty-six Hardy Boys books—in their original versions still clearly the best of the series. McFarlane, who moved beyond the Stratemeyer syndicate's limited plot and character formulas, *made* the books appeal to readers. McFarlane continued a tradition of Canadian mystery writing which later reached a flowering in the adult mysteries of Canadian Margaret Millar and her husband—the man *The New York Times* called "the greatest living mystery writer in America"—Ross MacDonald. MacDonald, whose real name was Kenneth Millar, was born and died in the U.S., but he grew up in Canada, and spent his formative years here. His novels and those of his wife, I think, can be seen to reflect the same kind of Canadian concern with the past, with the unravelling of one's relationships, with the psychological tracing down of one's origins and formative influences—including the influences of setting and physical propinquity—that permeates the work of such Canadians as Margaret Atwood, Margaret Laurence, Mordecai Richler, Robertson Davies, Marie-Claire Blais, Gabrielle Roy, and many, many others. However, I'm straying from children's literature—though it is significant that almost all of these adult authors have also written at least one children's book. Offhand I could mention over half a dozen other prominent Canadian writers for adults whose *opus* includes a children's book: Dennis Lee, James Reaney, Pierre Berton, Thomas Raddall, David Walker, Morley Callaghan, Tim Wynne-Jones, etc. (The adult author Richard Wright has even written a children's parody of the mystery story, titled *Andrew Tolliver*.) This phenomena seems—in terms of the statistical frequencies involved—to be an especially Canadian one—but why? I haven't reached any final conclusions on the matter, but I think it is because children and Canadians are concerned with some of the same questions about identity: Who am I? What does it mean to be me? What is my relationship to others around me? What do I want to be? What do I value in ethical terms? Children and Canadians also share some of the same needs: the need for more independence from outside control, the need for self-sufficiency, the need to assert and prove one's right to respect, the need to develop—*and live by*—a set of ideals. Coming to terms with one's place in time as well as in space, resolving the questions about identity that children—and less powerful nations—have: these are concerns characteristic of Canadian writers for both children and adults, and are reflected in the literary techniques—plot, character, symbolism, structure, fairy-tale elements, etc.—that they employ.

Finally, let's consider the genre of poetry. The most notable contribution to Canadian children's poetry is Dennis Lee's work: *Alligator Pie* (1974), *Nicholas Knock* (1974), and their successors. (Lee was also the 1972 winner of the Governor General's award for that year's best book of poetry for adults, *Civil Elegies*.) When he was reading *Mother Goose* to his children, he began to realize the distance between the verses and contemporary Canadian reality:

All we seemed to read about were jolly millers, little pigs, and queens. The details of *Mother Goose*—the wassails and Dobbins and pipers and pence—had become exotic; children loved them, but they were no longer home ground. (1974a, 63)

Home ground. That's what Lee is concerned with. That's what Canadian literature is trying to articulate. Lee deals with the definition of home ground in a variety of ways. Though a few poems show his fascination with the music of Canadian place names—"Kahshe or Chicoutimi" and "In Kamloops" are two instances—Lee is not usually this explicit. Generally his response is just to write, confident that home ground will emerge from the creative interaction of imaginative play with his Canadian roots, as is the case with so many of his poems. Lee's Ookpik poems, found in the first two books, provide a good conclusion for this discussion of home ground. As Lee said in a talk he and I adapted for publication in *CCL* in 1976,

Ookpik . . . is another of the vital figures that challenge how we are. He's a dancer, an embodiment of pure lyricism: harmless, pointless, irrepressible . . . . There are four Ookpik poems, and by the last one he has become a kind of totemic figure or tutelary god for the books. (1976, 52)

Ookpik: the "tutelary god" for the books. How does the last Ookpik poem end?

Ookpik,
    Ookpik
By your
    Grace,
Help us
    Live in
Our own
    Space. (1974b, 63)

Help us live in our own space. Lee's final word, then, is directed at the need for Canadians to inhabit—and thus give expression to, in life as well as literature—our own space, our country.

Incidentally, you may have noticed that, to this point, I haven't mentioned Canada's best-known children's book, L. M. Montgomery's *Anne of Green Gables* (1908), nor any of her later works. However, an item about *Anne* provides a good conclusion to my comments about the problems Canadian children's literature has faced on the world stage. It neatly illustrates international versus national factors, imperial versus local perspectives, and the importance and integrity of the concept of home ground. It is something that infuriated L. M. Montgomery—a scene from the first movie version of Anne, the rights over which she had (not surprisingly at the time) been cunningly deprived of by her American publisher, L. C. Page and Co. (whom she later sued for another copyright violation). The film scene? The Prince Edward Island schoolhouse Anne attended. Over it flew—an American flag.[2]

NOTES

1. John Sorfleet's commentary grew out of a panel discussion with Sandra Beckett, Tim Wynne-Jones, and Elizabeth Waterston at the Canadian Children's Literature Symposium.

2. Montgomery first saw the movie on February 20, 1920, after receiving negative comments from others about its presentation of her novel. See also Elizabeth Waterston's comments in *L. M. Montgomery: An Assessment* (19) and Montgomery's *Journals* (II: 373, 1920).

WORKS CITED

Lee, Dennis. *Alligator Pie*. Toronto: Macmillan, 1974a.

———. *Nicholas Knock*. Toronto: Macmillan, 1974b.

———. "Roots and Play: Writing as a 35-Year-Old Child." *Canadian Children's Literature* 4 (1976), 28–58.

Montgomery, Lucy Maud. *The Selected Journals of L. M. Montgomery. Volume II: 1910–1921*. Ed. Mary Rubio and Elizabeth Waterston. Toronto: Oxford University Press, 1987.

Waterston, Elizabeth. "Lucy Maud Montgomery: 1874–1942." *L. M. Montgomery: An Assessment*. Ed. John Robert Sorfleet. Guelph: Canadian Children's Press, 1976.

The Nature of Children's Literature: A Commentary

ELIZABETH WATERSTON

We HAVE BEEN TALKING ABOUT "Canadian Children's Literature"—that is, a stream of stories and poems for children, mostly in English and French, accompanied by a trickle of Aboriginal legends.[1] This specific literature rose roughly in 1750, swelled into some significance around 1850, and reached the proportions of a small tide roughly 1950.

But now we are to expand our focus. We are to consider the nature of ALL children's literature, children's literature in general—including I suppose everything from Aesop's Fables to a Ugandan ghost story or a Brazilian cyber-fantasy. And we are to theorize about the nature of everything literary that nourishes non-adults. We are to remember the prereaders who listen to parental reading of Zoom, and also the fifteen-year-olds, obsessed (we are told) by sexuality, violence, and self, but who need to develop the attributes that will serve them as they cross the threshold into the job world—industry, initiative, social responsibility, etc.

We are to assume that there is a "nature"—an essential quality, an innate character, a functioning force, a-social, in literature. A challenge, since most of us would agree that the nature of children's literature has changed between (say) *Beautiful Joe* in 1894 and *Angel Square* in 1984.

What is the nature of children's literature? What is the function of the books we write for children, the books that children read? Well, let's start by saying that we are not talking just about books but about *literature*. Carefully composed. Meticulously revised. Something permanent, something young readers can go back to for deepening experience. Or for the illogical joy of word play.

Can we agree about the literary aspects of children's literature? Can we assume that all children's stories and poems are rooted in myth (with the consequent benefits that Bettelheim postulates), even if the trace of myth is as tenuous as when a timid turtle feels disconnected from the tooth fairy? Children's literature is rooted in a universe of books, stories, fables, myths, and songs.

Can we agree that the style will communicate a joy in words, a thrill to rhythm, even when the story is very dark, dispiriting, or threatening? Let's agree that socio-psychological benefits are not the mark of literature, but that appropriate style is.

With Tim Wynne-Jones's permission, I could read a couple of sentences from *The Maestro:*

> When you were hungry in a fairy tale, an old hag would pass by with a magic bowl, or magic beans. Well, Burl had eaten what beans he could find, and when he awoke cold and damp in the morning, sure enough, the can was full again, but only with brown rain water. So he took a bite of the north wind for breakfast and headed out . . . . (1995, 31)

Agreed? That's literature.

Literature is not just a story about dysfunctional families, put together in a hurry, without singing phrases or rounded characters. And not just *Franklin,* in books, on TV, and in interactive CD-ROMs, a story without ragged edges or irony, a colourless validation of conformist non-threatening adjustment in small beings, whether turtles or children.

But we must go on to tackle the question of what children are, if we are to evaluate the literature produced for them, or, more important, perhaps, chosen by them. We must study some child-development theories.

When we ask, "How does literature fit into the development of the child?" our answer to that question has probably changed since yesterday. We have endured some horrific news stories from Kosovo that ask us to revise our sense of child development, and also our sense of the interaction between children and what they read, between their everyday life and the life of their imaginations. We had better think quickly again about the nature of childhood, and the proper and possible and actual functions of the literary fare, the imaginative diet that nourishes their development today.

I will begin with a case history of literary fare, by way of a metaphor. My daughter Charlotte is a teacher-librarian in a London elementary school. This being the modern world, her storage room is now full of computers, and she has become a teacher-librarian/computer resource person, spending less time dealing with books, more with the web and the CD-ROMS. And now, thanks to the cuts in educational funding, the librarian/computer resource part of her work is cut in half, and she is also teaching language arts to grade six and gym to grade four. In "language arts," she asked her students this spring to write reports on a book of their own choice. Here is the list of books they chose: a surprising array of texts. Out of a class of twenty-nine, there were no repeats, no duplications. There were no books the librarian had particularly recommended or worked with in the library side of her teaching. There probably were books that parents encouraged children to consider. But here is the list—perhaps a random, but certainly a suggestive sample of literature chosen by children at one stage of development (the authors in parenthesis are particularly popular, according to the librarian):

Sabrina the Teen-Age Witch	*Charlie and the Great Glass Window*
The Cartoonist (by Betsy Byars)	*Look Through My Window* (by Jean Little)
The Ear, the Arm and the Eye	*The Great Interactive Dream Machine*
The View From Saturday (by Konigsberg)	*Baby Sitters Club Series*
Charlie and the Chocolate Factory	*Harry Potter and the Philosopher's Stone*
The Acting Bug	*Blubber* (by Judy Blume)
The Inuk Mountie Adventure (by Eric Wilson)	*My Side of the Mountain*
Bunnicula (by James Howe)	*Clockwork Asylum*
The Chronicles of Narnia	*The Number Devil*
Summer Break	*The Dragon Slayers*
(Anything by Kit Pearson)	*Harriet the Spy*
Buffy the Vampire Slayer	*Left Behind*
(Dave Barry Books)	*Sweet Valley Twins*

But those books are merely a sample of the books children read when they are eleven or twelve years old. We know that children have different psycho-physical abilities at different stages of development. To define the nature of children's literature we must take account of those different stages.

We have watched enough *Nature* shows on TV to remember how young birds and animals change coat or plumage, develop digestive powers, develop musculature, bond, or differentiate from the pack or the pride or the nesting pair. Similarly, child psychologists and pediatricians have observed recurring patterns of growth which discriminate stages of human childhood. I used to structure my courses on children's literature—and I based my book, *Children's Literature in Canada*—on the formulations of childhood by Jean Piaget. Piaget discriminated sequential stages through which children develop into adult mentality. We can deduce what sort of books are appropriate at each stage.

According to Piaget, a child at the sensory-motor stage, with a limited sense of time and order, cannot follow a complex narrative. Capacity for symbolic thinking emerges later. Now the young child brings experience and imagination to the book, decodes it in a way that fits into a growing identity (in Norman Holland's sense), and concretizes it in terms that help make sense out of the impinging world. But a child at the concrete operational stage, between seven and eleven, develops two modes of thought: the intuitive and the rational. Binary thinking and the ability to form closures develop, but the love of magic, of heroic voyages, of quest, survives. The child at this stage enjoys tales of the divided self, the solo wanderer. Later, at the formal operational stage, children are capable of thinking abstractly about cause and effect. Children at the borderline of maturity have full cognitive power to decode, fill gaps, untangle disrupted time sequences, enigmas, and semantic oddities. Young adults will play more consciously with the occult and will also use dark realism to confront new experiences. They can handle a binary search for identity and they can recognize the complexities and fluidities of choices as they story themselves into their own space and time and family. At each age level, appropriate books preview and prepare for the next stage of development. (I was led to acceptance of Piaget by Laurie Ricou's *Everyday Magic*—a very important book, not as well known as his *Vertical Man, Horizontal World*.)

Not only did Piaget's ideas about the variants of childhood, from babyhood to young adulthood, make sense to me, they also made sense to the Ontario Department of Education, which issued directives and curricula based on Piaget's theory of stages. And who would argue with the Ontario Government when it reveals the depth of its understanding of education and childhood? Alas, Piaget is now as out of official style as classic Freudianism—though I still think that developmental theory is a good way to structure a course on children's literature, while remembering that experience with electronic technology has enabled the postmodern child to respond to readings in more complex ways than was possible before. I believe motor and mental skills have evolved in the cyber-kid, but the sequence of developmental stages remains the same.

Whatever theory we adopt, the meanings our cultural system assigns to childhood are sometimes at odds with what we perceive in our encounters with actual children. And we have to be ready to think again about the term "nature." I recommend an interesting article in a recent *CCL* by Mavis Reimer, which explores current confusion about the assumed power/powerless hierarchy between adults and children. Reimer begins her study with reference to James Kincaid's *Child-Loving: The Erotic Child and Victorian Culture,* which created a storm in 1992—clearly the question we are raising here is a troubling and important one, and the answers to it are fluid.

My only conclusions are:

- that the books we create for children, the books we "teach" to potential teachers and librarians, must indeed be *literary,* that is, the term "children's literature" implies quality, style, structure, theme;
- that it is essential that we learn to discriminate children's developmental stages so as to discriminate levels of children's literature. There is no such thing as "the child" in stasis;
- that whatever we conclude about children and literature, we must be ready to change our conclusions tomorrow.

And PS—if you want to see how Canadianness fits into the question of the nature of children's literature, a suitable background to John Sorfleet's preceding comments on the nature of *Canadian* children's literature, I recommend the two special 1997 issues of *Canadian Children's Literature/La littérature canadienne pour la jeunesse,* guest edited by Perry Nodelman, especially the second one, #87, in which forty important writers, editors, librarians, book-sellers, and teachers answer the question, "What's Canadian in Canadian Children's Literature?" Thought-provoking and fun.

NOTE

1.   Elizabeth Waterston's commentary grew out of a panel discussion with Sandra Beckett, John Sorfleet, and Tim Wynne-Jones at the Canadian Children's Literature Symposium.

WORK CITED

Wynne-Jones, Tim. *The Maestro*. A Groundwood Book. Vancouver and Toronto: Douglas & McIntyre, 1995.

Contributors

SANDRA L. BECKETT is a professor of French at Brock University. She is the editor of *Reflections of Change: The Last 50 Years of Children's Literature* (1997) and *Transcending Boundaries: Writing For a Dual Audience of Children and Adults* (1999), and is the author of numerous articles on fairy tales, legends, and folklore.

VIRGINIA A. S. CARELESS is a cultural historian and a research officer with the B. C. Ministry of Small Business, Tourism, and Culture. Her published works include articles on L. M. Montgomery, Mazo de la Roche, and Joanna E. Wood.

CECILY DEVEREUX is an associate professor of English at the University of Alberta.

IRENE GAMMEL is a professor of English at the University of Prince Edward Island. She is the co-editor of *L. M. Montgomery and Canadian Culture* (1999), editor of *Confessional Politics: Women's Sexual Self-Representations in Life Writing and Popular Media* (1999), and author of *Making Avonlea: L. M. Montgomery and Popular Culture* (2002).

LEE HARRIS teaches music at Concordia University.

BEVERLEY HAUN teaches at Adam Scott Collegiate and is pursuing graduate studies at Trent University.

AÏDA HUDSON is a sessional lecturer at the University of Ottawa.

KIM LA FAVE is an illustrator of children's books. His awards include the Governor General's Award for his illustrations to *Amos's Sweater* in 1988.

JANET LUNN is a writer, editor, and critic of children's books. She has won numerous awards for her work including the Canada Council Children's Literature Prize for *Shadow in Hawthorn Bay* (1986) and the Governor General's Award for *The Hollow Tree* (1997), as well as the Ruth Schwartz Children's Book Award for the picture book *Amos's Sweater* (1988). She has also written a biography of Lucy Maud Montgomery for young adults, *Maud's House of Dreams: The Life of Lucy Maud Montgomery* (2002).

GREGORY MAILLET is an assistant professor of English at the University of Regina.

ANDREA MCKENZIE is Director of Writing in the Disciplines at New York University.

JUDITH SALTMAN is an associate professor in Archival and Information Studies at the University of British Columbia and chair of the Master of Arts in Children's Literature Program. She is the author of *Modern Canadian Children's Books* (1987) and co-author of *The New Republic of Childhood: A Critical Guide to Canadian Children's Literature in English* 3rd ed. (1990).

HELEN SIOURBAS teaches English at Champlain Regional College.

MICHAEL SOLOMON is Artistic Director of Groundwood Books.

JOHN R. SORFLEET, associate professor of English at Concordia University, is now retired. He is a founding editor of *Canadian Children's Literature* and *Journal of Canadian Poetry*. His publications include *L. M.*

Montgomery: An Assessment (1976) and *Canadian Children's Drama and Theatre* (1978).

MARGARET STEFFLER is a sessional lecturer of English at Trent University.

ELIZABETH WATERSTON is Professor Emeritus of English at the University of Guelph. Among her numerous publications are *Children's Literature in Canada* (1992) and *Kindling Spirit: L. M. Montgomery's Anne of Green Gables* (1993). She is a founding editor of *Canadian Children's Literature* and the co-editor of the four volume work, *The Selected Journals of L. M. Montgomery.*

ALAN WEST is a sessional lecturer at the University of Ottawa.

TIM WYNNE-JONES is a writer of adult and children's fiction. His children's novels are *The Maestro* (1995), *Stephen Fair* (1999), and *The Boy in the Burning House* (2000). He won the Governor General's Award for one of his collections of stories, *Some of the Kinder Planets* (1993), and for *The Maestro* (1995). He has also edited works for children including the anthology *Boys' Own* (2002), and written radio plays, the book and libretto for the opera *A Midwinter Night's Dream*, as well as many picture books, including the *Zoom* books and *Ned Mouse Breaks Away* (2003).

REAPPRAISALS: CANADIAN WRITERS

Reappraisals: Canadian Writers was begun in 1973 in response to a need for single volumes of essays on Canadian authors who had not received the critical attention they deserved or who warranted extensive and intensive reconsideration. It is the longest running series dedicated to the study of Canadian literary subjects. The annual symposium hosted by the Department of English at the University of Ottawa began in 1972 and the following year University of Ottawa Press published the first title in the series, *The Grove Symposium*. Since then our editorial policy has remained straightforward: each year to make permanently available in a single volume the best of the criticism and evaluation presented at our symposia on Canadian literature, thereby creating a body of work on, and a critical base for the study of, Canadian writers and literary subjects.

Gerald Lynch
General Editor

Titles in the series:

THE GROVE SYMPOSIUM, edited and with an introduction by John Nause

THE A. M. KLEIN SYMPOSIUM, edited and with an introduction by Seymour Mayne

THE LAMPMAN SYMPOSIUM, edited and with an introduction by Lorraine McMullen

THE E. J. PRATT SYMPOSIUM, edited and with an introduction by Glenn Clever

THE ISABELLA VALANCY CRAWFORD SYMPOSIUM, edited and with an introduction by Frank M. Tierney

THE DUNCAN CAMPBELL SCOTT SYMPOSIUM, edited and with an introduction by K. P. Stich

THE CALLAGHAN SYMPOSIUM, edited and with an introduction by David Staines

238

THE ETHEL WILSON SYMPOSIUM, edited and with an introduction by Lorraine McMullen

TRANSLATION IN CANADIAN LITERATURE, edited and with an introduction by Camille R. La Bossière

THE SIR CHARLES G. D. ROBERTS SYMPOSIUM, edited and with an introduction by Glenn Clever

THE THOMAS CHANDLER HALIBURTON SYMPOSIUM, edited and with an introduction by Frank M. Tierney

STEPHEN LEACOCK: A REAPPRAISAL, edited and with an introduction by David Staines

FUTURE INDICATIVE: LITERARY THEORY AND CANADIAN LITERATURE, edited and with an introduction by John Moss

REFLECTIONS: AUTOBIOGRAPHY AND CANADIAN LITERATURE, edited and with an introduction by K. P. Stich

RE(DIS)COVERING OUR FOREMOTHERS: NINETEENTH-CENTURY CANADIAN WOMEN WRITERS, edited and with an introduction by Lorraine McMullen

BLISS CARMAN: A REAPPRAISAL, edited and with an introduction by Gerald Lynch

FROM THE HEART OF THE HEARTLAND: THE FICTION OF SINCLAIR ROSS, edited by John Moss

CONTEXT NORTH AMERICA: CANADIAN/U.S. LITERARY RELATIONS, edited by Camille R. La Bossière

HUGH MACLENNAN, edited by Frank M. Tierney

ECHOING SILENCE: ESSAYS ON ARCTIC NARRATIVE, edited and with a preface by John Moss

BOLDER FLIGHTS: ESSAYS ON THE CANADIAN LONG POEM, edited and with a preface by Frank M. Tierney and Angela Robbeson

DOMINANT IMPRESSIONS: ESSAYS ON THE CANADIAN SHORT STORY, edited by Gerald Lynch and Angela Arnold Robbeson

MARGARET LAURENCE: CRITICAL REFLECTIONS, edited and with an introduction by David Staines

ROBERTSON DAVIES: A MINGLING OF CONTRARIETIES, edited by Camille R. La Bossière and Linda M. Morra

WINDOWS AND WORDS: A LOOK AT CANADIAN CHILDREN'S LITERATURE IN ENGLISH, edited by Aïda Hudson and Susan-Ann Cooper